British Music Now

A guide to the work of younger composers

British Music Now

edited by Lewis Foreman

Paul Elek London

First published in Great Britain 1975 by
Elek Books Limited
54–58 Caledonian Road, London N1 9RN

Copyright © 1975 Lewis Foreman

ISBN 0 236 30933 1

Printed in England by
Latimer Trend & Company Ltd Plymouth
and set in Monotype Baskerville

Contents

Acknowledgements 6
List of Contributors 7
Editor's Introduction 11

The Problem of Communication—Two Solutions:
   Thea Musgrave and Gordon Crosse   *Leslie East* 19
Ronald Stevenson   *Colin Scott-Sutherland* 32
Alexander Goehr   *Guy Protheroe* 41
Hugh Wood   *Leo Black* 53
Harrison Birtwistle   *Meirion Bowen* 60
Peter Maxwell Davies   *Stephen Arnold* 71
Two Welsh Composers: Alun Hoddinott and William
   Mathias   *Michael Oliver* 86
Nicholas Maw   *Arnold Whittall* 97
Richard Rodney Bennett   *Christopher Palmer* and
   Lewis Foreman 108
David Blake   *Malcolm MacDonald* 120
David Bedford   *Carolyn Stokoe* 133
Two Traditionalists: Kenneth Leighton and John McCabe
   Harold Truscott 145
John Tavener   *Trevor Bray* 155
Miscellany: Justin Connolly—Jonathan Harvey—Roger
   Smalley—Anthony Payne—Tristram Cary—Anthony
   Milner—Christopher Headington—Robin Holloway—
   David Ellis   *Michael Oliver* 162
Postlude—A Note on Christopher Shaw
   Malcolm MacDonald 178

Other Composers 181
Select Bibliography 199
Sources of the Music 213
Discography 216
Index 238

Acknowledgements

Many people have helped with the writing of this book. My thanks are due to the contributors for cooperating with my scheme and for being so prompt with their contributions; to the composers who completed the questionnaires that I sent them to try to ensure the authenticity of the section entitled 'Other Composers', and to those who helped me decide which composers to include. To Malcolm MacDonald, for helping me to complete the section 'Other Composers'; to the promotion departments at Chappells and J. & W. Chester, to Chris Hayes who helped trace an obscure reference in *Melody Maker*, and the staff at Central Music Library who were particularly helpful and took the bulk of my repeated requests for runs of periodicals and obscure references; to Eric Hughes at the British Institute of Recorded Sound who helped check certain references in my discography, and the BIRS staff who also helped by playing me certain tape recordings not otherwise available; to Malcolm Walker; and to my editor, Antony Wood, who gave practical advice and made the published book a reality; to all of these my thanks.

LEWIS FOREMAN
Canonbury, October 1974

List of Contributors

Stephen ARNOLD. Born in 1946 in Cirencester, Gloucestershire. Educated at Cirencester Grammar School (where Peter Maxwell Davies was Director of Music), and then in Rome and at the Universities of Southampton and Nottingham. In 1971 appointed Lecturer in Music at the University of Glasgow, where he runs an extensive electronic studio.

Leo BLACK. Born in London in 1932. Learned the piano from the age of six. Studied music at Oxford University and joined the BBC Music Division as a producer in 1960 (since 1971 Chief Producer). He has translated books on Mozart and Schoenberg, also Schoenberg's essays for the enlarged edition of *Style and Idea* and many contributions to the series 'Die Reihe'.

Meirion BOWEN. Born in Swansea and educated at Birmingham University and at Cambridge. Since 1963 he has taught at various London art schools, and worked as a BBC producer; currently, he is musical director at Kingston Polytechnic. He has written extensively on music for *The Guardian*, *Music & Musicians*, etc. He runs a music group, The Electric Candle, specialising in percussion works and music-theatre.

Trevor BRAY. Born in London in 1944. Studied at Royal Manchester College of Music, Manchester University and St John's College, Cambridge. At present a lecturer at the Open University, and author of the published coursework in the music of the twentieth century. He has published a small book on Bantock (1973), based in part on his Doctoral thesis at Cambridge, and is writing a monograph on Frank Bridge.

Leslie EAST. Studied at King's College, London; teaches at the Guildhall School of Music, lectures and organises concerts at the City University, and is a contributor to *Music & Musicians*.

Lewis FOREMAN. A Chartered Librarian and Fellow of the

7

Library Association. Studied and then taught (part-time) at Ealing Technical College. Later obtained the London University External Diploma in the History of Music, winning the Robert Davies Roberts Memorial Book Prize. Contributes to programme planning and preparation of performing materials for several London semi-professional orchestras and operatic societies. His articles have appeared in a wide variety of the musical press, and he also writes programme notes and record sleeves. He edited *Havergal Brian—A Collection of Essays* (1969), and has since published *Discographies—A Bibliography* (1973), *Archive Sound Collections* (1974), and *Systematic Discography* (1974). He broadcasts frequently on BBC Radio London, and regularly reviews books for *The Gramophone*. He has recently completed a thesis for a master's degree in the University of Wales.

Malcolm MacDONALD. Born in Nairn in 1948. Read English and Music (in which he is otherwise self-taught) at Downing College, Cambridge. Now lives and works in London as a freelance writer on music. As 'Calum MacDonald' he has given radio talks and contributed to many periodicals. He is editor of *Tempo* and has published two books on Havergal Brian. His book on Schoenberg is in preparation as the present work goes to press.

Michael OLIVER. A technical journalist before becoming a freelance writer and broadcaster on music.

Christopher PALMER. Freelance writer on music. Author of *Impressionism in Music* (1973), and has just completed a full-length study of film music.

Guy PROTHEROE. Born in 1947. Received his early musical training as a chorister at Canterbury Cathedral, and later won a scholarship to Oxford to read music. A year at the Guildhall School of Music followed, since when he has worked freelance in London in many musical fields, concentrating on writing and conducting (he is Director of Spectrum and conductor of the English Chamber Choir).

Carolyn STOKOE. Born in Newcastle-upon-Tyne in 1946. Trained and worked as a teacher while studying harmony, counterpoint and piano with Dr Arthur Milner. Subsequently she read music at Newcastle University, graduating in 1974. Now writes freelance on music, and teaches privately.

8

Colin SCOTT-SUTHERLAND. The son of an artist, born in Fifeshire in 1930. Author of *Arnold Bax* (1973), and a shorter study of John Ireland is in preparation.

Harold TRUSCOTT. Principal Lecturer in Music at the School of Music, Huddersfield Polytechnic. He has broadcast piano recitals as well as regular talks on music since 1951, and his compositions have also been broadcast as well as receiving public performances. His articles have appeared in a wide variety of the musical press, and he contributed to *Studies in Romanticism*, *The Symphony* and the *Beethoven Companion*. Author of *Beethoven's Late String Quartets* (1969) and his book on Beethoven's Choral Symphony is in preparation.

Arnold WHITTALL. Senior Lecturer at University College, Cardiff, and editor of *Soundings*. His published articles include technical studies of Bartók, Britten and Stravinsky. He has written a BBC Music Guide on Schoenberg's chamber music and is currently working on a full-length study of music since the First World War.

Editor's Introduction

Few previous periods can have seen so much musical activity in Britain as the present. In the last fifteen years an exciting new generation of composers (and performers) has become established, and the young have changed the nature of the musical scene in a fundamental way. Composers are active in a wide variety of styles and traditions. Haunting and memorable scores are being produced by avant-garde and traditional composers alike. David Bedford, Peter Maxwell Davies and Harrison Birtwistle rub shoulders with a great variety of composers in more familiar styles. The variety is so great that a guide is necessary if any but the expert is to know what to expect from any given composer, and how to obtain the music of a writer whom one has found sympathetic. It is with the aim of guiding the listener to the new music that this book has been written.

When the book was conceived it was decided that it was to be about the younger generation of British composers (that is the post-Tippett-Fricker generation) and that a strict deadline would be chosen to qualify for inclusion in it. The cut-off date of 1 January 1924 included composers who were no more than fifty years old when contributions were commissioned. Of course these parameters mean that certain major figures are just excluded—Iain Hamilton, Robert Simpson and Malcolm Arnold on grounds of age, Malcolm Williamson on grounds of nationality and Don Banks on both counts.

However, this book is not intended as a chauvinistic demonstration of national achievement, but rather a demonstration of, and guide to, the unparalleled upsurge of creative activity in Great Britain since the Vaughan Williams-dominated generations and the cultural shock caused by exposure to the music of the Second Viennese School.

The change in outlook since the late Fifties is well-nigh incredible. For example, in a broadcast talk in 1959 (9)*, Peter Maxwell Davies asked:

If an audience laughs at early Schoenberg, how can it face the music of today? As yet, very few English audiences, specialist circles apart, have been invited to listen to new music. I suspect the English have been living in a fool's paradise, in complete ignorance of recent or even distant musical developments.

In an earlier article Maxwell Davies had pointed to the real root of the trouble as far as composition in this country was concerned:

Perhaps even more insidious . . . is the reactionary, who rejects all recent developments, and produces music which is often a pale imitation of some revered idol. This mentality still flourishes in Britain, and is largely responsible for the teaching of composition. It would not be so terrible if these teachers knew something about older music, but almost invariably they know no more than the most commonplace superficialities. Their taste is based exclusively on conditioning and prejudice, and they normally dote on one of the better—or occasionally one of the worst—who lived earlier this century, admonishing their students to write in a similar style. . . . (10).

In October 1961 the *Musical Times* published a carol by Peter Maxwell Davies (*Ave Maria*) as one of its musical supplements. It was a piece that today would be accepted without comment. However, at the time it prompted an outcry, and some of the comments were published in that journal two months later. Typical remarks were: '. . . it is high time someone made a firm stand against this unnecessarily unpleasant music . . .' 'Personally I think it is an affront to God . . .' 'A choir, above all a church choir, which would persevere with it after a first reading must be a very rare thing indeed.' 'Is this a hoax by the *Musical Times*?'

That the public's ears have been opened is shown by Maurizio Pollini's performance of the entire piano ouevre of Schoenberg to a *sold out* Queen Elizabeth Hall in October 1974. Certainly the European classics of the twentieth century are now played and have a much wider following than hitherto. Also, recent music is now performed more successfully than the recent music was in the twenty years after the Second World War.

However, the problems resulting from the variety of composing styles are important ones. There are still all too few critics and writers, not to say ordinary concertgoers, able *and willing* to appreci-

* Throughout this book numbers in brackets refer to sources in the Bibliography.

12

ate objectively the incredible variety of styles of today. It is difficult to get away from the romantic concept of 'high art music' on the one hand and entertainment music on the other. There is no reason to evaluate a film score by criteria different from those applied to a concert work. Richard Rodney Bennett is reputed as having said that if one is to be a professional composer one must be able to write in any style with complete sincerity (80).

In this book, the criteria of what constitutes a major composer are the Editor's and there will obviously be readers who will disagree. There has not been the space to treat at length all the composers whom one would have wished. This problem has been tackled by paring the space devoted to some major figures, and by including a composite chapter on ten or so further composers and a ready reference section on about seventy others. The text, together with the extensive bibliographical and discographical apparatus, should enable the reader to trace any composer under fifty with any claim to be of importance today.

The claims of certain vigorous pressure groups for different avant-garde and experimental composers have been considered, and it is hoped that a balance has been achieved. I believe that most of these changing groups may be important by their example but their actual music will amount to very little. They will probably be seen historically as more important as pamphleteers than as composers *per se*. Probably the cause most vigorously fought in this respect is for Cornelius Cardew and his 'school', of whom something is said in the ready reference section, and there are further references in the Bibliography. The Scratch Orchestra and its progeny is clearly of some historical importance but has very little place in the mainstream, or mainstreams, of musical development now. This is not to belittle Cardew as a composer, for he has produced worthwhile music (try the Leo Brouwer guitar record). The wasteland of indiscipline and politically inspired changes in the very nature of music itself is more insidious than the stylistic problems of the Fifties when strict serialism was found not to be the liberating influence many had hoped it to be.

It must be increasingly difficult for a characteristic voice to emerge and establish itself in the way Vaughan Williams or Walton or Britten did in the past. The composer today has the internal personality problem of finding himself and his style in relation to the major historical figures of the twentieth century and to developments abroad, seen from a country that until very

13

recently was traditionalist by temperament. This stylistic problem can be seen for example in the music of Hugh Wood. By comparing his songs and quartets on the Argo record listed in the discography the reader may gain some practical insight into the problem in one composer's work.

The dominating influence of Britten must also be a great problem for the composer whose musical inclinations tend to be tonal. I would see this influence as a serious flaw in a work like Crosse's *Changes*. However, many less ambitious works written in this tradition, for example Robin Stephenson's *The Four Seasons*, can be supremely successful. It is instructive to compare early works by Bennett and Maw. Bennett's *The Approaches of Sleep* (which features a quartet of voices and ten instruments), and his slightly later *A London Pastoral*, hold the attention in performance but although very skilfully written, and for all the former's powerful closing section with all the voices together, they are comparatively unmemorable, while the *Nocturne* by Nicholas Maw, a series of four poems each with an instrumental interlude (written at the same time as Britten's *Nocturne* but freed from excess influence by sheer force of personality), haunts the imagination long after the music has ceased, particularly the gorgeous *Cantilena* for horn and harp after the first song. It is also interesting to remember that Maw followed up the success of the *Nocturne* with the beautiful Webernesque *Chinese Songs* of 1959.

There are so many composers writing today that they tend to militate against each other's chances of success. For example, of the composers noted in the ready reference section, about twenty-five have written song-cycles for voice and orchestra. Similarly, a huge number of concertos have been written for most instruments in the last twenty years. So very often one will know a given composer closely through only one or two works, and each listener will have his own favourites, almost invariably encountered fortuitously.

A case in point is Trevor Hold whose *The Unreturning Spring*, a beautiful work for soprano, baritone and small orchestra, demonstrates how the problem of style can be successfully tackled within a dominating tradition and with an individual voice and personality. Yet this composer has not established himself as a national figure. Further examples of isolated works of quality are the violin concertos by David Morgan and Christopher Headington, and the delightfully convincing *Sinfonia da Caccia* by Jeremy Dale

Roberts. Indeed the latter work is worth considering here in some detail, so typical of the kind of success here discussed is its adaptation of traditional stimuli to composition with new means of expression.

The *Sinfonia da Caccia* was commissioned by the Morley College Concert Society for the 1967 Thaxted Festival. In the event the work was not played on that occasion. However, it dictated the composer's approach to the work for the orchestration was limited to what would have been the available resources, a Haydn-size orchestra of double woodwind, two horns, tympani and strings. While the Stravinsky of the Second World War period may occasionally be heard in the music (notably at the beginning), the work as a whole is deeply rooted in the composer's native Gloucestershire, but totally without resource to folksong or anything like it. It is an excellent example of how a composer can stretch and develop a tradition, without having to do so in a given overt style. The music is inscribed 'to the memory of Ivor Gurney, war poet and composer of Gloucestershire'. Some of the materials that Jeremy Dale Roberts uses in it are taken from a projected song-cycle based on the poems of Ivor Gurney and on letters that he wrote from the Western Front and from hospital. (At the end Gurney was confined in the City of London Mental Hospital at Dartford, Kent.) The music is in three sections with the central one forming a refuge, as it were, from the urgency and pace of those enclosing it. 'The title may be thought to refer not only to the terror and beauty of the hunt, but to all forms of pack and all forms of quarry.'

A number of major new choral works have appeared, but in this traditional form Alexander Goehr (in *Sutter's Gold*) in particular seemed to experience some stylistic problems, and later Alun Hoddinott's *The Tree of Life* seemed somewhat forced. However, in the more recent major choral works—David Blake's *Lumina* and Jonathan Harvey's *Ludus Amoris*, for example—the mainstream of the choral tradition has been renewed and in a brilliantly successful rapprochement with the new and the old in *Star Clusters, Nebulae and Places in Devon*, David Bedford has shown the vast possibilities inherent in new vocal procedures, and how they may be successfully realised on the popular concert platform.

On the other hand, in the more traditional field of opera, in spite of unprecedented opportunities, the composers who have accepted the challenge have not all shown themselves to be suited

15

to it. Probably the most successful to date has been Maw in his second opera *The Rising of the Moon*. The work's strengths were unerringly pointed out by Winton Dean in the *Musical Times* (September 1970) at the time of the first production:

Maw's score shows a far more assured sense of dramatic timing than his first opera . . . This is one of the keys to operatic success, not least in comedy . . . Music and drama play consistently into each other's hands. Much of the music is very fast (not just slow music warmed up); there are numerous lively ensembles . . . and in the second act some scenes of striking lyrical beauty. Constant Lambert once declared an atonal comic opera to be unthinkable. Maw, though his idiom retains tonal references, has disproved this . . . the opera is an excellent entertainment.

The general interest in writing opera or music drama would seem to augur well for the future vitality of the musico-dramatic stage. Recently there has been something of a flood of new operatic ventures. These haven't been altogether successful; the development of a British operatic tradition has been hard won. British composers have long been fascinated by opera as a medium, but between the Wars works such as the operas of Goossens, Collingwood's *Macbeth*, Coates' *Pickwick* and even—a precursor of Britten's *Curlew River*—Clarence Raybould's chamber opera based on *Sumida River*, achieved performances but never established themselves. No one would dispute the importance of Britten's achievement in establishing a viable operatic tradition since the Second World War, and this is the background against which the emerging generation has been writing with *performance* in mind in a practical way.

Problems with libretti have been causes of a number of operatic failures. Neither Richard Rodney Bennett nor Gordon Crosse has lived up to early promise, though Bennett's *The Mines of Sulphur* is a gripping and stageworthy piece that has been successfully toured abroad. Thea Musgrave's recent *The Voice of Ariadne* was beautifully scored and featured a sensitive use of electronics, but ultimately failed dramatically and the libretto must bear the blame. On a more modest scale, however, those composers who have written children's operas—Bennett, Crosse, Williamson, Bryan Kelly, Trevor Hold—have had considerable success. Many composers have written operas, and achieved the occasional broadcast (such as Philip Cannon's *Morvoren*) and more frequent but less publicised local performances. These include David Barlow's *David and Bathsheba*, Francis Burt's operas (performed

16

in Germany), David Dorward's *Tonight Mrs Morrison* and John Purser's *The Undertaker* and *The Bell*.

It is most encouraging to learn of a number of major operatic projects while preparing this book. Derek Bourgeois' *Rumpelstiltskin*, David Barlow's *The Selfish Giant* (for school children), Christopher Steel's *Odysseus* and Thomas Wilson's *Confessions of a Justified Sinner* are examples of works in progress from tried and respected composers. Nor should the new and vital development of music-theatre be ignored. Taking their cue from the work of Maxwell Davies and Birtwistle, other music-theatre works such as Nicola Lefanu's *Antiworld* (given in London at the Cockpit Theatre in 1972) and Bernard Rands' *Serena* show that musico-dramatic ambitions can achieve practical outcome in an economical way and with the composer fully involved in the practical problems of composition and production.

Having watched a composer develop over a period of time, one has to make a constant effort to adjust one's assessment of him in the light of his latest work. For example, I remember how exciting Goehr's *The Deluge* seemed at the time it appeared, but as Guy Protheroe points out, how comparatively unsuccessful this and other early works now seem in the light of the whole oeuvre. Goehr has become a major international figure. An American critic reviewing a recording of his String Quartet No 2 in *High Fidelity* wrote recently: 'the Olympian world of Beethoven's last quartets is reborn here in modern guise'.

If the uninitiated listener were to try to get to grips with the younger generation of composers via the wrong work, he could well be deterred rather than encouraged to further investigation. For example, Bedford's *Piece for Mo* came as a major shock to me when I first heard it, and it is still not a piece that I can listen to with any pleasure. It highlights a problem of some importance when dealing with the avant-garde. With some very noisy or dense avant-garde scores the limits of many listeners' physical receptivity to the proceedings may be a problem not sufficiently appreciated.

Highly talented performers of new music have emerged in the last decade, and it is almost solely owing to their efforts that the present quantity of new music is heard: groups such as the London Sinfonietta and the Fires of London, and solo performers such as sopranos Dorothy Dorow (who moved abroad and is no longer active in Britain), Mary Thomas and Jane Manning, clarinettist

Alan Hacker, and a variety of talented pianists some of whom are also composers, such as Roger Smalley, John Ogdon, Roger Woodward, John McCabe and Robert Sherlaw Johnson. The BBC continues to present a large range of new music, and local radio is also beginning to feature the music of local composers—this has been an experiment particularly successful in the Humberside area (12). Of course, universities and colleges of music are also continuing sources of activity. Particularly encouraging is the continuing rapprochement between 'pop' and 'serious' styles.

Although the unprecedented number of composers now writing in this country (a recent estimate put it at about five hundred) (22) are achieving performances, their work is making little impact on the regular repertoire of our orchestras, and this is probably the most problematic aspect of an otherwise encouraging scene. Even conductors who might consider playing such works are put off by the sheer volume of available music and lack of time. And although a good selection of works has been recorded commercially (as may be seen from the discography in this book), a large number of outstanding scores still require attention. In particular it is less than satisfactory that no major works by David Blake, David Ellis, Jonathan Harvey or Robin Holloway are available, and I am surprised that no one has given thought to recording Philip Cannon's outstanding prize-winning String Quartet.

Even as this book was being prepared, other new composers have had significant works performed, notably John Buller and David Rowland, while Barry Guy is making an important contribution in both jazz and composed styles. These composers will surely feature in any later edition of this book, and the lesson to the reader is to take an active interest in all new music.

In this book you are offered nearly a hundred composers of quality, writing in a great variety of styles. They all have music of value to offer. In most cases with a little effort it will be possible to hear at least some of the music on tape or disc. Do so. Your musical horizons will be pleasurably enlarged. If you are a performer, you will be expanding your art and helping the tree to continue fruiting. This is an exciting musical age.

L.F.

The Problem of Communication—Two Solutions: Thea Musgrave and Gordon Crosse

LESLIE EAST

For the composer who adopts serialism or any type of genuine atonality, the problem is the same, whether he or she is a Musgrave, a Crosse or a Schoenberg. Remove the articulative procedures of tonality and the traditional forms are no longer viable: the dramatic essence of tonal structures will have disappeared.

The search for an equally dramatic alternative has been a fundamental concern of many British composers who emerged in the Fifties and Sixties. The solution could not be imposed, it had to grow from within the composer's idiom. Many intuitively recognised that the dramatic essence of conflict and reconciliation existed in the original meaning of 'concerto', to strive or struggle, implying, in particular, a contest between unequal forces.

Thea Musgrave (born in 1928) and Gordon Crosse (born in 1937) are two composers for whom the concerto format provided a liberating influence. Both were blessed with an outstanding gift for lyricism; both adopted serialism as an essential discipline, adapted it to their needs and then abandoned its strict application; both have graduated, when it suits them, from a precisely notated ambience into a more luxuriant, more fluid orbit of free tempi, indeterminate pitches and random note orders. The abstract drama that both have explored in purely instrumental pieces seems to have eased their way towards the natural outlet of opera. Investigation of the ways and means of abstract instrumental drama has enabled both Musgrave and Crosse to find and develop an independent voice, an individualism that will—in fact, already has done in Musgrave's case—reap the benefits in further operatic essays.

Thea Musgrave took more than a decade to find a truly individual voice; once discovered, it proved to be a voice of uncommon richness and strength. As so often with composers, an opera provided the turning-point, in this case Musgrave's first full-length opera,

The Decision (1964–5). In the succeeding eight years, Musgrave's individual vein of musical resource nurtured a body of works remarkable as much for the variety and freshness of the invention as for the consistency and integrity of the musical thought behind it. The dozen-or-so major compositions from the second and third Chamber Concertos of 1966 to the opera *The Voice of Ariadne*, premièred in 1974, represent a unique achievement in the music of her generation. The works in the canon are concerned with a common ideal: the search for and exploration of a viable dramatic form for abstract instrumental music. This ideal has been pursued with great single-mindedness and the result has been a strongly integrated corpus with well-defined lines of development, culminating and coalescing in an operatic outlet. Nevertheless, each constituent work proposes an individual slant on this ideal, and develops the implications of the ideal in its own terms, according to the size and character of the medium.

Integrity is the keynote of Musgrave's artistic development. For a composer born in 1928 and raised in the rather conservative and insular atmosphere of a British university music department (Edinburgh), the explosion of styles and techniques that marked the early Fifties—the Webern discovery, the 'Darmstadt experience'—could have proved more of a debilitating than an inspiring influence. When Musgrave went to Paris in 1950 on a postgraduate scholarship, Stravinsky and Bartók were as new to her as Schoenberg, Webern and Dallapiccola, let alone Stockhausen and Boulez. That she was moved by such rapidly widening horizons yet able to remain untainted by the more extreme fashionable elements is as much due to her own strength of character as to the sobering influence of Nadia Boulanger's teaching. Since those apprentice years, Musgrave has always enjoyed a familiarity with and full understanding of vanguard experiments and discoveries, yet has never needed to jump onto the bandwagon nor indeed slavishly to resist its temptations. Instead, she has incorporated and adopted such techniques—serialism, free tempi and rhythm, and the use of electronic tape—only when her natural development has led her that way and the expressive need arisen.

Her early works, for instance, show a gradual movement towards serial technique. She started with a thorough grounding in compositional craft from Hans Gál in Edinburgh and Boulanger in Paris. From Boulanger, Musgrave learnt the fundamental principles of discipline and economy, 'the importance of every bar' as Musgrave herself has acknowledged. (239) With an acute sense of colour and textural balance and secure in her technique and the structures to which it was applied, Musgrave was able to indulge the natural pull towards free chromaticism.

In the works following the diatonic and tonal *Cantata for a Summer's Day* (1954), her first major success, chromaticism was rooted by tonal centres and ostinato patterning; melodic lines became more angular and less consciously 'singable' so that for a short period Musgrave's instrumental lyricism carried more conviction than the vocal variety. In the terse three-movement String Quartet of 1958, the leaning towards serialism is tempered by a Bartókian exploration of closely interweaving chromatic cells, from which distinctive ostinato motifs are natural offspring. The melodies, such as they are, are rigorously instrumental in character. Yet Musgrave's first fully serial piece (still tinged with tonal triads and reverberating held pedal notes) was a setting for high voice and piano of a poem attributed to William Dunbar, *A Song for Christmas* (1958), a colourful declamatory dramatic *scena*; and she followed this with the equally colourful *Triptych* for tenor and orchestra (1959). This strongly contrasted setting of Chaucer's 'Merciles Beaute' immediately shows the composer's personal adaptation of serialism. The absence of literal repetition in the first part is compensated by the more intuitively perceived unifications of serial technique: the simultaneous presentation of the twelve-note series and its inversion at the opening, and the use of the inversion of the original melodic line for the return of 'Your eyen will slay me suddenly' (compare figure 10 in the score with figure 2). In the second part, the demands of the text dictate the distinctly unserial repetition of single notes by the tenor and it is left to the orchestra to create the chromatic atmosphere by reinterpreting the single-note repetitions as block chords in a climax of considerable force. If the third part, a lighter scherzo movement, is less convincing it is perhaps because of its more colouristic background, an exotic percussive continuum which threatens to undermine the solo's lyricism, yet is thwarted by some warm sustained writing for horns and trumpets.

Musgrave's next two important works, the *Colloquy* for violin and piano and the Trio for flute, oboe and piano (both 1960), have long-term significance for reasons other than the fluid serial application which they display, but, since it is this very application and the idiom it creates that is the cornerstone of the distinctive style that emerged later, it may be useful here to highlight some of its crucial features. First, Musgrave is very careful to define subjects or themes by rather more than their intrinsic intervallic character. She does this by means of distinctive dynamics and rhythms so that, while the repetitions allowed by serial technique may be backwards or upside down or both, they remain immediately perceptible. Secondly, such strong characterisation of subjects that develop through the variation techniques of serialism makes the ritornello structure employed in the Trio and in movements I and II of *Colloquy* (as well as the first part of *Triptych*) more vital. Thirdly, both works reveal a fascinating and remarkably successful reconciliation of the extreme limitations of the material—and the devices of canon and inversion with which it is treated—with the composer's natural lyricism.

The strict serial phase lasted no more than two years. Yet it was the natural outcome of Musgrave's development until that time and it provided a discipline of lasting value. It also revealed the first seeds of Musgrave's dramatic instrumental style as the use of a serial idiom had demanded strongly contrasted musical gestures in both the definition of motifs and themes and the formal structuring of a composition. In the outer movements of the String Quartet, for example, two subjects are distinguished by their own intervallic and rhythmic characters which alone would have provided ample conflict; Musgrave compounds this, however, by violently contrasting the tempi of these ideas, thus creating a more dramatic development through their confrontation. In the third episode of the Trio (figure 12 in the score) there is a sharp contrast made between the piano's percussive style and the soothing, sustained flute and oboe counterpoints. Such confrontations are taken further in the compositions that followed. The *Monologue* for piano (also dating from 1960) introduces the String Quartet's accumulative climactic feeling into the more variously contrasted sectional form of a fantasia on a twelve-note theme; the conflict arises out of the theme's different treatments and the tensions created by the apparent acceleration through the piece to a 'tumultuous' rhetorical coda. The Serenade for flute, clarinet, harp, viola and cello (1961) for the first time presents contrasting tempi simultaneously, or rather creates an illusion of contrasting tempi by offsetting jerky, ostinato-based passages against sustained, lyrical ones in the first movement, and melisma against held notes in the second movement. The First Chamber Concerto (1962) again takes the alternation of contrasting tempi as its main generative agent in a one-movement structure.

The period 1961–65, though distinguished by some well-written pieces, does mark a hiatus in Musgrave's development. This came about through force of circumstance rather than any temporary loss of direction. It was a period when she gave extra-mural lectures for London University; when two substantial choral works were commissioned from her (*The Phoenix and the Turtle* for the Proms in 1962 and *The Five Ages of Man* for the Norwich Triennial Festival in 1964); when she produced some attractive music for children; and when her imagination was fired to embark on her first full-length opera without commission or prospect of performance, yet virtually to the exclusion of everything else for two years. *The Decision*, to a libretto by Maurice Lindsay, may have fulfilled a need at that time to write something 'all-consuming', to get something out of her system. Certainly she admits that it was a struggle to maintain stylistic consistency in completing the opera.

The Decision has little to do with what came after. It has perhaps only one feature in common with the series of concertos that followed—the E flat pedal note that heralds the opera's unique flashback scenes; pedal notes are an important element in the concertos and E flat happens to be the prominent pedal in both the Concerto for Orchestra (1967) and *Night Music* (1969). However, the wrestling with concrete dramatic problems in *The Decision* obviously contributed to the desire to explore dramatic qualities in abstract instrumental terms.

In an article in the *Musical Times* (245) Musgrave has explained the origins of this concern and described how it was developed in different works. The succession of concertante pieces was not preconceived and the elements of the new style were not new except in the way they were combined. Looking back from the Viola Concerto of 1973 to the Second and Third Chamber Concertos of 1966, it is possible to see not only that, rather obviously the different works in the canon have something striking in common and that different aspects are developed in various ways from piece to piece, but also that the freedoms, the innovations that Musgrave explored grew naturally out of the 'seeds' in the pre-1966 works as well as logically out of musical sounds and situations she wished to exploit.

The dramatic concept varies from work to work. Musgrave has said that 'in several works there is almost a theatrical element

23

which uses the players like *dramatis personae*'. In the Second Chamber Concerto (scored for the versatile *Pierrot Lunaire* combination), a 'sophisticated argument' is constantly interrupted by the Rollo figure (of Charles Ives's invention) represented on the viola, which trivialises motifs by turning them into popular tunes, provoking the other instruments into 'joining' rather than 'beating' him in order to assuage the conflict. The rebel in the Concerto for Orchestra is the first clarinet which impudently interrupts and gradually subdues a frenetic orchestral climax; in order to entice other soloists to join the rebellion he offers tasty morsels of suitable musical material (distinctively characterised motifs) that the others fall for and swallow. The Clarinet Concerto (1968) develops this principle in setting up a sort of battle of wits between soloist and conductor for control of different orchestral sections. The orchestral violas in the Viola Concerto, already promoted to the first violins' station, are so inspired by their solo compatriot's virtuoso prominence that they become first subversive, then domineering, and neither soloist nor conductor is able fully to quell their enthusiasm.

In this and the other later concertante works, the drama grows less out of such explicit conflicts and more from the subtle contrasts of matching tone colours and the different types of musical material and gesture to which they are suited. The chamber orchestral *Night Music* features two horns first in close lyrical partnership, then in dramatic opposition in which other instruments are caught up. This contrast is emphasised by the horn players' physical movement from a central position to opposite sides of the orchestra for the conflict and eventually one hornist disappears from the platform, still playing, reluctant to give up his declamatory style to the returning *Andante misterioso* which began the work. This striking physical manifestation of the musical idea sprang from simple beginnings in the Third Chamber Concerto in which the dominance of one instrument over its fellows at any one point is emphasised by the player standing; Musgrave felt that, where standing was possible, the player would respond with more freedom and virtuosity. The clarinet rebel in the Concerto for Orchestra stands to heighten the effect of his rebellion and the Clarinet Concerto has the soloist actually moving to the different concertante groups he has to play with—though this grew out of the purely practical need for ease of coordination. The force of the contrasted musical ideas is increased by their emer-

24

gence from specifically localised areas on the platform. The Horn Concerto (1971) goes further with this spatial effect, capitalising on the idea in *Night Music*, by relating the soloist's virtuosity to the music of the orchestral horns: under the soloist's command they form a breakaway concertante group and, after one has played offstage, three move out into the auditorium to enhance the effects of space and distance on horn timbre. The soloist's identification with the orchestral violas in the Viola Concerto encourages a similar exploration of matched tone colours.

As a sidelight on this concern with subtle colour contrast, Musgrave has produced two works for solo instrument and pre-recorded electronic tape. Both *Soliloquy I* (1969) for guitar and *From One to Another* (1970) for viola pit live soloist against the processed sounds of the same instrument on tape. As if to emphasise that the processing was necessary and the use of tape not merely a gimmick, *From One to Another* grew out of a purely instrumental duo, *Elegy* for viola and cello, written when Musgrave was Guest Professor at the University of California in 1970 and, like all the solo viola pieces, dedicated to her husband, Peter Mark. All the material for the tape piece comes from *Elegy*—notably the recurring chord motif that opens both pieces (and appears again in *The Voice of Ariadne*)—but, developed anew, it sounds quite different. Musgrave creates a dramatic dialogue between past (the tape) and present (live soloist) ranging from blatant confrontation to gentle interweaving and vitalised by the tensions of coordination with the tape by the soloist. (In her Beethoven bi-centenary tribute, *Memento Vitae* of 1969–70, there is another past/present conflict in the form of a commentary on and development of quotations from Beethoven's works, the timpani this time acting as anarchist.)

The initial impetus for Musgrave's use of tape came from the subject of the ballet *The Beauty and the Beast*, which she wrote for the Scottish Theatre Ballet in 1969, where the supernatural element is represented on tape amid an otherwise straightforward orchestral score. The viability of tape in expressing the 'other-worldly' is more cogently exploited in the chamber opera *The Voice of Ariadne*, composed between 1971 and 1973 for the Alde-burgh Festival. A Henry James story was transformed by Musgrave and her librettist, Amalia Elguera, into a suitable vehicle for the natural use of taped sound as a dramatic extension of one character's mental agonisings. The Count, infatuated with the ideal of

25

the perfect woman, the abandoned Ariadne, the pedestal of whose statue has been discovered in his garden, is reconciled with his wife only when he realises the parallel predicament of Ariadne and the Countess and when the dramatic musical conflict between past and present, imagined and real, taped voice (Ariadne) and live voice (the Countess) is resolved in Act III.

Significantly, *The Voice of Ariadne* contains a synthesis of Musgrave's compositional concerns of the previous decade, a decade in which she established and developed a voice unique in British music. The logical use of tape for dramatic means, the prominence of particular solo instruments to underline some aspect of character or illustrate the conflicts of a particular situation, the freedom of timing that so enhances expressive moments in the drama and the impressive grasp of act-long structures in which theatrical tension is built with unerring judgement—all these are the product of Musgrave's dramatic gestural style.

At the root of this style's success are three important interrelated factors. When Musgrave had evolved a natural musical idiom by the early Sixties, she was brave enough to undo the metrical fetters that held her imagination in check and ingenious enough to devise and go on inventing new time controls through clear notational innovations. Yet the new freedom of her stratified musical thought, its dramatic implications and the fresh, uninhibited attitudes it provoked in performers, had still to be kept under control lest anarchy destroy the coherence of her larger structures. She achieved this by always maintaining the harmonic control of her early Sixties idiom. Look carefully at any page of free-tempo notation in the solo concertos, the Concerto for Orchestra, *Night Music* or the Second and Third Chamber Concertos, and one will see that the harmonies, no matter how complicated in themselves or apparently diffused in their deportment, are constructed so that the freedoms will work without destroying the intended harmonic impression. Allied to this harmonic control is an individual structural sense that almost unfailingly captures the right proportions of balance and progression through a multi-sectioned, single-movement form. The way the rebellious clarinet and its fellow concertante conspirators propel the still-protesting orchestra into the final, breathless *Presto* of the Concerto for Orchestra is a splendid example of this sensibility. Finally, Musgrave is possessed of an acute ear for orchestral balance, textural clarity and novel tone colours—the matching of clarinet

26

with piano accordion in the Clarinet Concerto is particularly arresting—and her immediately attractive, sensuous scoring does much to clarify the thematic processes and natural lyricism of her music.

If *The Decision* was a hiatus or a turning-point in Musgrave's evolution, then *The Voice of Ariadne* was both an end and a beginning. It will be fascinating to see if and how Musgrave's sure dramatic manner will develop further.

Ariadne is more than a coincidental link between Musgrave and Gordon Crosse. Like Musgrave's opera, Crosse's Concertante for oboe and twelve players, premièred at Cheltenham in 1972, is a product of a phase of strong individualism; but, unlike its partial namesake, *Ariadne* marks what one hopes is the beginning of that phase. Again, an opera provided the turning-point. Crosse's *The Story of Vasco*, first performed in March 1974 by Sadler's Wells Opera but composed between 1968 and 1971, proved to be rather over-indulgent, weak in dramatic tension but full of warm lyricism. Yet it may be its very over-indulgence that is Crosse's salvation as there are signs that in *Vasco* Crosse came to terms with and reconciled the disparate influences on his creative personality. That he was able to do so is due to two thoroughly individual strengths: a consistent ideal of the drama to be obtained from the conflict of widely differing musical elements or styles; and his natural inclination towards unification through an all-pervasive motivic development.

The roots of the latter are to be found in his earliest models. Bartók, Webern and the medieval techniques that Crosse developed in common with Peter Maxwell Davies (drawing strength from Davies's example), all worked on unifying principles involving exhaustive exploration of the possibilities inherent in small melodic cells. The earliest recognised pieces, dating from 1959 to 1961, work out the specific influences while developing this technique in Crosse's own terms. This bore fruition in the *Corpus Christi Carol*, Op. 5 (1961, revised 1963) where the miniature tension/resolution situation created by the cell of minor third-tritone-minor third pervades the appropriately sparse vocal line, leaving the discreet accompanying forces to explore the full implications of the basic cell in more dramatic intervening commentaries. The drama is relative, however, to the fragility of the vocal part. It was Goffredo

27

Petrassi, with whom Crosse studied at the Accademia di Santa
Cecilia, Rome, for a short period in 1962, who pointed out the
limitations of this particular vein and suggested trying something
as different as Crosse knew possible in the scherzo of the *Concerto
da Camera*. The result, in Crosse's words (in a note accompanying
the recording), was 'violent, spiky and dynamic' and 'the remain-
der of the concerto became a kind of dialogue' between this and
his earlier 'calm, lyrical and static' manner of the first movement.
Something of the dramatic opposition of styles in the Concerto
can be seen in many of Crosse's more successful works of later
years; it is an external structural impetus that complements the
internal motivic workings. A seven-note series forms the basis of
all the Concerto's material and Crosse's constructional techniques
—including canon so close as to border on heterophony and overlapping sonorities that could almost be a colouristic equivalent—
clarify its development and underline its unification in a manner
reminiscent of Dallapiccola. The contrast of 'lyrical' violin with
'spiky' wind and percussion seems relatively unimportant here
but is one which Crosse returns to explore in the Violin Concerto
No. 2 of 1970.

On his return from Rome, Crosse undertook research into
fifteenth-century music—an interest entirely in keeping with the
development of his own music—with the eminent scholar, Frank
Harrison, but from there his career took off on a different track
when he was appointed Tutor Organiser to Industry by the
Workers Educational Association in 1963. With hindsight it is
possible to see that this and Crosse's association with Britten
through the Aldeburgh Festival combined to introduce a new
influence on his music. The experience of teaching (he also became
extra-mural staff tutor at Birmingham University in 1964) and of
writing music for children—especially the disarmingly tuneful
yet harmonically tough *Meet My Folks!* (1964), written for
Aldeburgh—undoubtedly led him to seek a broader-based popular
appeal without compromising his personal idiom. His successful
reconciliation of direct appeal—memorable melody, bright and
exciting instrumental textures—with his quasi-serial motivic
technique produced just the right balance of simple surface and
sophisticated depths to make further works for children—*Ahmet
the Woodseller* (1965) and *The Demon of Adachigahara* (1968)—and
the 'nocturnal cycle' *Changes* (1965–66), for amateur and semi-
professional choir and orchestra, immediate in language yet taxing

28

and rewarding to perform. *Changes*, a celebration of and meditation on the 'resonances' of bells in life and death, is significant in this respect. Its first part, tightly argued and symphonic, is none the less full of brilliant attractive sonorities and the whole work is laced through with and ingeniously unified (yet diversified) by the treatment of an ascending five-note figure heard at the outset and thematically recognisable at many later points.*

In *Changes*, Crosse's admiration for Britten's music was shown, despite the work's evident individuality, in the manipulation of diverse texts, of children's voices and in some aspects of word setting such as phrase repetition—though the latter had been more noticeable in *For the Unfallen* (1963), emphasised by the Brittenes-que tenor, horn and strings combination. Where Britten had a decided influence on Crosse was in Crosse's first opera, *Purgatory* (1966), which set W. B. Yeats's play with only minor cuts in the text. *The Turn of the Screw* 'was an inevitable and very conscious model' and in *Purgatory* there is a parallel with the model's tonal use of a twelve-note series. The idiom, however, is more distinctly Crosse's own, his two fundamental strengths ensuring cogency through apt musical/dramatic parallels. The threads of tension in Yeats's 'already musical' drama are mirrored in Crosse's pervasive motivic building, the moments when the root of the drama is suggested being underlined by the motifs' coalescence into a full twelve-note series (e.g. vocal score, bars 545–50); and the renewed tension, after the old man kills his son in the forlorn hope that this act will release his own mother's soul from purga-tory, is created in the dramatic conflict of tonal triads gradually infiltrating the predominant atonality.

Purgatory is an impressive achievement for a composer under thirty: a first opera rare in its sustained theatrical potency. All the more disappointing then that the works immediately follow-ing—among them *Purgatory*'s companion one-acter, *The Grace of Todd* (1967)—should so neglect the organic fusion of idea, develop-ment and dramatic gesture that is *Purgatory*'s strength.

The Story of Vasco—drawn from Georges Schehade's play with an extra lacing of Ted Hughes's black humour—does little to retrieve the situation; Crosse chooses to pigeonhole characters with a particular type of music, declines to develop the majority as anything other than 'cut-out' figures, and, consequently, there is

* For a fuller discussion of this, see notes by Crosse and Anthony Payne accompanying Argo recording, ZRG 656, 1970.

a minimum of the dramatic character interaction that opera needs. The one exception is Vasco's interrogation scene based on a sequence of variations. The enterprising dramatic conflict and variation processes in *Some Marches on a Ground* (1970), using material from *Vasco*, suggest that Crosse felt the need for further expansion.

During the composition of *Vasco*, however, Crosse managed to complete his Second Violin Concerto (1969), this time scoring for full orchestra, and it is the Concerto far more than the opera that seems to point a way ahead based on a synthesis of established strengths. For instance, the bipartite Concerto presents dramatic opposition of different elements or styles on various levels: unassertive first part against aggressive second; lyrical against bravura writing for the soloist; motivic contrasted with thematic presentation of material; mosaic opposed to rhapsodic development, static to dynamic. Then there is the formal organisation, an amalgam of medieval carol (Refrain I-Verse-Refrain II) and variation form for the first part, more fluid, linked fantasias on material from each carol section for the second. The whole culminates in a quiet epilogue in which Ockeghem's chanson, *Ma Maîtresse*, is quoted with its original harmonies, thus clarifying (some say unnecessarily) the derivation of a six-note *cantus firmus* in the carol form's Verse section. The Concerto's basic material (some of it from *Vasco*)—three or four short motifs in Refrain I, the Verse's *cantus firmus*, and two 'simple tunes' in Refrain II—is strikingly economic, yet Crosse's invention never flags thanks to the familiar all-pervasive motivic working and the revitalising formal expansion and dramatic contrast provided by part two. Crosse avoids the heroic virtuosity of the traditional concerto but finds viable dramatic substitutes on several levels.

With the Violin Concerto, Crosse made stylistic incongruity a positive virtue for dramatic ends. After the completion of *Vasco*, he wrote two major works, both in effect dramatic *scenas*, that benefited enormously from this achievement. The first was *Memories of Morning: Night*, a monodrama for mezzo-soprano and orchestra, commissioned by the BBC and finished in July 1971. The text, drawn from Jean Rhys's novel *The Wide Sargasso Sea*, is a study of the madness of the first Mrs Rochester in *Jane Eyre*, set against first a West Indian background, then the Thornfield fire. The text's subjective intensity and the opportunity for 'local colour' which took the shape of an orchestral equivalent of the Mexican

'Mariachi' band, inspired Crosse to produce over a thirty-minute canvas a vivid projection of a single character, made the more vivid because all the composer's developmental powers and orchestral eloquence is concentrated on a single aspect. The dramatic content is underlined by an abstract musical conflict between local colour (band) and conventional forces (horn and strings), between the first part's dance rhythms, melodies and phrase lengths and Crosse's development, distortion and expansion of these in the Interlude and second part (a process directly related to that of the Violin Concerto). Elements of improvisation, of spatial platform setting, of non-musical participation by the players are not quirks of fashion but integrated reinforcements of Crosse's singular vision.

So successful was this vein that Crosse was able to produce, in *Ariadne*, a purely instrumental extension of it. The solo oboe is the protagonist; the conflicts of the Ariadne legend are musically reflected in the conflict of diatonic and chromatic harmony; local colour (this time an extraordinarily evocative re-creation of Cretan folk music) reverberates against atmospheric background and motivic blocks of sound with fragmented solos. Unifying the multi-sectioned, basically slow-fast-slow structure is the long-limbed lyricism of the oboe's solo lines, distinctly diatonic despite occasional twelve-note aspirations (as at figure 59).

In *Ariadne*, *Memories of Morning: Night* and the Violin Concerto, drama, colour and organisation are inextricably fused; the charge of undigested eclecticism is dispelled, an ear for the apt musical gesture or colour in a particular situation recognised. Crosse's next venture into full-length opera could not have better credentials.

31

Ronald Stevenson

COLIN SCOTT-SUTHERLAND

The artist of talent links the present with the future. The truly great artist, the visionary, relates the future to the past. The thought, a profound one for which I claim no credit since the words are, I think, Hans Keller's, has some significance in a book devoted to the present trends in British music. It has considerable relevance in an evaluation of the work of the Scottish composer Ronald Stevenson, whose music reflects a deep understanding of the inexhaustible powers of the system of tonality that has developed over the years of the great masters and its continuing importance in the context of an era of discovery that has brought not only new and troubled discord but disorientation, disintegration and the fashion for the spectacular at the expense of truth.

Stevenson's output is profuse, and includes an epic Choral Symphony, two Piano Concertos, a Cello Concerto, several song cycles and choral cycles and the longest single movement in contemporary piano literature, to say nothing of well over two hundred songs. All these works demonstrate a mature creative intellect as well as prolific inventive powers. The originality of his work lies not in its strangeness, but in its individuality in an age of conformity, and in its sheer musicality.

Ronald Stevenson was born in Blackburn, Lancashire, in 1928 into a working-class background with antecedents both Scottish and Welsh. From these origins has been born a social conscience that ranges widely and is expressed in all his work from *Anger Dance* (for guitar) to *The Continents* (Piano Concerto No. 2). His earliest musical experiences were of the singing of his father, a fine amateur tenor, and of recordings of John McCormack. He began piano lessons at the age of eight, and composition (settings of the words of Moore, Scott and Byron, a choice significantly unusual) at fourteen. In his studies at the Royal Manchester College of Music and the Accademia di Santa Cecilia, Rome, to which he gained scholarships, piano and composition developed simultaneously, with reciprocal benefits manifest in the power and brilliance of his own piano writing and in the bravura and expressive rubato of his playing.

Most of his earliest compositions were written for the keyboard, although several were later orchestrated or scored for other instrumental combinations. They include three Sonatinas for piano which show clearly the development of an individual strength of character and an original instrumental technique; and such pieces as *Variation-Study on a Chopin Waltz*, two *Eclogues* (*Sumer is i-cumen in* and *The Ploughboy*), Chopin's two A flat Waltzes transcribed one for right hand alone, and the other for left hand alone, then combined (the affinity with Godowsky is even more apparent in the later piece, *Canonic Caprice on 'The Bat'*, a fiendishly difficult work).

Early in his student days he encountered the music of Busoni (on whose work he has since written a deeply penetrating book) who became a kind of master *in absentia*. Stevenson's practical knowledge of the piano and the influence of Busoni's music and aesthetics proved to be the principal forces guiding the early progress of his creative work up to the point where the present survey begins. Amongst these early compositions are a three-movement Violin Sonata (based on a twelve-note row), numerous settings of Blake, *Berceuse Symphonique* for orchestra, *Prelude, Fugue and Fantasy* (of which the First Piano Concerto is a reworking), *A Twentieth Century Music Diary* (fifteen aphoristic movements including two-part inventions, strict canon in quadruple tonality, quasi-dodecaphonic variations and serial rhythms, each illustrating, with reference to Busonian aesthetics, the paths of twentieth-century music), and some strikingly original piano transcriptions of music as diverse as that of Bach and Van Dieren, Mozart and Alban Berg. A recent example is the *Peter Grimes Fantasy* in fantasy-fugue form.

On Christmas Eve 1960 Ronald Stevenson conceived the idea of a variation structure built on the musical fragment D E flat C B, (D S C H—a nucleus derived from the initials of Shostakovich to whom the completed work is dedicated), using the virtuosic form of the passacaglia. The first few variations, conceived as pure polyphony without the piano primarily in mind, revealed extensive possibilities and, as so often in his work, the cell-like fragment assumed a subtle motivic significance, begetting a huge and urgent creative expansion. Although the origins of the passacaglia form lie in the dance, great keyboard masters such as Frescobaldi and

Buxtehude used it as a vehicle for the display of contrapuntal skill. In the same way the completed *Passacaglia on DSCH* which by the Spring of 1962 had become an eighty-minute-long single movement for piano demonstrates a command, rare enough today, of polyphonic device, fugal structure and harmonic complexity. The idea of a work of such dimensions, based throughout on a reiterated four-note ground, is a forbidding one: yet its ingenuity, its technical skill and masterly handling of the keyboard drew the attention of musicians, while the first performance drew an enthusiastic and immediate response from the listeners. Both Walton and Alan Bush wrote warmly of the work, 'at the conclusion of which', wrote the latter, 'I was so carried away that I could scarcely speak at all.' (272)

With the introductory statement of the kernel of the work, the ground bass, the composer constructs thereon a vast architectonic framework in which the strictest and freest forms are combined in an enormous fresco. A Sonata, whose three-movement form is telescoped, with second movement becoming second subject, is followed by a Waltz-Intermezzo in Rondo form (with variety of key in the episodes). An eight-part dance suite, with repeated jig, concludes with a Polonaise and leads to a Dirge (based on the seventeenth-century Scottish piobearachd (pibroch) 'Cumha na Cloinne' (Lament for the Children) by Patrick Mor MacCrimmon —a dark flowering of un-polemical nationalism drawn from the wellsprings of Scottish cultural history. This slow movement continues with a quiet set of arabesque variations and a Nocturne (with bitonal elements) from which emerges a passage of syrinx-like *glissandi* played first on the keys, and then on the strings, of the piano. *Arpeggi-glissandi* (a pianistic innovation achieved by *glissandi* between and over silently depressed superimposed thirds) end the slow section which is disturbed by a clamorous fanfare. The massive warlike section that follows like a scherzo makes use of nationalist elements drawn from Africa, from Asia (the march theme derived from the speech intonation of the classical slogan of 1917 Russia 'Peace, Bread and the Land') and from Spain.

A series of piano studies central to the whole work and employing almost every technical device succeeds this, culminating in a triple fugue, with BACH and the Dies Irae as second and third subjects. The Passacaglia concludes with an extended *adagissimo barocco* set of variations with the theme finally given out in block

34

chords. The peroration is broken off and the work ends in quiet reflection.

The *Passacaglia on DSCH* stands bridging an important moment in the composer's life—his return to Scotland from South Africa where he had occupied the post of senior lecturer in music at Cape Town University. It is difficult to avoid some kind of symbology for, consciously or no, the DSCH motif, like the keystone set in the arch of a bridge, relates the music on either side of the composition and epitomises, with its mirror-like reflection in the rising and falling semitone, the harmonic and melodic character of Ronald Stevenson's earlier music, and prophesying much that was later to develop in his work. From this nucleus the work unfolds, Janus-like, touching at some point almost all the motivating experiences encountered in his work and foreshadowing the liberating influences that he had already begun to derive from folk sources and which form a perfect foil to the obsessive tensions of the semitonal step which mark his earlier work. Of the necessity for such a release the composer himself was not unaware, though perhaps unconsciously. For the first work to follow the Passacaglia was a choral cycle *Songs into Space* to words of Whitman. And after beginning the equally panoramic Second Piano Concerto with the DSCH motif (and ironing out its semitonal tensions deliberately in the final bars by raising and lowering the second and fourth notes of the motif), he wrote the expansive song cycle *Songs of Quest* (John Davidson).

To the conception of a 'world music' that he had embodied in the Passacaglia Ronald Stevenson returns in the Second Piano Concerto subtitled *The Continents* which was commissioned for the 1972 season of Promenade concerts. Like the Passacaglia it has links with South Africa. Its inspiration is found in the poem 'Die Kind' (The Child) by the Afrikaans poet Ingrid Jonker, and, remembering the tragedy of Sharpeville, voices the idea that as the dead child represents the nations of all humanity, so the coalescence of the music of all the continents is the expression of humanity. The five sections of the concerto, with prologue and epilogue, are interlinked in one movement. Its obsessive rhythmic opening, swarming with drum sounds, echoes the DSCH motif and leads, through unharmonised 'droned' pentatony, to the more complex western music of fugal polyphony. A brass fanfare announces the Russian march which is followed by the highly coloured American and Latin American sections in brilliant orchestral dress. The

35

various musics are intertwined in the final section which ends with the DSCH motif broadened to whole tones. 'This concerto,' writes the composer in a programme note, 'is an attempt to write polyglot music in the way that Ezra Pound, T. S. Eliot and Hugh McDiarmid have written polyglot poetry.'

Both the Passacaglia and the Second Piano Concerto show Ronald Stevenson's command in handling large formal structures. But at the same time we are conscious of a care for the minutiae of fine detail which shows the hand of a craftsman. Such songs as 'To the Future' (Soutar), 'Ae Gowden Lyric' (McDiarmid) and 'The Rose of all the World' (McDiarmid) are exquisite miniatures, between ten and twenty bars in length. This care for detail is not confined to the musical content as a glance at any of his finely drawn manuscript scores (in the Scottish Music Archive, Glasgow) will show. I have in my possession a charming piano miniature, some twenty-five bars long, written with elegant clarity on the back of a postcard.

Other facets of his work are reflected in the Passacaglia. His particular concern for the child, in the laments of the Passacaglia and the programme of the Second Piano Concerto, is expressed, with the keen contrast of size and medium, in the short pieces such as *A Wheen Tunes for Bairns to Spiel*, *Three Scots Fairytales* and in the Soutar song '*Day is Dune*'. There are too the simple transcriptions of Delius; the careful editing and transcribing of *The Young Pianist's Grainger* (Schott); and the volume of harp arrangements, *Sounding Strings* (composed for his younger daughter and published by the Welsh Harp Society), which convey to the child, with the skill and touch of a born teacher, his own infectious delight in all that is music.

Stevenson has also evinced an especial concern for the handicapped child. At Garvald School for children in need of special care (at Dolphinton in Peebleshire not far from his own home at West Linton), he has arranged music for the instruments and young players locally available for the annual Christmas concert given to the children. He has also set, in his own translation (itself evidence of his understanding of the needs of these children), a poem of Morgenstern as the school song ('One and All' (1965) for unison children's choir, descant recorder, violin, cello and guitar). He is enthusiastic about the Kodaly concept of music education and has written part-songs for the St Catherine Singers of Blackpool embodying Kodalyan principles. Their conductor, Margaret

Holden, a Royal Manchester College of Music colleague of Stevenson's and a leading exponent of Kodaly, deepened Stevenson's interest in the Hungarian master.

Stevenson's return to the Scottish Border country focused his creative energies on the openly nationalist element in Scottish music. In William Sterling's *Cantus Part Book* of 1639 he chanced upon a melody that contained yet another quasi-symbolic motif which, with its expressive upward leap of a seventh, formed the perfect foil to the semitone. Firstly embodied in *Ne'erday Sang* (piano and later scored for string quartet), this melodic fragment F G E flat became the motivic germ of a work for orchestra, *Keening Sang for a Makar*, in memoriam Francis George Scott (whose initials the fragment also aptly delineates). Originally scored for piano, this was followed by two companion pieces forming a kind of Scottish trilogy: *Heroic Sang* for Hugh McDiarmid, the opening notes of which ring out through the silently depressed bottom octaves of the keyboard with the echoing proud and lonely magic of the Scottish hills; and *Chorale Pibroch* for Sorley MacLean.

Arnold Bax once commented that the professors had done everything in their power to emasculate folksong. It is certainly true that Scottish folksong, with its so often artistically deplorable trimmings, has suffered more than most. To those unrecognised folk origins in Gaelic and Lowland song and in classical pibroch, the music of the pipes, Stevenson directed his energies, finding therein not only an expressive poetic language but one that derived from a virtuosic instrumental tradition. This music, with its gapped scales and microtonal colour, showed links with other musics of Europe and with the East. An earnest of this had also appeared in the Passacaglia, in the pipe lament for the children inserted into its framework shortly before the first performance. MacCrimmon's lament, with its dignity, breadth, nobility and emotive power, foreshadows those aspects of Scottish nationalism —the heroic and the virtuosic—that Stevenson found most significant. The contemporary appositeness of the medieval element lay in its melodic basis and in its virtuosity. And as in the Passacaglia the pibroch's eloquence is controlled by the unifying element, the *urlar* or ground of its variation structure. Thus in the contrasting strains of the pipe music, with its pentatonic and microtonal proclivities, and in the wide leaps of Scottish traditional song, he found unity in diversity and relationships with his own conception of the virtuoso keyboard technique of the nineteenth century which

37

had been influenced in him by Busoni (who, it will be remembered, found like sources of musical inspiration in the culture of the American Indian).

This nationalist element, with its characteristically dour and granitic quality, is expressed in the choral cycle *A Medieval Scottish Triptych*, employing in one song the rarely used Locrian mode. As well as several Scottish folk music settings, the vital *Scots Dance Toccata* for orchestra (in which several traditional dance tunes from Neil Gow's *Repository* are drawn out of an opening *haar* into a Paganini-like polytonal reel of Ivesian complexity), and a pibroch for bagpipe *Calum Salum's Salute to the Seals* (written in Tiree), he has composed several suites for piano based on the folk music of South Uist, Ireland, China and Ghana. All these elements knit into a wider concern for humanity are to be found in the two largest-scale works.

Apart from a fine Harpsichord Sonata (commissioned for the 1968 Harrogate Festival by Alan Cuckston), and a Duo-Sonata for harp and piano (written for Ann Griffiths), Ronald Stevenson has more recently concentrated on works for voice. His songs include early settings of Blake, the *Songs of Innocence*, of which there are nineteen, listed as a cycle for SATB, solo and final chorale, with piano or flute and string quintet; they date from 1948, although the cycle was not finalised until 1965. There are also settings of words by Poe, Tagore, Ho Chi Minh (*Vietnamese Miniatures* for voice and harp), Morgenstern, Emily Brontë, Lancashire dialect poems, and nine delicate Japanese *Haiku*. Scottish poets he has set include Robert Louis Stevenson, Hogg, Alan Bold, Sidney Goodsir Smith, John Davidson, Robert Garioch, and William Soutar. The Gaelic poet Sorley Maclean's *Anns an Airde as an Doimhne* he has set in the original Gaelic in response to a commission from the Greenock Gaelic choir. But the Scottish poet with whom he has shown most affinity is Hugh McDiarmid, a poet in whose work are felt the same contrasts, the flashes of granitic power and lyricism expressed in lines of childlike simplicity. He has chosen to set not so much the early lyrical verses (which Francis George Scott also set), but the later poems. 'I find McDiarmid's later poems full of possibilities for setting in exploratory techniques,' he writes. 'They have a kind of musical dialectic of their own and often build concepts out of emotions, which is what music does.' In 'The Skeleton of the Future' Stevenson relates the four chords of traditional harmony (major, minor,

38

diminished and augmented), to four colours mentioned in the poet's description of Lenin's tomb:

> Red granite and black diorite
> With the blue of the labradorite crystals
> Gleaming like precious stones
> In the light reflected from the snow

The chords are laid out in such a way that the sum of their notes equals a Schoenbergian tone row, but at the same time the wide leaps of the melodic line in ninths (the antithesis of the semitonal step) are influenced by Lowland song types. There is something of both the harshness and the softness of the Scots character in all these songs. The 'sharp sweet smell' of the little white rose permeates 'The Rose of All the World'. A similar melodic line with its eloquent leap of a tenth is found in 'Ae Gowden Lyric'—and at the words 'nane for thee a thochtie sparin'' in 'The Bonnie Broukit Bairn'. 'Bubblyjock' and 'Cophetua' contrast, with their grotesque imagery, with the delicately spun melody line, accompanied by a fragile piano figuration of descending demisemiquavers, of 'The Bobbin Winder', a song of bewitching beauty. One of the biggest of the McDiarmid settings is 'In the Fall', lines from 'In Memoriam James Joyce', in which the poet desires that his lines should, even in inclement times, gleam like the bare hawthorn tree, tinselled with snow like 'a candelabrum of oxidised silver', a line which Stevenson sets in an iridescent pattern of tremolo chords.

Hugh McDiarmid's words are the text of two song cycles: *The Infernal City* (a setting of six songs—one of which uses Sorley Maclean's poem 'Calvary'—with scornful reference to Glasgow) and, one of Stevenson's most lyrical works, *Border Boyhood*. The score of *Border Boyhood*, commissioned by Peter Pears for the Aldeburgh Festival, is inscribed in memory of the patroness Tertia Liebenthal and is a setting of six prose extracts with a central piano intermezzo. The words are a glorification of the sensual beauty of the countryside seen, with the poet's characteristic clarity of vision, through the eyes of youth. The music in turn expresses the composer's own delight in the sharply felt delights of youthful freedom with the nostalgia of retrospect. (*Retrospect* was the title of a very early piano piece.) The cycle opens with a piano figure containing both the upward leap (C sharp/A) and the semitonal tension which seems to represent, coiled like a spring,

39

the pent-up eagerness and joyous energies of youth and the liberating impact of the countryside in late summer and autumn. This opening figure, like Stevenson's other basic germ patterns, is motivic and is the source of the development. The first song sings of 'going through fields hedged in honeysuckle and wild roses, through knee-deep meadowsweet' and at the words 'to the wood' (A/E flat) we sense the mystery of the pristine encounter, the magic experience of youth. If these are the 'occult regions of experience', they are fresh and positive; the pleasures recollected are simple, the music full of a complex simplicity that is inexpressibly beautiful. 'Even the robin hushes his song in these gold pavilions': this eloquent line is echoed in a central piano solo, a nocturne in mood, full of delicate chiaroscuro marked in the score 'spellbound' and redolent of the poetry of the woods of the Langfall. An energetic scherzo, full of rough humour and spirit, is succeeded by the final fugue, 'The Nook of the Night Paths'.

And what of the future? The recently completed *Songs of Quest* (John Davidson) await evaluation after their first performance in Vienna in 1974. And important works are in progress. A Violin Concerto, commissioned by Yehudi Menuhin, has long been formulating in the composer's mind, while the Choral Symphony *Ben Dourain* (using as text McDiarmid's translation of Duncan Ban McIntyre), begun in 1962, is still to be completed.

What qualities make Stevenson what he is? What attributes set him apart? A few facts are incontestable. Since Havergal Brian he is the only nationally known composer of industrial proletarian parentage. He shares the people's and the children's love of melody in an age when most composers renounce it. He is the only composer working in Scotland from folk roots to internationalism. He is one of the few composer/pianists in Britain and the only one in Scotland. He is a 'fugalist' of austerest mastery, yet a colourful harmonist. He is an aristocrat of the mind who also heartily embraces the truly vulgar, the essentially popular: this duality makes him misunderstood. Taking his atavistic apprehension of remote Celtic history as his cultural base he aspires to voice the future of Scottish culture. He is convinced that art reflects and transforms historical reality. If a new realisation of Scottish nationhood is growing, as it appears to be, Stevenson's music will contribute to it; and, in contributing, it may yet link past and future and be assessed as visionary.

Alexander Goehr

GUY PROTHEROE

From the first Alexander Goehr was destined to be a serial composer: in his childhood he was inured in the music of the Second Viennese School, at a time when only a handful of British composers had even begun to come to grips with Schoenberg's developments—and this was in the early Fifties, when the continental avant-garde was already plunged deep into the intricacies of total serialism. Goehr's father, the conductor Walter Goehr, had been a pupil of Schoenberg, and had left Berlin to come to England as a refugee, shortly after his son's birth in 1932.

By the time Alexander Goehr went to study with Richard Hall at the Royal Manchester College of Music, he was able to act as something of a mentor to his fellow-students, Harrison Birtwistle and Peter Maxwell Davies, who were both determined to escape from the hermetic atmosphere of English music at the time. Goehr's first published work, the Piano Sonata, Op. 2 (1952), shows an immediate fluency of style and ease in handling serial technique. The piano writing is warm and attractive, but lacks a specific individuality; and one of the prominent features of its eclecticism is a rhythmic patterning which bears the stamp of Messiaen, whose music had recently burst upon the English scene. To pursue his enamoration, Goehr contrived a year's study with Messiaen in Paris, from 1955 to 1956, and this was to prove a vital influence in the emergence of his own musical character. Messiaen had also nurtured the young Parisian avant-garde, led by Boulez, and Goehr's flirtation with their ideas spawned two works—one written in fact before his spell in Paris: the *Fantasias* for clarinet and piano, Op. 3, and one after his return: the *Capriccio* for piano, Op. 6. Both are written in a terse, intricate and rather anonymous style, aping the latest idioms; then, having culled what was of use to him, Goehr discarded the rest and moved on, abandoning in his wake an incomplete first string quartet.

His next composition bears a much stronger mark of individuality, and was the first to establish his reputation with the musical

41

public. It was *The Deluge*, a cantata for soprano, contralto and a small ensemble of eight instruments, with a text derived from a 'model' shooting script by Eisenstein. *The Deluge* is conceived by Eisenstein in dramatic visual terms—the macrocosm of universal chaos characterised by a succession of scenes where the camera lens zooms in to pick out groups of creatures, each fighting for their lives against incalculable forces. Goehr's musical language advances by strides in this work; but ultimately his score fails to grip the listener—the power of Eisenstein's conception, and of that of Leonardo da Vinci, on which he based his script, lies in its fundamentally objective viewpoint of humanity in a state of subjective terror. Goehr's music seems to be suspended in mid-space not knowing whether to become involved or not. An interesting comparison can be made with a cantata written some four years later for a very similar group of performers—the *Leopardi Fragments* by Peter Maxwell Davies. Leopardi's verse is essentially subjective and psychological, and Maxwell Davies's musical language is entirely at one with this mood, and balances it perfectly, building its structure and momentum through a series of developing variations. But of course Maxwell Davies is an essentially subjective composer, and Goehr has been most success-ful in objective, 'pure' musical forms.

His next work was in fact written in variation form, the form which has become the most prevalent in his subsequent works. The Variations for flute and piano were followed by a small work which succeeds through its reserve—the *Four Songs from the Japanese*, Op. 9. The epigrammatic poems evoke an economy of style and expression, which work best, symptomatically, in the bleakness of the fourth song. After this, Goehr returned to Eisenstein for another shooting script, this time with a more promising structure: the story of *Sutter's Gold*, which he set in a large-scale cantata for solo bass, chorus and orchestra. The first performance, at the Leeds Triennial Festival of 1961, was disastrous, and the cantata unfortunately has never had a chance to prove its merits; but, apart from a few striking moments, it does suffer from the harmonic sterility which was then undermining the composer's musical language.

In *Hecuba's Lament*, Op. 12, Goehr reached the nub of his stylistic dilemma. The work contains music assembled from an unfinished opera, a version of Euripides' play *The Trojan Women*, and is scored for a large orchestra with an extensive percussion section.

It begins with a fertile two-part invention, but rapidly the impetus is lost, and the music contorts itself in febrile expressionist gestures, supported by gauche percussion sallies. Perhaps the disjointed argument of the music had a purpose in the opera, but as a separate work it waves its arms in a vacuum: compare his other operatic abstraction, the *Three Pieces from Arden*, with its closely-bound, integrated material.

It must have been a relief for Goehr to work, in complete contrast, on a commission from the Melos Ensemble. The Suite, Op. 11 (it was conceived after *Hecuba's Lament*, though completed before it) is an attractive, gritty work, distinguished by its neat instrumental writing, economy of material, and clarity of line. Goehr has become concerned for the listener: the opening section is repeated, to familiarise the ideas, before he embarks on what is really a series of variations. A short, restful Intermezzo succeeds, and launches into a brittle Scherzo, mainly in just two parts, with a Trio for violin, cello and harp, and a final echo of the Scherzo. A short Arietta features a flute melody, commented on by strings, to the accompaniment of a three-note rocking horn figure; then the final *Quodlibet* is a witty dissertation on ideas from the previous movements, punctuated by a recurrent horn call, and it contains diverting cadenzas for flute and harp.

This lucidity was carried over into his next orchestral work, the first of his series in concerto form—the Violin Concerto, Op. 13. The first movement is a series of chorale variations, with the *Cantus* always clear and indicated in the score. But in both this movement and the second, a sonata-like structure, there are impassioned orchestral climaxes which are simply not supported coherently by their musical substance. The second movement contains some extraordinary passages in which the orchestra, with brass glissandi, alternately heaves and slumps, in a tempo marked *feroce*. If the concerto does ramble, and if the solo violin part does contain much conventional virtuoso figuration, there are also episodes of a quiet lyrical beauty, which make it the sadder that, in the end, all is sacrificed to a trite, *moto perpetuo* coda, a capitulation to an outworn tradition which this original work had otherwise stoutly withstood.

The *Two Choruses*, Op. 14 wear Messiaen's *Cinq Rechants* emblazoned on their sleeves, and in them suddenly blossomed a new sonority, the result of a new organisation of serial harmony that Goehr was to bring to fruition in his first masterpiece, the *Little*

Symphony, Op. 15. In its most basic form, it is a method of generating new harmonies and new note-rows by superimposing the two halves of a twelve-note series. Each of the six intervals formed by the six pairs of notes is taken as a self-existent factor, and each of these six factors is in turn applied to each note of the original twelve-note series. This creates twelve new series, all related, and each contains a certain amount of repetition of notes, resulting in a tonal flavour—Goehr regards this as a useful bridge between regular dodecaphonic rotation and more limited tonal areas. The first of the *Three Pieces for Piano*, Op. 18, is designed as an almost didactic example of this technique, employing just the first four factors above-mentioned.

Much of the strong character of the *Little Symphony*, Op. 15 is owed to these tonal suggestions. The opening movement is a slow, simple chorale of nineteen bars, with one chord per bar, played by the strings. When one note is removed from each of these chords, the chorale proves to consist of five triads of E major, three of G minor, five augmented triads on A, and six diminished on C—a total of only four different chords. The character of this simple arrangement impinges immediately on the aural memory; but even more important than this harmonic colouring is the little melody formed by the highest notes of the first four chords—E, down to B, up to G sharp, which relaxes down to G natural. This sensation of a major-minor resolution permeates the whole symphony. The eighteen variations which comprise the second movement comment on the chorale in a wide variety of instrumental groupings and rhythmic patternings, working from solo groups to tutti, and from extreme high and low pitches to the centre. This tutti centre is reached at the thirteenth variation, which bears more than a passing resemblance to the opening of Tippett's Second Symphony (Tippett's influence seems often apparent in the symphony, as in the writing for horns, and the working of contrasting blocks of material in the last movement—in fact, Tippett was a friend of Walter Goehr, and a frequent visitor to the Goehr family home). The seventeenth variation reduces the orchestral scope again, and the movement ends with an echo of its beginning. The third movement is a lively scherzo, full of zest and rhythmic vitality, with a more relaxed trio. The jubilant ending of the movement, where high woodwind and strings chatter over vibrant brass chords in broken phrases, to resolve onto a final rich C major chord, displays Goehr's sudden maturity in handling the orchestra. The final movement is one of Goehr's favourite types, combining features of slow movement and finale. Elements from previous movements are juxtaposed and played off, with *recitando* commentary from solo instruments. In the centre of the movement the music breaks down, and works the choral chords round to a short quotation from Schoenberg's *Chamber Symphony*, Op. 9 (a favourite of Walter Goehr, to whose memory the *Little Symphony* is dedicated). The last bar of this quotation contains (in retrograde at the fifth in the strings) the very same four-note melody on which the symphony is based, and with a short canon on which it hauntingly ends.

In the *Little Music for Strings*, which followed the *Little Symphony*, Goehr explored much the same territory, though in miniature; but his next large orchestral work, written in 1965, refers back to the earlier world of *Hecuba's Lament*. The title of the *Pastorals*, Op. 19, does not refer to the English pastoral tradition, but to that of the classical world, and it dates from a time when Goehr was writing incidental music for stage productions of Sophocles' *Oedipus Rex* and *Oedipus in Colonus*. The mood of the work reflects that of the plays, in which violent events take place in a pastoral landscape. The outbursts of *Hecuba's Lament* are here also, but rigidly controlled and balanced. The orchestra is divided into groups which present the ideas in blocks, and the tension is built up by juxtaposition and superimposition rather than by any principle of development. The one-movement structure is divided into two sections: the first is a set of variations on a duet stated by alto flute and clarinet, then a transition leads into a fugal movement, inspired by the polychoral music of Giovanni Gabrieli— the material is divided between a choir of four horns and tuba, two choirs of two trumpets and trombones, two four-part violin choirs, and three four-part choirs of cellos, the whole supported by a percussion battery.

In the following two years appeared two chamber works: the Piano Trio, Op. 20 (1966), and the Second String Quartet, Op. 23 (1967). In the quartet the first movement is the most substantial, an extended set of double variations. The idea for this movement originated in a viola melody which now comes two-thirds of the way through, answered itself by three variations in a synchronised but non-metrical structure. When the composer discovered he could redesign the melody as a rising theme answered by its inversion, descending, he used this idea as the basis for the main set

45

of variations, which now encase the smaller set. The variations cover a wide range of string techniques, concentrating, as does the following scherzo, on neo-Schoenbergian contrapuntal devices. The third movement is a slow, absorbed study of the harmonic implications of the chorale which is built up at the opening.

Among the few piano trios written this century, Goehr's certainly stands among the best, and it is not an extravagant claim, as made by a number of commentators, to place it beside the great legacy of the two previous centuries. The writing for the three instruments is perfectly calculated, totally controlled and poised, with every note crucial, and every moment of silence integral. Again a set of variations constitutes the first movement, and the subject-matter comprises four sections. The first is a pithy dance theme for violin and cello, displaying its gypsy heritage in its use of scordatura—the violin G string is tuned up to A flat for the whole movement. This is repeated, then answered by a sequence of ringing piano chords, repeated in turn. The two ideas are then combined in a varied form, and rounded off in a coda, after which the whole of this exposition is played again, without the internal repeats. In the course of the variations Goehr employs polymetric systems— where the rhythmic pattern of a passage is in a different metre from the main tempo—but he always provides a complementary scheme of reference to the main tempo, so that he can maintain strict vertical, therefore harmonic, control. In the second movement a slow, pensive cello melody of three phrases, each soaring higher, is accompanied by irregular groups of piano chords; the violin then comments on a varied repetition. The two string instruments continue in introverted, desolate duet, sliding four-part harmonies through langorous micro-intervals in a spiritual disintegration. At last the piano rudely interrupts, stirring them to brief action—but only for a moment; so it tries again, and again, and eventually woos them to new territory. Yet it is hardly scouted before it is abandoned again. Goehr's most perceptive observer, Bayan Northcott, sees in this passage an anticipation of what might have been the Trio's finale, had it needed one, and the music gently withdraws into itself, and closes.

Concurrently with the conception of the Piano Trio Goehr's major concern was with his opera, *Arden Must Die*, based on the Elizabethan play *Arden of Faversham*. The libretto for the opera was by Erich Fried, who concentrated not on re-creating a historical situation, but on a portrayal of the characters and events in the

46

nature of a morality play. Hence the characters are treated as symbols of types rather than as human beings, and the story is of the results of interactions between these character-types. All the characters are 'black'—even Arden himself, a hardened capitalist, whose one moment of magnanimity (inviting the rest of them to supper) ironically gives the final opportunity for his murder. The only character without a direct hand in his death is Mrs Bradshaw (an invention of Erich Fried) who constantly protests her innocence and even instigates the murderers' arrests; yet in her cowardly self-righteousness she is as evil as the others. Fried's libretto reinforces the starkness of the plot with bland rhyming couplets in ballad-style, owing much to Brecht. Goehr meets it with a dry, sinewy music remarkable for its variety of styles which highlight each scene: the impressionist music for the foggy marsh, the romantic surge of Alice's last phrase as her lover Mosbie carries her up to bed, the chorale-style ensembles, the atmosphere of a London street, where the tradesmen sing out phrases of Gibbons' *Cries of London*, and the lute-song which Susan, the maid, sings while her master is being murdered (a true historical detail). Yet Goehr constantly unifies his material by relating it to the two-bar phrase that opens the opera. The original production, in Hamburg in 1967 (in German, as *Arden Muss Sterben*), emphasised the relevance of the plot to modern times, and the various parodies of Nazi songs were directed as a protest against the neo-Nazis. If this is of little consequence to an English audience, Fried's determination to alienate his audience from the characters is more far-reaching, and indeed so successful that it inhibits any emotional involvement of the audience in the progress of fate. The artificiality of Fried's libretto encouraged Goehr to some rather wooden word-setting, especially apparent in the English version; and he also had no chance of rescuing the final trial scene from an impression of static inconsequence.

But for a first opera, *Arden* displays some remarkable talents, and Goehr has explored the world of the stage since in three music-theatre pieces, written for the Music Theatre Ensemble, which he formed in 1967 for the Brighton Festival. *Naboth's Vineyard* (1968) was the first, and takes its subject from the Book of Kings. Naboth has a vineyard which Achab, the king, covets, but Naboth will not sell it to him. Jezebel, the king's wife, schemes to have Naboth killed by stoning, so that Achab can take possession of the vineyard. When Jehovah sends his prophet, Elijah, to reprimand him,

47

Achab repents, but is allowed to retain his ill-gained prize. Again, Brecht's political theatre looms large in this allegory, in addition to such diverse influences as the Japanese Noh theatre (which also inspired a more recent piano piece, *Nonomiȳa*), and the dramatic madrigals of Monteverdi, especially *Il Combattimento di Tancredi e Clorinda* (upon which Goehr was to write a *Paraphrase* for clarinet in 1969). The narrative of the story is told in English by a miniature chorus, formed by contralto, tenor and bass soloists; and the direct speech of the characters is sung in Latin by the individual soloists, in recitatives and arias reminiscent of Stravinsky's 'ritualistic' Latin word-setting. Each of the main arias is accompanied by an obbligato instrument from the small ensemble of flute (doubling piccolo and alto flute), clarinet (doubling bass clarinet), trombone, violin and double bass. The ensemble is always associated with the singers, who stand with it, and the action is portrayed by mimes with masks, accompanied by piano duet. Goehr's music, pellucid and supple, might appear inadequate by itself, but it perfectly complements the visual element to create a powerful theatrical experience of a type quite opposed to the cult expressionist form of music-theatre, dominated by Peter Maxwell Davies, which began to proliferate in England during the Sixties. *Naboth's Vineyard* was followed in 1970 by *Shadowplay-2*, based on a passage from Plato's *Republic*, which examines the nature of illusion and reality through the allegory of the prisoners in the cave. Goehr reacted with a self-conscious heavy-handed attempt to convey all the levels of meaning inherent in Plato's involved symbolism, with the result that this is by far the least satisfactory of the triptych. *Sonata about Jerusalem*, written in the same year, is based on Hebrew texts from the twelfth century, and concerns the fate of the persecuted Jews in Baghdad. A false messiah persuades them to put on green clothes (the colour of paradise), climb onto the roofs of their houses, and try to fly to Jerusalem. They fail, and a small boy mocks them: 'to fly, you must have wings'. In this work Goehr returns to the more felicitous objective treatment of *Naboth's Vineyard*, though the rather obscure symbolism of the story unfortunately impairs its full potential impact.

Most of the Music Theatre Ensemble's appearances have been at the City of London and Brighton Festivals, and for the latter Goehr has written three works in concerto-form: the *Romanza* for cello and orchestra, Op. 24 (dedicated to Jacqueline du Pré) in 1968, and two works for piano and orchestra (both first per-

formed by Daniel Barenboim): the *Konzertstück*, Op. 26 (1969)
and the Piano Concerto (1972). Each of the three, in its own individual way, consciously avoids the overpowering nineteenth-
century virtuoso concerto tradition, to which his earlier Violin
Concerto had in part succumbed. The *Romanza* is a long instrumental aria in one movement (lasting some twenty-five minutes),
and in it Goehr seeks to rediscover, within the context of the modern
Viennese tradition of composition, some of the romantic tradition
of performance: the background language, which is unwritten,
but which creates a performance; the use of more or less bow; the
colouring of a note by means of smaller or greater vibrato and
instrumental tone-colour; what happens *between* the notes. The
cello rocks over repeated patterns, gradually picking up new
material in its course to propel it along. The orchestra takes up
the cello's message, and together they build up to a climax of
repeated staccato wind chords, answered by a series of Goehr's
extraordinary orchestral glissando slumps (compare with the
Violin Concerto, Op. 13), here given grotesque prominence by a
Lion Roarer. A discussion in harmonics ensues between soloist
and orchestra, and this leads back to a purely orchestral scherzo.
The cello joins again for the trio, but there is no repeat of the
scherzo, and a second development leads into a *lento* section,
consisting of a series of short accompanied cadenzas, which evoke
some of Goehr's most imaginative instrumental effects (especially
the string ensemble's glissandi harmonics). A third development
section leads to the recapitulation, where the original cello melody
now appears heavily decorated, in the style of the ornamentation
Chopin uses in some of his Nocturnes. At the last the soloist finds
rest amid the serenity of sustained woodwind chords.

   The discursive and expansive lyricism of the *Romanza* emanated
from the nature of the cello itself as an instrument; so, in the
Konzertstück, faced with writing for a small classical chamber
orchestra (the English Chamber Orchestra) and solo piano, Goehr
produced a work which, in its compact, refined style, its polished
elegance and Stravinskian dry humour, demonstrates the composer at his most individual and characteristic. This likewise
comprises a single continuous movement, but for the structure
Goehr returns to his favourite variation form. There are a number
of sections (the first is repeated), each of which is characterised by
its own rhythmic structure and thematic material; and each section is followed by a development of itself, in which one element

49

of the rhythmic structure is changed. This results in thematic and textural variation, and ultimately in a transformation of the original. The idea for this construction came from the ancient Chinese oracle the *I Ching* (Book of Changes), in which a change in the grouping of the six lines of a hexagram brings about a new image and a new meaning—and he adapted this idea to his serial hexachords in a way that has little to do with traditional serial technique.

Goehr's next orchestral essay was again in an all-embracing single movement—the *Symphony in One Movement*, Op. 29 (1970), a powerful, uncompromising work. Its inspiration was similar to that of the second movement of the *Little Symphony*: here Goehr envisaged a protracted ascent, followed by a descent—each instrument of the orchestra literally moving from the highest to the lowest pitch available to it, until the music falls into silence. The subject-matter for the whole symphony is the melody which a solo viola unfolds over a quiet orchestral backcloth. Expansion of the melody into two-, three- and four-part polyphony constitutes the exposition which culminates in a melodic (though not rhythmic) transformation of the original melody which is used cyclically throughout the work. A development follows, in which the lower instruments divide into two groups: low strings, bassoons and tuba ponder over the main melody, while woodwind and brass add intermittent counterpoints in a different metre. The ascent begins, a sustained build-up of tension that goes on and on climbing until it reaches a nervous teetering peak, with whooping horns and pealing bells. Immediately the descent begins, in a measured tread of constant tempo, with each step of the descent shorter in time than the previous one, so there is an acceleration to a silence. Mahlerian growlings ensue, out of which grows again a cello and bass recitative which leads into the faster central section, a kind of scherzo. And again an ascent begins, gradually building up through three successive sections to a high string chorale counterpointed by a distorted march. But still the tension increases, and still more, until the march freezes in a series of mercilessly hammered-out brass chords. Exhausted, the music collapses into lugubrious mutterings. After a strenuous effort it manages to reassure itself by rediscovering some of the original material, but the mood at the end is one of only partial reconciliation.

Goehr's two most recent works, at the time of writing, move away from the one-movement form which had been preoccupying him. Both works bear the title concerto—Op. 33 is the Piano Concerto, but Op. 32 is a different sort of concerto. *Concerto for Eleven* is in the mixed chamber ensemble tradition popular in Eastern Europe. Goehr saw the eleven instruments he uses here on an old photograph of a Russian Jewish wedding band (an inspiration reminiscent of Stravinsky and his Octet): flute (doubling piccolo), two clarinets (the second doubling bass clarinet), two trumpets, small tuba, percussion, two violins, viola and double bass. The spirit of Stravinsky is present in the outer movements, and the Schoenberg of the Serenade and Suite (Op. 29) lies at the heart of the whole conception. The composition is based on two related, but significantly different twelve-note rows, coupled so that they form a continuous circuit of twenty notes, which provides unifying features for the work. It is in a traditional four-movement plan: the scherzo comes second, and has a trio *quasi folkloristico* which is itself a set of variations on the opening of the concerto. Apart from some harmonic sections in the *Adagio*, the texture is primarily a fragmented contrapuntal invention between the eleven players, with an idiosyncratic employment of percussion that might have seemed impossible in the light of his early works.

The Piano Concerto dates from 1972, and finds its solution to the challenge of concerto-writing, in contrast to the romanticism of the *Romanza* and the neo-classicism of the *Konzertstück*, in the rich tradition of Mozart's mature piano concertos. Goehr considers its form an advance on that of his other full-scale concerto, the Violin Concerto, in that there is no direct repetition of any kind—in fact an adherence to a stricter serial practice. Of the two movements, the first consists, in most basic terms, of two forms of structure, the one homophonic and the other polyphonic; the movement juxtaposes them, and moves from one to the other. The second movement is an *Adagio* which, characteristically, incorporates a scherzo, in a proportionally related tempo. Throughout there is a Mozartian lucidity and warmth, and fluent, brilliant writing for the solo instrument (Barenboim is an ideal apostle in his poetic interpretation). There are no cadenzas, though there are many lyrical, introspective passages for solo piano—Goehr has said his ideal of piano writing would be a cross of Bach and Debussy, something in the nature of a 'polyphonic impressionist'. The orchestra includes double woodwind and brass, though he omits horns and trombones, to create a bright 'Italianate' luminosity in the harmony. The careful balance of the structure and the fertility

51

of musical invention combine to make this one of the composer's most satisfying and fascinating works.

In recent years Alexander Goehr's time has become increasingly occupied with concerns other than composition, most notably with his responsibilities as Professor of Music at the University of Leeds, a position he has held since 1971. (In addition, in 1976 he succeeds Lord Harewood as Artistic Director of the Leeds Festival.) Between 1972 and 1974, no new works were performed after the Piano Concerto of 1972, until three were scheduled for premières in November 1974: a large orchestral work, *Metamorphosis/Dance*; *Chaconne* for wind instruments (a mixed band of eighteen woodwind and brass); and *Lyric Pieces* for seven instruments (four woodwind and three brass).

As Goehr continues steadily to add to his corpus of works, still very few seem to have found their way into the regular performing repertoire. He seems neglected both in concert and on radio, though at last a number of his works are becoming available on records. His type of progressive conservatism has not the charismatic quality by which the contemporary musical public is so easily seduced; but the uncompromising integrity of his music may be expected to ensure its survival in posterity.

Hugh Wood

LEO BLACK

Hugh Wood was born in 1932 at Parbold, near Wigan, Lancashire, the younger of two sons in a music-loving family. He was educated at Oundle School and later, after national service which at one point took him to Egypt, at New College, Oxford. Although from the age of sixteen, after his first visit to the early Bryanston summer school (forerunner of Dartington), he had sensed that he had to be a musician, the resolve to act upon this did not come until after the end of his three years at Oxford. There he made a good deal of music, notably in the amateur theatre, but read history. He then settled in London, where he learned the rudiments of music systematically. Those who greatly helped him at that time were Dr W. S. Lloyd Webber, Iain Hamilton, Anthony Milner and the late Mátyás Seiber; he has been responsible for the article on Seiber in the sixth edition of Grove.

During the late Fifties and early Sixties Hugh Wood earned his living by teaching, music-copying and writing. The teaching began at the bottom with supply teaching in London schools, then moved on to lectures for the Workers Educational Association and Morley College, through a brief spell at the Royal Academy of Music, to more recent work in Glasgow and Liverpool. He has been a prolific writer of articles and programme notes, and has made memorable broadcasts, notably about Beethoven and Schoenberg. He was in London from 1954 until the end of 1970, though for the final four years of that period he was the first composer in residence (Cramb Research Fellow) at Glasgow University. In 1971 he moved to Liverpool, where he had taken up a lectureship at the University, which continued on a full-time basis for two years.

His first work to appear in print was the Variations for viola and piano. Gradually he extended his range and succeeding works were scored for three instruments (Trio for flute, viola, piano), and then four (*Logue Songs* for voice, clarinet, violin, cello; First String Quartet).

53

These works led up to his first composition for symphony orchestra, with two singers, *Scenes from Comus*, first heard at the 1965 Proms. Many features of *Scenes from Comus* are found equally in the chamber works that preceded it, and in the *Three Piano Pieces*, the second of which was written while the composition of *Comus* was under way. For example, the *Logue Songs*, First String Quartet and *Three Piano Pieces* all manifest at their start a similar pattern of extended introductory section in a tempo that is sostenuto if not actually slow, leading to a quicker Scherzo or dance-like movement. But *Scenes from Comus* proved a landmark. It was on a larger scale than any previous work of his, and for the first time he had composed, with remarkable success, for orchestra.

Whether Hugh Wood composes for full orchestra or for a couple of instruments he is always concerned with form, with continuity; with momentum and a sense of direction. In his major works one may well be amazed at the end that so much time has passed so quickly. This continuity, this unfolding of a discourse that is passionate but rational, has been a major preoccupation with him, as has what he calls 'the manifoldness of symphonic movements'. If this sounds like the integration of strong contrasts familiar to us in Viennese classical music, the assonance is no accident. Hugh Wood has been called, mostly with pejorative intent, a traditional-ist composer. He undoubtedly is that, and there is no doubt as to which view he favours in the running debate about the constella-tion 'music-time-form'.

Perhaps a majority of reflecting musicians would agree that one of the things about music most to be valued is its power to make one forget the passage of clock-time. Disagreement begins when one considers how this can be done. Broadly, and trying to avoid value-judgements on either side, one could identify two present attitudes, each with its sympathetic points. First, that in view of the suspen-sion of time while serious music is going on, the art itself can be static, one in which (to misquote Schoenberg's quotation from Balzac) there is neither up nor down, before nor after, no succes-sion: music as a building or picture gallery, through which one wanders creating form through what one does and sees or hears. The one essential is the right state of mind: due awareness, con-centration. The other attitude is that all this is too metaphorical. Time does persist, things in music must by definition occur one after the other, and the impression of time's suspension comes about precisely because of the relationships, the unity, that a

54

composer creates and the listener in turn senses within a train of events whose principal dimension is clock-time. What are for convenience given the poetic designation 'timeless moments' may be the basis of much that is most serious and valued in art or life, but they are granted, rather than created. And they are moments. They stand outside the creative process, at one end or the other. A timeless twenty-five minutes would be a contradiction in terms, one not to be argued away by invoking the word 'static'. The task of the composer with this second, more classical attitude would be to organise a period of clock-time, by hard-learned techniques of composition, requiring the listener not to add anything but rather to keep up as best he can. Here the composer would find many great men of the past or present to guide him, each of them having learned in turn from his own predecessors, and each having performed the task in his own way, inimitable but still to be learned from. The successiveness of events in clock-time imposes obligations and offers opportunities, among these the manifold techniques of thematicism. Hugh Wood firmly believes in and practises thematicism, which in its technical aspect is a rational process.

As another part of a general concern that the passional inspiration should be brought to fruition by musical rationality, Hugh Wood will often begin a piece with something basic and simple: a single note, around or against which others gradually cluster, or an unfolding line, possibly over a pedal-note. Harmonically there may or may not be the sense of a distant key-note, though if there is, one may be kept rather too busy to work out what it could be. Wood's harmonies are gaunt, astringent or purposefully harsh; at other times, of a complexity more clearly linked to that of the sensuously chromatic models provided by late-romantic music. I have implied that he has learned much from past composers, taken in some respect as models; looking for models and resemblances one's eye strays naturally to the composers of the Second Viennese School, whose music he knows very well indeed. One senses little natural affinity with Webern's terse austerity, but a fair amount of the 'in-there-fighting' quality of Schoenberg, as of Berg's melancholy sensuousness. For many years Hugh Wood has used the twelve-tone method: he acquired it as he acquired any other musical resource, by passionate study and the best kind of imitation. He has written of the twelve-tone method, 'What I understand of its technical means has become part of my ideal too', and 'to me it's neither a religion nor a science'. It is not

55

something to be used lightly: it takes on the obligation to make
sense of great complexity, and almost any alternative mode of
thinking makes things in some way easier for composer and listener
alike. Perhaps (heretical thought) its function nowadays is to be
there as a composer's iron rations, for the kind of emergency which
throughout Schoenberg's career generated his music.

The initial impulse towards Hugh Wood's next major work after
Comus, the Cello Concerto, came within weeks of the former's
première, but completion took nearly four years. The work was
one of three concertos composed between 1965 and 1971, and
after its first performance (Zara Nelsova and BBC Symphony
Orchestra, 1969 Proms), he went on to produce a Violin Concerto
(Manoug Parikian and Royal Liverpool Philharmonic Orchestra,
1971) and a Chamber Concerto (London Sinfonietta, also 1971).
In the format of *Comus*, each lasts a good twenty-five minutes,
with the Chamber and Violin Concertos falling into clearly characterised movements. The Cello Concerto is a 'single-movement'
work in the true sense, with no scherzo section. As Wood's music
has steadily worked out the opposites in his make-up, an essential
has usually been the element of dance. 'Scherzo' could suggest a
joke, but lightness of heart is not what seems to lie behind this
impulse to dance. What, then? An assertion of vitality against
some unspecified odds? A vigorous gesture of protest? Didn't
Stevie Smith's most famous poem have the title 'Not Waving but
Drowning'? Be that as it may, Hugh Wood's music dances, and
here it continues a distinguished British line—Vaughan Williams,
Holst, Tippett—even though its way of achieving its aims by quite
simple combinations of two and three, in compound metre, has as
much in common with Bartók or Stravinsky. The vein of dance-
scherzo runs from the playful 'Bargain My Love' (*Logue Songs*) or
the 'schattenhaft' Scherzo of the First String Quartet (which he
has described as the result of 'liking Mendelssohn and liking
Roberto Gerhard and perhaps making some unholy compôte') to
the less metrically regular dances such as the pagan orgy that
forms the central section of *Comus*, and the Scherzo of the Violin
Concerto. The second of the *Three Piano Pieces* is noticeably like
the central section of *Comus*, and was written at about the same
time. The Chamber Concerto contains a more worldly, sophisticated piece in this genre, with echoes of jazz rhythms and an
amplified pizzicato double-bass.

Both the Cello and Violin Concertos seem to have been composed under extreme inner pressure. A principal means toward Hugh Wood's continuity has always been the repetition of basic ideas within an unfolding line, by appropriate use of sequence and variation. He could be called a rhetorical composer. In the two solo concertos the basic material is worked very hard indeed. The one for cello carries no comforting message, it simply reports. Its eventual quotation from the Elgar Cello Concerto needs very apt, rather detached performance, as does the comparable one from *Tristan* at a similar point in Berg's *Lyric Suite*. This is not the only instance of quotation in Wood's work: the harmonic pattern of Beethoven's 32 variations in C minor occurs at the end of the viola variations, and in the *Chamber Concerto* there are tributes to the memory of Roberto Gerhard in the form of brief figures from his music. The Violin Concerto runs toward a close as desolate as that of the cello work, but then something remarkable happens, which may in retrospect appear to have been a breakthrough for this composer. It has puzzled well-disposed people, who find such a 'happy ending' hard to credit. They cannot feel it to have been inevitable. Well, indeed (to compare great things with lesser ones), why should Mozart have tagged on that complacent D major coda at the end of his tragic D minor piano concerto, or Beethoven that skittish prestissimo in the major after the grim struggles of his serious String Quartet in F minor? These are mysterious matters, in which it may not be good to claim too much understanding.

Hugh Wood has written a good deal for the human voice. He loves the imaginative use of words and has been drawn to some distinguished texts: the elegant Milton of *Comus*, fellow-Northerner Ted Hughes, part of the Sirens chapter from *Ulysses* (probably his favourite book in prose), D. H. Lawrence, Yeats, Robert Graves, the quietly thoughtful Edwin Muir and the spikily passionate Christopher Logue (both in that poet's own right and as the 're-composer' of love-poems by the late Pablo Neruda). Five Laurie Lee settings were composed and although put away in the late Fifties were resurrected and performed in 1971. The Neruda cycle had its first performance at London's Round House in 1974 (Morag Noble and members of the BBC Symphony Orchestra). Whereas the early Logue songs were pure chamber music the Neruda cycle is in effect a concerto for voice and a sizeable chamber orchestra. This is a problematic genre: the Swiss composer Othmar Schoeck left several rather successful examples, but the problems are evident. A concerto soloist can occasionally accompany, but it is very hard for a singer's line to be anything but the principal part, at least in the kind of work where the text is treated as a rational communication rather than purely as material for musical elaboration. To compose twenty-five minutes of accompaniments and interludes is a challenge, and one temptation will be to overload the orchestral parts to the detriment of the singer's chances of being heard. This was obviously a problem at the Neruda cycle's first performance. Its wealth of colourful invention and its structural continuity, so typical of the composer, were just as obvious. The two sets of songs with piano from the mid-Sixties show that certain musical ideas were consistently in Hugh Wood's mind from then until 1973, notably those that convey the 'leaping and springing . . . of an adventurous bird' (third song of *The Rider Victory*) and the stationary turning of enormous masses held in a precarious balance ('Pennines in April', second song of *The Horses*).

Hugh Wood's music is challenging for singers, because another essential of his passionate style is the use of wide intervals for emphasis and expression. Just as his music dances, so too does it leap and swoop. Its restless phrases might be plain enough to sing if one or two notes of a phrase could be transposed to the more obvious octave, but then the very life of the phrase would disappear with its shape and its difficulty. A composer writing in this way must at all costs remain aware of what a well-trained and beautiful voice can and cannot do, if the challenge to the singer is to prove a profitable one. In a well-written twelve-tone work it may well be that things are made a little easier because certain patterns of intervals are bound to keep recurring.

One sizeable work so far not mentioned is the Second String Quartet, commissioned, like the first, by the BBC and performed in 1970. It stands a little aside from the rest of Hugh Wood's work, since he deliberately made it more fragmentary than any composition before or since. An article by him in the *Listener* (302) told how in 1969 and 1970 his mind had turned toward an alternative to the musical rationality which for over a decade he had been at pains to cultivate. 'Obsessive cleanliness keeps the irrational and primitive from the door', he wrote, and he reflected on painters 'with the courage to draw a rough circle with one stroke of the hand, and leave it'. The 39-section Second String Quartet he described as 'my first attempt at rough circles'. It is in no important sense in any 'free form', nor does it greatly differ in its continuity and shapeliness from the composer's other works, but it relies less on thematic development and more on abrupt juxtaposition than is usual with him. Only time will show whether this, the only work in which he has come even within sighting distance of an alternative attitude to music and time and form, was an isolated foray into strange country or the harbinger of a future line of development.

At the time of writing Hugh Wood has in mind another large-scale orchestral work, for the BBC Northern Symphony Orchestra (his sixth BBC commission), and he hopes to compose more songs with piano. Whatever he writes, it will be done with passion, just as his students will need to continue to share his conviction that music is something crucially important, that it is hard but rewarding work for all concerned, and that there are no short cuts. All of which could be found a little old-hat, a little boring: but then one definition of a composer is a man who, when you ask him 'How are you?', tells you a little, and then refers you to his music.

Harrison Birtwistle

MEIRION BOWEN

Everything about Harrison Birtwistle bespeaks a son of the soil. Pay him a visit at his Twickenham home, and you are likely (at least in summer) to find him curled up asleep like a hedgehog in a corner of the garden, covered in leaves and bits of grass. Prod him with conversation on any subject, and he is by turns docile and prickly: he digresses easily from music and other professional matters to talk of trees, birds and insects, which absorb him just as much. Born in 1934, he spent most of his childhood on a farm, and his voice still carries more than a trace of the accent of his birthplace—Accrington, in Lancashire.

At the bottom of his garden is a gazebo-like place in which Birtwistle composes, as odd a shape as anything to be found in his music. But he is not a character straight out of *The Wind in the Willows*, nor could you associate him with this century's English pastoral school, seeking refuge from the stresses and rigours of an increasingly urbanised culture in the simple delights of folk-music-based composition. He could, in fact, be described as a hedgehog in another, entirely different sense—that popularised by Sir Isaiah Berlin in his famous essay on Tolstoy, which takes its starting-point from a fragment of Archilochus: 'The fox knows many things, but the hedgehog knows one big thing.' The whole of this composer's output seems to gather itself together into a gigantic statement concerning the nature of music and musical expression. Why sing, or play? he seems constantly to ask. The summatory work that may well produce an answer—at least at this stage of his career— is likely to be the opera *Orpheus* (due to receive its world première at Glyndebourne in 1976).

At the time of writing, Birtwistle has reached the point where music, text and presentation amount to so personal a conception that he can only hint that it will be a comprehensive affair, embracing many interrelated issues. Birtwistle has laboured long on this opera, and it has undergone many modifications and metamorphoses. Like Tippett, writing *A Midsummer Marriage*,

60

Birtwistle has felt strained to the limits physically and psychologic-ally in the creation of this major work. Its focal point is the myth of Chronos, and it portrays the primeval Chaos out of which is born the human species that discovers the need to sing. The action shows a progress from dumb-show to singing, almost as an explanation of the nature of opera: an operatic composer (in Birtwistle's view) must show *why* his characters sing instead of merely speaking or whatever. The work draws together a number of themes which have preoccupied Birtwistle from an early period: we shall encounter some of these in the course of this chapter.

The hedgehog-like convergent thinking that underlies Birt-wistle's creative personality was manifest from an early age. He started composing as a child, almost as soon as he acquired a clarinet, at the age of seven. He continued doing so into his teenage years, and his efforts—right through into student days at the Royal Manchester College of Music and Royal Academy of Music—were conducted independently of the musical education he received. Classroom training at school tended to centre on the customary massed-singing sessions: these were irrelevant to his way of thought. At the Manchester College (to which he won a scholarship, and where he studied with Richard Hall), composi-tion lessons were based largely on what Birtwistle calls the 'goal-orientated' tradition of European music, clashing with his own ambitions and motivations: thus he found his creative vitality virtually numbed. Indeed, he stopped composing for a while and concentrated on clarinet studies and performance in general. The instrument was to become essential to his very idiosyncratic scoring, especially from the time of his acquaintance with the clarinettist Alan Hacker: much of the pungency and violence that characterises works like *Tragoedia* and *Punch and Judy* springs from his fondness for sending clarinets and other wind instruments up into their highest registers. He met Alexander Goehr and Peter Maxwell Davies—two undoubted foxes, very divergent musical minds by comparison—and together they formed the Manchester New Music Group which played a wide selection of contemporary music, including much that one might not have expected to hear even in London at that time (1953), let alone Manchester: Messiaen, Berg, Webern were all featured.

After two years in the army, Birtwistle enrolled as a clarinet student at the Royal Academy of Music, and promptly began

C

composing again with renewed energy, manifesting once more the absorption with the raw materials of music that he had displayed as a child. Since then, nothing has diverted him from this creative stance. Several years' teaching (e.g. from 1962 to 1965 as Director of Music at Cranborne Chase School near Salisbury), visits to America (he resided in the United States for two years on a Harkness International Fellowship, and he has been back several times since), where latterly he has found himself conducting a college orchestra in Tchaikovsky and Mahler—this has all primarily served to provide financial grist for a mill that otherwise only grinds more slowly, such is the fate of English composers who are dependent upon commissions and royalties, and who do not use the composition of film-scores to keep the wolf from the door. Even his association with the Pierrot Players—which he co-directed with Peter Maxwell Davies until the group disbanded in 1970, and re-formed as The Fires of London—did not ulti-mately serve his particular creative purposes, and was probably a cul-de-sac in his career. He had scope to experiment, but the limitation of the group to the sort of ensemble Schoenberg had employed in *Pierrot Lunaire* constituted a considerable straitjacket. He was not happily employed updating medieval and Renaissance motets—as Maxwell Davies has been—and, generally, makes a better impression when he can move some distance from his models. He had much earlier, for instance, produced a set of six instru-mental movements, entitled *The World is Discovered* (1960), the offshoot of a canzonet by Heinrich Isaac, and very much an independent composition. Indeed, the work is an early example of his use of verse forms. He needed, furthermore, to move away from his models, so that he could introduce them, where appro-priate, as 'found objects'—like the Bach chorale in *Medusa*, or the old dance-forms (gavotte, allemande, etc.) that occur in *Punch and Judy*.

Once in a broadcast Birtwistle said that he felt he was continu-ally writing the same piece. Thus there are not only motifs and techniques that pervade his output, but strong connections between many of the individual works. The compositions themselves are open-ended, and he has revised some simply by extending them. *Medusa*, for instance, grew considerably between its BBC première (November 1969) and its first live London performance (March 1970). The *Four Interludes from a Tragedy*, for basset clarinet and tape (1969), are re-workings of interludes—originally for various

62

solo instruments—from the earlier *Monodrama* (1967), and are absorbed into *Medusa,* where the clarinet line is a 're-composition' of the musical material from the *Interludes*. Their appearance in a continuous programme that included *Medusa* (*Spring Song,* presented by the Pierrot Players at the Queen Elizabeth Hall, London, in March 1970) emphasised the fact that the short *Interludes* are now to be heard as an extension of the larger work.

Likewise, *Entr'actes and Sappho Fragments* (1962) grew from a small-scale conception into something more substantial (1965). Originally a set of pieces for flute, viola and harp—*A Song Book for Instruments* (1962) which comprises entr'actes 1, 2, 3, 5 and the coda of set 1 of the final structure—it acquired a further entr'acte (no. 4) the following year. By the time of its publication the work had grown into its present form, with a second set of pieces, which increased the ensemble by the inclusion of an oboe, violin and percussion, as well as soprano. Interwoven, here, with variants of the entr'actes are settings of fragmentary lyrics by Sappho—*Canti*—finishing with a variant of the Coda. From those entr'actes that do not reappear (nos. 1 and 4) Birtwistle lifts certain seminal motifs for quotation in the vocal movements. But even after all that revision and rethinking of the largest and smallest elements in the design, Birtwistle has lately begun to feel dissatisfied with the work, and countenanced the possibility of withdrawing it from circulation. Such an outcome may be more common amongst the efforts of contemporary painters and sculptors than amongst composers. Certainly, his music throws up far more analogies with the visual arts than with the literary models that come to mind in connection with most European music over the last hundred and fifty years. Instead of music conceived to move forward inexorably towards some particular goal or apotheosis, we find with Birtwistle something more comparable with mobile sculpture or film. In musical terms, we are concerned with relationships between geometric shapes and planes as observed from different angles or in transition from one set of perspectives to another. Open-ended, capable of further change or elaboration, his past work might well seem to him at times to contain wrongly selected paths which ought to be disowned, or certainly discarded in favour of something entirely different, even though his basic motivation was always the same.

In any of Birtwistle's works, his main reference point is the image of music burgeoning from a primal source: hence his habit

63

of allowing everything to flower from a single note or phrase, or of placing a single melodic line or motif in the foreground and letting that grow in all directions, expand, contract, acquire new thematic branches, shed subsidiary material, and so on. His musical fingerprints are quite basic. He has always been obsessed with the possibilities of repetition, the developing monodic line, above all, symmetry. The sources of these particular preoccupations are, on the other hand, diversified. They comprise a vast body of experience and observation, some of it explicitly stated—and having its roots right outside music—and some of it implicitly, but not necessarily deducible.

His earliest published work, *Refrains and Choruses*, for wind quintet (1957), manifests his early fondness for verse forms, a feature of all his music. It derives not so much from any specific interest in pre-classical music as such, but rather from its intrinsic value as an archetypal form. For Birtwistle, music by its very nature exists in a time-continuum, and therefore has to have a beginning and an end. Composer and listener become aware of 'modes of change' in the sound-materials deployed within that continuum. Repetition is one means whereby these modes of change attain coherence. The verse form in *Refrains and Choruses* is rather freely treated. Its seven short sections are closely interwoven, manifesting a kind of idiom related to dodecaphony yet actually more instinctive, making up its own rules as it proceeds.

In later compositions, where the thematic units are generally much smaller, the sections proliferate, taking in a wide gamut of sonority and texture: the repeating forms are more tautly organised. A particularly fine example is *Verses for Ensembles* (1969), in which formal elements of repetition and symmetry are given emphasis by a theatrical disposition of the twelve players involved. The players are split into smaller, self-contained groups clearly articulated in relation to their musical material and function, and their spatial distribution. There are seven playing positions in all. The separation of groups, in distinct antiphonal writing, solo outbursts or interventions, for example, is only a surface indication of another of Birtwistle's elaborately sculptural groundplans. Thematically, the starting and finishing points are two pairs of articulated notes, horn with oboe or two trumpets, respectively, which recur to initiate activity at any stage and are finally resolved in an AED chord on the final rising accelerando. Within the framework of a series of characteristic interchanging

64

and colliding blocks of thematic material, there are cadenzas or solo interruptions, which take the music onto a different geometric plane—an idea accentuated by the performing layout. The two trumpets intervene from their stereo-style separated positions at one such point in the midst of antiphonal exchanges. Elements of repetition—canons, ritornelli, verse forms—proliferate throughout the work. Moreover, the range of possible geometric metamorphosis is enhanced by the use of aleatory elements in the notation: these are not a substitute for invention, but a stimulus to its unfolding.

Already it will be observed that Birtwistle's conception of musical form is of something that shapes itself spontaneously, without depending upon techniques or traditional models from the immediate or distant past. In this respect, his work has much in common with that of Edgard Varèse. Like Varèse, also, he has evolved structural patterns from natural observation. In *Medusa*, for example, the title refers not only to the Greek myth of the Gorgon's head, but more importantly to a species of jellyfish that has eight identical parts, each of which is a microcosm of the whole. The jellyfish reproduces itself not by fertilisation but by detaching one part, which then grows into a fully matured jellyfish. Birtwistle draws this analogy because likewise, *Medusa* contains musical material that can continue in relation to the whole or can divorce itself, lead an independent life of its own, or disappear altogether. Such a process is commonly found in Birtwistle's music. Here amplification of the instruments, and electronics, give it extra scope. *Medusa* employs two tapes: one a recording of a distorted saxophone sound, the other, synthesised sounds. It also needs a specially devised electronic instrument (performed by the keyboard player) which extends the percussion sonorities. The colour-spectrum in *Medusa* is thus vast. The composition is superbly manipulated in a format whose enormous ternary shape is reflected in the large number of small segments it comprises.

Birtwistle often links an intensely abstract formal and sonorous exploration to a specifically devised dramatic presentation. This is one important sense in which he develops the musical conception of Varèse. Only very gradually did he evolve an idiosyncratic notion of the connection between music and drama. It starts as an investigation of the relationships between words and music. In *Monody for Corpus Christi* (1959), the stature of the voice is very

65

different at the start from what it becomes in the course of the piece. Its role is only vaguely defined at first, then evolves to the point where, after a climax, it is accompanied only by the flute almost to the end of the first section, highlighting the words 'Corpus Christi' with long single notes, surrounded by a halo of ornament, and a separate *quasi parlando* treatment of the words 'written thereon'. *Ring a Dumb Carillon* (1965), a setting of words by Christopher Logue, goes a stage further, and in doing so enunciates a *corporeal* as opposed to *abstract* concept of music-making. That is to say, the act of creation is the product primarily of a physical need, secondarily of objective, cerebral pattern-making. The interplay of voice and accompaniment here illustrates the matter well.

The piece starts typically with single notes for voice and clarinet, with the intervallic elements that are the seed of the whole work soon introduced. At first the percussion fills a subordinate role, providing mainly punctuation. Then as the music gets under way, there is a closer integration of voice and percussion parts, while the clarinet enjoys a cadenza-like freedom to ruminate. The music subsides to nothing, and starts again in a similar fashion, gathering momentum to a point where the soprano herself has to play on suspended cymbals, signifying thus her total physical involvement in the act of music-making.

In compositions such as these, Birtwistle seems to be insisting that music springs from within ourselves as vital physical organisms, and from our speech-inflexions. For him these are its ultimate source, whether the outward manifestation is vocal, instrumental or theatrical, and he has maintained this outlook throughout his music. Outstanding amongst his more recent vocal works is his study preparatory to his next opera, called *Nenia on the Death of Orpheus* (1970), modelled on the ancient Roman funeral song (Nenia is also the name of the goddess invoked on such an occasion). A setting of a text by Peter Zinovieff, it is a dirge that runs the full gamut of vocalisations, from separate, spoken monosyllables to elaborate melismata. Three bass-clarinets, piano and crotales envelop the voice, until it wrests itself free to project overtly and eloquently important names like *Euridice* and *Orpheus*: the *need* for expressive vocalisation is experienced by the listener—and the music ultimately fulfils it.

Nenia figures amongst those works Birtwistle has written over a period of about nine years as basic research material, so to speak, upon which to raise the complex edifice of *Orpheus* itself. These compositions include dramatic pieces, like his first opera, *Punch and Judy* (1966–67), the dramatic pastoral *Down by the Greenwood Side* (1969), and a number of instrumental pieces. The greatest leap forward in his early development was, in fact, *Tragoedia* (1965). This not only brought about a refinement of the slightly more amorphous forms and textures of his earlier works, but introduced a toughness and corrosive power into his idiom that makes the experience of his music genuinely cathartic in the classical sense. It is closely related in sound and structural format to *Punch and Judy*, making a kind of savage frontal attack on the listener; yet together with the violence it is possible immediately to recognise an iron grip on the formal outline of the music.

In *Tragoedia*, each movement, and every section of each movement, bears the title from some formal feature of Greek drama. (The title itself indicates only the origins of the headings Birtwistle uses and does not connote any particular tragedy; literally *tragoedia* means 'goat-dance'.) The scoring has a theatrical alignment comparable to that in *Punch and Judy*. *Tragoedia* employs two groups of instruments—wind quintet and string quartet—with a harp acting as go-between. *Punch and Judy*, similarly, contrasts and links a stage ensemble (wind quintet) and pit band (strings, trumpet, trombone, harp, percussion). Both works are in essence studies in bilateral symmetry, wherein the formal layout and scoring lend force to each other. Larger symmetries contain much smaller symmetries, or departures from symmetry. In *Tragoedia*, the *Prologue* stands outside the work proper, as a separate essay in symmetry. The core of the piece is contained in two movements entitled *Episodion*, separated by a *Stasimon*, introduced by a *Parados* and followed finally by an *Exodos*. In the first *Episodion* two types of texture are contrasted: solo versus group in the outer subsections (horn against strings, then cello against wind), and the two soloists together in the middle section. *Episodion 2* reverses the character of the subsections of *Episodion 1*, but freely modifies the scoring and content. Moreover, in the central *Anapaest* of *Episodion 1*, the *Antistrophe* of *Episodion 2*, and the final *Exodos*, the performers on flute, oboe and clarinet take up claves—as with the soprano at the end of *Ring a Dumb Carillon*, symbolising their complete physical involvement in the drama. The end of the whole work is to be found quoted in *Punch and Judy*, and the violent repeated notes of the *Parados* and *Exodos* recur in Punch's war-cry.

But the analogies of formal shape and scoring are more significant. The opera has its own Prologue and Epilogue, and is organised into a series of four Melodramas, each corresponding to a murder, the third of which is interrupted by a Nightmare episode. Each Melodrama contains a sequence of short sections that precede the music for the actual slaughter, the latter being varied on each recurrence.

These two compositions crystallise some of Birtwistle's most typical musical gestures. On the one hand, we have a proliferation of ostinato figurations, repeated notes and chords, pungently scored thematic blocks; on the other, a diaphanous lyricism, mobile and refreshing (as in Judy's 'Be silent, strings of my heart', or the 'mediatory' music for the harp in *Tragoedia*).

Punch and Judy, which has an obtuse, over-written libretto by Stephen Pruslin, eschews any particular myth, and is in fact an open-ended opera—a 'source' opera—based on one of the oldest of stage legends, whose central allegory represents man in search of his own identity. The successive murders, the ritualistic portrayal of Punch and his abandonment of conventional personal and social ties, all are part and parcel of this quest. Pretty Polly, whom he ultimately attains, stands for his goal of self-integration. Mediating in and commenting on the action are the combined voices of the Doctor, Lawyer, etc., but above all Choregos, who is both showman-commentator and the alter-ego of Punch himself. In sum, Choregos represents music itself. In a Coronation scene, he is crowned with trumpet, drum and cymbals (the tools of his trade), only to be bowed (or sawed) to death later as he sits inside a bass viol. This rejection by Punch even of his own better qualities signifies the full extent to which he is prepared to go to assume his most distinctive identity.

This opera succeeded, but *Monodrama* (written for the first Pierrot Players concert in 1967) failed, at least, to unite the music and stage-presentation. Again, we find here an odd conflation of expressionistic and classical dramatic forms: another sort of dramatic source book, in short. It was suggested by an early form of Greek tragedy in which a single actor took on numerous functions. The soprano protagonist here passes through a prodigious range of vocalisations from speech to melodramatic singing. As in *Punch and Judy*, there is a Choregos combining the functions of alter-ego to the protagonist and outside chorus. The four *Interstices* are the most impressive musical episodes in a work whose

68

composer seemed uneasily here trying to turn from a hedgehog into a fox.

Of Birtwistle's projects for the Pierrot Players, the most enduring is the *Cantata* (1968), whose text is compiled from tombstone inscriptions and free translations from Sappho and a Greek anthology, and which reintroduces a theme that harks back to earlier phases of Birtwistle's career: the idea of regeneration, of rebirth. This is the central preoccupation in his unaccompanied choral work, *Narration: The Description of the Passing of the Year* (1964); it underlies Punch's quest to east, north, south and west in *Punch and Judy*; and is the central idea in *Down by the Greenwood Side*. The last-named is a subtly allusive work. Its text, by Michael Nyman, is drawn from two sources: the popular ballad *The Cruel Mother*, passages from various mummer's plays, rural folk-drama. The ballad itself is sung by Mrs Green, while the actors and mime perform the play, the whole being accompanied by an ensemble which is a slightly expanded version of the Cornish Floral Dance band:

> Cornet, Clarinet, Big Trombone
> Fiddle, Cello, Big Bass Drum,
> Bassoon, Flute and Euphonium.

Underlying the conflation of the two traditional stories here is the equally traditional rite of spring, and the Easter resurrection. The characters are amalgams of various mythical figures including St George and Father Christmas. Here again we meet the two polarities of Birtwistle's idiom in the contrast between Mrs Green's songs (lyrical at first, but becoming progessively wilder until the act of killing itself, which is sung *dolcissimo*), continually punctuated by folksy refrains ('Fine flowers of the meadow', etc.), and the coarse, deliberately banal and at times shriekingly dissonant music that accompanies the declamations of the actors. It is both moving and very funny.

During the last few years, Birtwistle's obsession with the idea of rebirth and the 'eternal return' has given way to a confrontation with another important theme—that of the transience of existence, and the inevitability of death. The two collide in the new opera. In two other studies for *Orpheus*, *The Triumph of Time* (1971–72) and *Grimethorpe Aria* (1973), we enter a new sound-world as far as Birtwistle's music is concerned. Both share a predominantly adagio pace, and the natural efflorescence of the musical material in his early music is now attained with much greater sense of effort and strain. *The Triumph of Time*, an extended orchestral prelude, takes its cue from a Brueghel engraving—although Birtwistle had already conceived the music before he encountered it. (His earlier *Chorales* for orchestra (1962–63) was also a response to Brueghel, though nowhere near as assured in its handling of the orchestra or in thematic manipulation.) He takes from the painting both detailed imagery and its central image of Time, an old man, riding on a cart, bearing the globe itself, hung with zodiacal signs. For the first occasion in Birtwistle's music, we are made dramatically aware of the temporal factor. In this, his first major goal-directed work, we are ever conscious that Time is passing, bringing Death. There is a three-note soprano saxophone motif that hovers throughout the music like the angel trumpeting Fame: it is the source of some other thematic ideas, transposed variants occurring on trumpets and on horns. There is more than one climax, the central one shattering in its impact simply because every strand in the instrumentation has contributed to the slow ascent towards it. Some of it is not remote in character from Mahler's Ninth Symphony. Of all Birtwistle's works, *The Triumph of Time* seems to have cut across most barriers and succeeded in convincing the music world at large of his significance and stature.

Certainly, here, we have Birtwistle shifting his horizons somewhat. His handling of the death motif has now been projected onto a larger, more objective plane. In many previous works this was not the case, for Birtwistle appeared constantly to be exorcising a personal trauma in the numerous infanticides featured in his dramatic pieces (something sparked off by the first film he ever saw, *Alexander Nevsky*, whose opening image of children being thrown into a fire he has never forgotten). He has reconciled himself to the notion of Time in music by giving it a special significance. In doing so, he has drawn closer to the European cultural inheritance, yet the creative direction he takes is still very much his own.

Peter Maxwell Davies

STEPHEN ARNOLD

Peter Maxwell Davies was born in Salford in 1934. Although he received piano lessons from an early age, he was in other respects self-taught musically until he left school and went to Manchester University in 1952. The University could not offer him real encouragement in composition, and it was at the Royal Manchester College of Music that he found more enlightened tuition and fellow-students who shared and developed his interest in new music. These included Alexander Goehr, Harrison Birtwistle, Elgar Howarth and John Ogdon, the student composers and performers who formed the Manchester New Music Group, and who were among the first in Britain to benefit from the renewed European interest in the suppressed music of the Second Viennese School.

Davies's early works were written for members of the group, the Sonata for Trumpet and Piano (1955) for Elgar Howarth and the *Five Pieces for Piano* (1956) for John Ogdon. Both works require considerable virtuosity in their execution, and, as well as showing the Second Viennese influence in their contrapuntal tautness, they also reveal a familiarity with the recent rhythmic practice of French music, and of Messiaen in particular. Davies states in his preface to the libretto that he started sketching the opera *Taverner* at this time. In this connection it is interesting to note that, for all the development of his musical language that took place before the opera was completed, the Sonata for Trumpet and Piano, Op. 1, was written in a style at times strongly foreshadowing that of the trumpet writing in the series of *Taverner* compositions where the small D trumpet is frequently required. A comparison of the first few bars of both the sonata and the opera suggests that this predilection for a high 'last trump' kind of writing is not the only similarity, and that the earlier work had a more specific influence on *Taverner*, at least in its preliminary stages (Ex. 1). The trumpet motif apparently even predates the Sonata for Trumpet and Piano. Davies's unpublished juvenilia make use of

71

it, which throws an interesting light on the evolution of the musical material now associated with *Taverner*.

Ex. 1A. Sonata for Trumpet and Piano

Ex. 1B. *Taverner*, Act I

In 1957 Davies was released from military service to take up an Italian Government scholarship which enabled him to study composition with Petrassi in Rome. It was under Petrassi's guidance that the sonata for seventeen wind instruments, *St Michael*, was written, and his insistence on the precise handling of musical material so that each musical event is justified in terms of overall structure has had a continuing effect on Davies's music. This influence is at its most obvious in Davies's first acknowledged orchestral work, *Prolation* (1958). The title derives from the terminology of medieval music, but the structure clearly owes much to the experiments in total serialism of the European avant-garde: a set of five durational values (10, 4, 7, 6, 5) governs not only local events but large-scale durations of movements, sections and sub-sections, while a set of five pitch classes (G, F, D flat, A, G sharp) generates all aspects of the pitch argument.

Prolation is probably the nearest that Davies's music ever approached to the mainstream of European music. Already he was turning from the obsessive search for a new, common musical language that was the preoccupation of so many of the younger European composers at the time, and drawing inspiration from plainsong and medieval music. Thus *Alma Redemptoris Mater* (1957) derives from the Dunstable motet of the same name, and *St Michael* (1957) makes use of plainsong from the *Requiem* mass, while the meditative fifteenth-century carol *To Many a Well* is the source of the *Ricercar and Doubles* (1959). The characteristics of canon, *cantus firmus* and elaborate *melismata*, while perhaps not as pronounced as they were soon to become, nevertheless showed the individual, not to say idiosyncratic, position Davies was adopting. His involvement with medieval music extended to a creative interest in all aspects of medieval cultural life, which manifests itself time and again throughout his musical output. To explain this involvement is not easy, but clearly Davies's feeling that all artistic activity at that period was closely integrated into the entire social fabric (dominated as it was by the powerful edifice of Christianity) has some significance, especially when the general situation of the present-day artist is contrasted. Yet, somewhat against the odds, Davies aspires to create works that are as directly related to our society as were the wall paintings of a medieval church to medieval society. In addition, he believes that the symbolism of the medieval Church still has great power today, and he freely draws upon it to project his own philosophical concerns, while on the specifically musical level, his use of many early musical procedures is not merely method, rather mandalas in music.

When in January 1959 Davies went to Cirencester Grammar School as Director of Music, a more direct relationship with early music seemed to provide the best answer to the practical problems of music-making in a country school. These problems involved finding a repertoire for an inexpert choir and orchestra to perform, a choir and orchestra most of whose members had very little experience or appreciation of the 'standard classics'. Davies quickly discovered that the school arrangements of composers such as Haydn were still too difficult (especially for strings), that new music written specially for schools tended to be too condescending, even bad, and that to adjust available material to suit the raggle-taggle collection of instrumentalists in the school was a time-consuming and thankless task. He therefore began a series of original arrangements which, by the time he left the school in 1962, included music by Attaignant, Byrd, Gabrieli, Monteverdi, Couperin, Croft and Clarke, and Stravinsky, Bartók, Satie and Milhaud. After a few months in Cirencester Davies produced his first composition for school orchestra, *Five Canons* (1959), which were stylistically not far removed from the Stravinsky and Bartók that the orchestra had already tried. A new departure, however,

73

was the introduction in Canon 3 of improvised melodic parts based on a given set of notes suiting the particular harmonic context. The set of orchestral pieces that followed continued to make use of a certain amount of improvisation: these were the *Five Klee Pictures* (1960), each of the five short movements being an impression of an evocatively titled work by the artist Paul Klee. (Ein Kreuzfahrer—A Crusader, Garten im Orient—Oriental Garden, Die Zwitschermaschine—The Twittering Machine, Heilige aus einem Fenster—Stained-glass Saint, Ad Parnassum—Ad Parnassum.)

The school choir, meanwhile, was being introduced to a wide range of medieval and Renaissance works, including both religious and secular music by Dunstable, Palestrina, Victoria, Byrd, Gibbons and Dowland. Encouraged by the enthusiastic response to earlier music and finding that two *a capella* works by Stravinsky, *Ave Maria* and *Pater Noster*, were within the grasp of the choir, Davies began his own series of choral compositions in a style which, while clearly of the present century (indeed owing not a little to Stravinsky), drew heavily on medieval carols for their inspiration with regard to both music and texts. The four carols he wrote for Christmas 1960, *O Magnum Mysterium, Haylle Comely and Clene, Alleluia pro Virgine Maria* and *The Fader of Heven*, form a set which is interspersed with two instrumental sonatas. These are based on the thematic material from *O Magnum Mysterium*, and were originally performed by members of the school orchestra. The cycle is concluded by a large-scale working-out of the first carol in the form of a *Fantasia* for organ, a carefully paced, arch-like structure with a well-judged and shattering climax. This dramatic handling of large-scale forms has developed into one of Davies's greatest compositional skills.

For the carols, Davies employs a more or less modal basis of his own devising, the chief characteristics of which are flattened third, fifth, sixth and seventh scale degrees, with occasionally a flattened supertonic and double-flattened seventh. (The flattened third and fifth are very common in most of Davies's subsequent choral works written in his carol style.) The main tone centre of the cycle is F, although the burden of *Alleluia pro Virgine Maria* is on A with the verses on B flat. The first instrumental sonata, *Puer Natus*, is in a straightforward ternary form with an elaborated repeat of the opening section. The *O Magnum Mysterium* melody is here presented more as a set, with many repeated pitches (extraneous in an instrumental context) being omitted. This set is timbrally partitioned and octave-displaced in the Webernian manner. Such translation and transformation of material from one context to another is a procedure that Davies has since used on countless occasions. The second instrumental sonata, *Lux Fulgebit*, comes to a climax with the most extensive controlled improvisation the composer had yet tried, an experiment which he followed up in his next work for the school singers and instrumentalists, *Te Lucis ante Terminum* (1961). Having tested controlled improvisation in his school works, Davies quickly extended its use to compositions written for professional performers, such as the String Quartet (1961), the *Frammenti di Leopardi* (1961) and the *Sinfonia* (1962). In these cases the improvisatory aspect is restricted to allowing a certain metrical and rhythmic flexibility in 'decorative' melismata which overlay more slowly-moving *canti firmi* which generally, although not always (cf. the second and last instrumental interludes in the *Frammenti*), maintain a strict metre.

In a number of other respects Davies's compositions and arrangements for Cirencester Grammar School had an influence on his subsequent works for professional musicians. In the metrically 'free' sections of *Te Lucis ante Terminum* (Sections C, D and E of Instrumental Verse II), is to be found an instrumental timbre—glockenspiel, guitar and pizzicato cello—which recurs, slightly varied, in *Antechrist* (sections K, L), *L'Homme Armé* (bars 270–80) and *From Stone to Thorn* (cf. from the Third Fall). Even the 'feuriger Regen' at the end of *Offenbarung und Untergang* (1965–66) has its antecedent in the Cirencester work. The experience Davies gained in arranging extracts from the Vespers of 1610 by Monteverdi bore fruit, as is well known, in the String Quartet, the *Frammenti di Leopardi* (for soprano, contralto and chamber ensemble) and the *Sinfonia* (for chamber orchestra). The first movement of the *Sinfonia*, for example, with its obbligato wind parts over sustained string chords and interspersed recitando sections, has a strong affinity with the opening *Deus in Adjutorium Meum* of the Vespers. A more obscure influence, however, is to be found in the large orchestral work, the *Second Fantasia on John Taverner's 'In Nomine'*, where an instrumentation first tried in the school arrangement of Monteverdi's *Sonata sopra Sancta Maria* was again employed. This involved string parts engaged in an antiphonal exchange being doubled alternately by glockenspiel and xylophone. In the *Second Fantasia*, completed four years after the Monteverdi arrangements in 1964, the same idea is re-used in the outer sections of the fourth ternary group of the Scherzo (cf. bars 718–33 and 740–59) and, following the Trio (bars 760–865), in the varied restatement of the Scherzo, this time in the outer sections of the third and fourth ternary groups (cf. bars 942–51, 956–66; and bars 971–86, 993–1,008).

One important aspect of the musical life of Cirencester Grammar School has not yet been mentioned. Throughout Davies's time there, many of the children began to write music of their own. These compositions sometimes evolved from exercises set in class, but just as many pieces came from pupils who were not studying music formally. Although the children were clearly infected by Davies's own enthusiasm for composition, it is a striking fact that their music, in spite of benefiting from certain aspects of his technique (notably the use of plainsong and *cantus firmus*), hardly ever imitated his style. This was not so much because of lack of skill—the technical accomplishment of a few of the pieces produced is beyond question—but rather because each composer was remarkably self-assured in his or her musical imagination. Whatever the crudities of detail, the essentials of the musical ideas were refreshingly original and always strikingly projected. In the main, these student compositions were performed by fellow-pupils. They included choral works, works for chamber ensemble and solo instrumental pieces and songs. Joint projects were also carried out, notably the incidental music to two school plays, *Peter Pan* and the *Secunda Pastorum* from the Wakefield cycle of mystery plays.* The Musical activities of the school became well-known, and the school musicians were invited to perform at various festivals and on radio and television. But this thriving and varied musical life did not evolve from any theory of music education which could be learned and reapplied elsewhere; neither was it the case that the children possessed anything beyond average musical ability. It is more likely that it derived from the fact that Davies's talents as a schoolteacher at that time fed his own compositional needs, and that the alchemy of the interacting personalities of the school community resulted in a vigorous but, at the same time, simply moving group of pieces by both master and pupils.

* A recorded selection of the music composed by pupils from Cirencester Grammar School, and Davies's own account of his time there, may be found in *Music in Education* (edited by Willis Grant), the Colston Research Society, London, 1963.

Throughout his busy three-and-a-half years as a schoolmaster, Davies frequently had to work through the night to meet his commitments as a professional composer. In these circumstances, it was hardly possible for him seriously to embark on the project that had been evolving in his mind since his student days, namely the opera *Taverner*. A meeting with Aaron Copland led to the suggestion that Davies should join the Graduate School in the University of Princeton as a Visiting Student in the Department of Music. Copland was shrewd enough to realise not only that the extra composing time would be invaluable to Davies, but that the dedicated attitude of the faculty composers and their rigorously conducted seminars in composition and analysis could be of immense importance in his development as a composer. A Harkness Fellowship made the whole venture a practical proposition and Davies sailed for America in September 1962. At Princeton he first revised the *Five Motets* of 1959, the revision consisting chiefly in supplying supporting instrumental parts to the existing vocal lines. Three groups of singers and instruments are used, and their discrete timbral characteristics and wide spatial separation recall the antiphonal layout of the *St Michael* sonata, but the revision itself may involve a re-application of the procedures adopted in his arrangement for the Cirencester Grammar School musicians of Giovanni Gabrieli's *Canzon Noni Toni* from the *Symphoniae Sacrae* of 1597.

Before leaving Britain, Davies had completed his first composition based on the music of the early sixteenth-century English composer John Taverner. This was the *First Fantasia on Taverner's 'In Nomine'*, an orchestral work first performed at a Prom in September 1962. Its style and form are clear and incisive, and, perhaps thinking ahead to the problems of the operatic presentation of his musical ideas, Davies seemed concerned that the work should make as immediate an impact as possible. Certainly, the relationship of the opening bars (Ex. 2Ai) and of the principal theme of the sonata section (following the first *recitando* section) (Ex. 2Aii) to the *In Nomine* theme (Ex. 2B) is unmistakable, while the brass chord (Ex. 3) that introduces and underpins both the first and second *recitando* sections (framing the sonata) takes on a crucial and sinister dramatic function in the opera.*

* For a discussion of this chord in the opera and of the contents of the scenes, see Stephen Arnold, 'The Music of Taverner', *Tempo*, Summer 1972.

The idea for the opera *Taverner* came from the few biographical details collected by E. H. Fellowes and published in the introduction to *Tudor Church Music*, Volume I (1923), and expanded into an entry for the third edition of *Grove's Dictionary of Music and*

Ex. 2Ai. Opening of *First Fantasia*

Ex. 2Aii. Opening of sonata section

Musicians. Briefly, this version of the life of John Taverner has it that in 1526 he was appointed by Cardinal Wolsey 'informator' of the choristers at Cardinal College (now Christ Church), Oxford, was in 1528 implicated in a Lutheran heretical group and im-

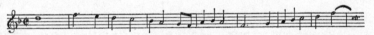

Ex. 2B. *In Nomine* theme (cf. the Mulliner Book, *Musica Brittanica*, Vol. I)

Ex. 3

prisoned, only to be pardoned by Wolsey on account of his valuable musical abilities. Fellowes states that Taverner 'abandoned music under pressure of religious conviction', quoting John Foxe's remark that Taverner 'repented him very much that he had made songs to popish ditties in the time of his blindness'. He left Oxford in 1530, moving to Boston in Lincolnshire, becoming an important agent of Thomas Cromwell and a 'fanatical persecutor' of religious institutions which indulged in 'idolatrous worship', even to the extent of martyring his religious opponents.

(One of Taverner's surviving letters is the sole evidence for this latter allegation.)

This version of Taverner's biography has now been discredited.* But it is important to realise that the ideas Davies wishes to convey making use of this story are ultimately unaffected by its strictly historical shortcomings. As he puts it, 'My opera *Taverner* projects onto the life and mind of . . . John Taverner certain perennial preoccupations of my own, notably with the nature of betrayal at the deepest levels.'† The uncorrected history of Taverner's life provides the perfect vehicle: a great composer, creating marvellous music for the Church of Rome, finds that his religious beliefs are leading him away from Catholicism. Persecuted, but later pardoned, for these beliefs, he forsakes his musical activities to become a persecutor of Catholics when the political climate swings in his favour. The betrayal involved is on many levels: betrayal of the Roman Catholic Church, which he worshipped through his music, betrayal of his family, but, above all, betrayal of his own creativity and individuality of spirit as expressed in and by his music.

However, Taverner is in fact *not* in a position to make a rational or moral choice: he is completely subservient to the authority of the idea that drives him to morally indefensible acts. That normal people *do* submit to such authority, disregarding normal moral constraints, has been at the root of many disasters in human relations throughout history. The authority for which Taverner betrays himself is the Lutheran doctrine which denies his creativity, and in the name of which he becomes a destroyer.

Act I of *Taverner* was completed in Princeton, New Jersey, in 1964. Act II was completed in 1968, with part of it being reworked from the sketches in 1969 following a fire in Davies's cottage in Dorset. The first performance took place at Covent Garden on 12 July 1972.

The opera is divided into two acts of four scenes each. Act I deals with the events leading up to Taverner's conversion, which takes place during Act I Scene 4, while Act II, which largely parallels or parodies Act I, sees the working out of this conversion, culminating in Taverner's presiding over the execution of the White Abbot in Act II Scene 4. There is no overture, but the scenes are separated by orchestral transitions which have the musical

* David Josephson, 'In Search of the Historical Taverner', *Tempo*, Summer 1972.
† '*Taverner*—Synopsis and Documentation', *Tempo*, Summer 1972.

function of reflecting on the previous, but preparing the next scene.

The representation of Taverner's gradual conversion and corruption in Act I Scene 4 is accomplished musically by means of the gradual transformation, or conversion, of previously established 'sets'. 'Set' is Davies's own term for a complex of pitches yielding both melodic and harmonic compositional entities. Although 'set' is normally associated with twelve-tone music (being roughly synonymous with 'row' or 'series'), Davies in *Taverner* uses sets of eight, nineteen, eleven and seven pitches. Compared with 'row' or 'series', there is less implication of a fixed *order* associated with 'set': *content* alone may define a set.

It is worth examining Davies's set-transformation in some detail because, apart from being crucial in the context of the opera, the process is important in the wider context of Davies's development as a composer.

In section 1 for John Taverner and the Jester (Death) (bars 1–53), the intervals of the 'main' set of the opera (cf. Ex. 1B, opening of Act I Scene 1) are progressively expanded or contracted by fixed amounts for each set statement, the transpositional levels of which are determined by the successive elements of the set. As Table A shows, the durations are similarly varied, but the timbral partitioning and general contour are constant, as are the intervallic relationships between ringed pitches, the first, second and third of which also retain fixed durations. The overall duration of each set statement becomes gradually longer, while over the section as a whole there is a registral move from low to high. (In the third transformation, the final pitch is altered to D natural to avoid repeating the preceding D flat.)

Section 2 (bars 54–90) is cast in the form of a baroque *da capo* aria, a duet for two monks (A: bars 54–71; B: bars 72–82; A: bars 83–90). As in section 1, the flute, oboe and clarinet are treated as a timbral group. The same cycle of transformations, order inverted, is assigned to them as in the previous section, but the transpositional level reached at the end of section 1, namely C, is preserved for each transformation. While the timbral partitioning remains essentially the same as before, the systematic treatment of durations is abandoned in favour of a freer rhythmic surface which seems to allude to the style of some of the obbligato instrumental writing to be found in, for example, Bach's cantata arias. Table B refers to the opening section of the aria: it does not show its many repeated notes and permutations of order.

TABLE A

(In Tables A, B and C, integers between pitches denote intervals in semitones; integers below pitches denote duration in quavers)

bar	register	clarinet		bassoon or oboe		flute	duration of cycle
1	LOW	$(Gb)^9\ Eb\ ^4(G)$ 6 · 2 · 2	7	$D\ ^{11}\ C\#$ 4 · 2	10	$(B)^{10}\ A\ ^3(C)$ 4 · 2 · 2	$= 24\,♪$
5		$(Eb)^8\ Cb\ ^5(Eb)$ 6 · 3 · 2	6	$Bb\ ^1\ Cb$ 6 · 3	9	$(G\#)^{11}\ G\ ^2(A)$ 4 · 3 · 2	$= 29\,♪$
10		$(G)^7\ D\ ^6(Ab)$ 6 · 4 · 2	5	$C\#\ ^3\ E$ 8 · 4	8	$(C)^1\ Db\ ^1\ D$ 4 · .4 · 3	$= 35\,♪$
15		$(D)^6\ Ab\ ^7(Eb)$ 6 · 5 · 2	4	$G\ ^5\ C$ 10 · 6	7	$(G)^2\ A\ ^{11}(Ab)$ 4 · 5 · 4	$= 41\,♪$
21		$(C\#)^5\ F\#\ ^8(D)$ 6 · 4 · 2	3	$F\ ^7\ C$ 12 · 6	6	$(F\#)^3\ A\ ^{10}(G)$ 4 · 6 · 4	$= 44\,♪$
27		$(B)^4\ Eb\ ^9(C)$ 6 · 8 · 2	2	$D\ ^9\ B$ 14 · 8	5	$(E)^4\ G\#\ ^9(F)$ 4 · 8 · 6	$= 56\,♪$
35		$(A)^3\ C\ ^{10}(Bb)$ 6 · 10 · 2	1	$B\ ^{11}\ A\#$ 16 · 10	4	$(D)^5\ G\ ^8(Eb)$ 4 · 10 · 8	$= 66\,♪$
44	HIGH	$(C)^2\ D\ ^{11}(Db)$ 6 · 12 · 2	11	$C\ ^3\ Eb$ 18 · 12	2	$(F)^6\ B\ ^7(Gb)$ 4 · 12 · 10	$= 76\,♪$

TABLE B

(Notes in brackets omitted in score)

Bar ref.	clarinet		oboe		flute
54	$C\ ^2\ D\ ^{11}\ Db$	11	$C\ ^3\ Eb$	2	$F\ ^6\ B\ ^7\ G$
57	$C\ ^3\ Eb\ ^{10}\ Db$	1	$D\ ^{11}(C\#)$	4	$F\ ^5\ Bb\ ^8\ Gb$
59	$C\ ^4\ E\ ^9\ Db$	2	$Eb\ ^9\ C$	5	$F\ ^4\ A\ ^9\ Gb$
61	$C\ ^5\ F\ ^8\ Db$	3	$E\ ^7\ B$	6	$F\ ^3\ Ab\ ^{10}(Gb)$
63	$C\ ^6\ Gb\ ^7\ Db$	4	$F\ ^5\ Bb$	7	$F\ ^2\ G\ ^{11}\ Gb$
65	$C\ ^7\ G\ ^6\ Db$	5	$F\#\ ^3\ A$	8	$F\ ^1\ F\#\ ^1\ G♮$
67	$C\ ^8\ Ab\ ^5\ Db$	6	$G\ ^1\ G\#$	9	$F\ ^{11}\ E\ ^2\ Gb$
69	$C\ ^9\ A\ ^4\ Db$	7	$Ab\ ^{11}\ G$	10	$F\ ^{10}\ Eb\ ^3\ Gb$

81

In the middle section of the aria, this instrumental combination is not used, and at the varied, shortened *da capo* only the first and last transformations are used (bars 83–85 and 86–90).

Because of the transposition of the cycle to C natural, and because of the accumulation of other details of variation, the gradual return to the original set is not a musical 'regression', but rather a working-out of some of the musical possibilities. This point is borne out by the fact that the cellos (Table C) take up the most distant transformation of the flute-oboe-clarinet group (section 1, bars 44–53, and section 2, bars 54–56) and *further* systematically transforms it until the inversion of the main set is arrived at in bar 83, the beginning of the *da capo* section. This cycle is non-transposing and confirms the tone centre of the aria as C natural. By repeating the inversion of the main set on F sharp (bar 86), the original transpositional level of the opening of both scene and act, Davies anticipates the reintroduction of this level in the following section of the scene.

The remaining layers of the first two sections of Act I Scene 4 do

TABLE C

Cellos, Act one, Scene four, section two

Aria sections	Bar ref.								
A	54	C_6 $^2D_{12}$	$^{11}Db_2$	$^{11}C_{18}$	$^3Eb_{12}$	$^2F_4$	$^6B_{12}$	$^7F\sharp_{10}$	
	* 64	C_6 $^2D_8$	$^{11}Db_2$	$^{11}C_{10}$	$^3Eb_{12}$	$^2F_4$	$^6B_{12}$	$^7F\sharp_8$	
B	72	C_6 $^2D_6$	$^{10}C_2$	$^1Db_8$	$^2Eb_8$	$^3Gb_4$	$^4Bb_2$	$^8F\sharp_4$	
	78	C_6 $^2D_4$	$^9B_2$	$^3D_6$	$^2E_4$	$^2F\sharp_4$	$^4A\sharp_2$	$^8F\sharp_4$	
A	83	C_6 $^3Eb_2$	$^8B_2$	$^5E_4$	$^1F_2$	$^2G_4$	$^2A_2$	$^9F\sharp_2$	
(da capo)	86	$F\sharp_6$ $^3A_2$	$^8F_2$	$^5Bb_4$	$^1B_2$	$^2C\sharp_4$	$^2Eb_2$	$^9C_2$	

* Although this set instance repeats the preceding one, its contour and durations are varied.

not involve the transformational procedures just outlined. The vocal lines derive from the *In Nomine* melody (cf. Ex. 2B) modally adjusted to suit the prevailing harmonic context. Thus, in section 1, the vocal parts are based on the succession D, F, E flat, D, C, B flat, A flat and its transpositions by minor thirds. These are echoed by string melismata which grow from already sounding pitches. In section 2, this succession is inverted and again intervallically altered: D, B, C, D, E flat, F, A flat. This tightens up the crab canons which are sung by the two monks at the beginning, middle and end of the aria. In this case the transpositional levels are determined by the original vocal line itself, the successive vocal entries for the first part of the aria being on D, B, C, E flat, F and A flat. The *In Nomine* theme as presented in section 1 of the scene is also the source in section 2 of the cor anglais and bassoon parts, which form a timbral unit in the fashion of the flute, oboe and clarinet. Another such timbral unit is formed by the lower brass instruments in section 1: although the pitches they articulate are derived from the main set (the transpositional levels of each instance being determined by the set itself on G flat but in retrograde), they are not presented in order and are treated rather as collections defining harmonic areas. Thus the fourth transposition on D flat (bar 15) coincides with Taverner's words 'Death! A thief!' and projects the whole-tone tetrachord as superimposed major thirds D–F sharp; E–G sharp (cf. Ex. 3).

In the two sections discussed, then, there is both transforming and non-transforming material. In the case of the transforming sets, instead of having available the normal forty-eight set forms, Davies has, in addition, finely graded steps between (say) a prime and its inversion, so that the original set gradually loses its intervallic identity only to acquire that of its inversion, just as Taverner loses his identity and acquires another that is the inversion of all that he implicitly stood for by being a creative artist.

This process is capable of considerable extension beyond what it has been possible to describe here. For Davies, it has been a kind of philosopher's stone enabling him to transform any musical idea into any other at will. In the opera, for example, the three subsidiary sets are made to transform into each other, and disguised quotations of other people's music are gradually distorted back into *Taverner* material. At other times, for example in the opening section of *Revelation and Fall* which is based on the same set material as the opera and the *Second Fantasia on John Taverner's*

83

'*In Nomine*', there is no stabilising non-transforming material and several sets are simultaneously transformed.

From the dramatic point of view as well, *Taverner* is a key work exerting considerable influence over Davies's subsequent theatrical compositions. This influence has been negative in the sense that Davies clearly feels more at home with the less prescribed, music-theatre genre than he did with all the formalities of the conventional, proscenium-arch opera house. (It will be surprising if, in his next opera for Covent Garden, *Resurrection*, he does not attempt to overcome the over-neat, framing effect of such buildings, which too often effectively remove the audience from the immediate experience of contemporary operas.) But music-theatre works such as the *Eight Songs for a Mad King* (1969), *Vesalii Icones* (1969) and *Miss Donnithorne's Maggott* (1974) continue to explore the idea of 'betrayal', the representation of people and their mental condition in a state of (usually sinister) change. Davies sees it as a moral question, as he put it in a programme note for *Vesalii Icones*, 'a matter of distinguishing the false from the real,—that one should not be taken in by appearances'. This also applies to *Revelation and Fall* (1965–66) and to the *Missa super L'Homme Armé* (1968) which are not strictly of the music-theatre type, although staged versions of these works have been given. It is in the light of these dramatic developments of the philosophical concerns of the opera that the staggering broadening of Davies's stylistic terms of reference should be viewed. Whereas quotations in *Taverner* are mostly disguised (in fact, there are two literal quotations of Taverner's music, one in Act II, Scene 3 and the other in Act II Scene 4), in later pieces they tend to become explicit, all the apparent stylistic discrepancies being allowed to stand. 'Because the music contains disparate, opposed elements, the total effect of these elements can be interpreted by the listener in different ways and on different levels, according to his means,' writes Davies in the above-quoted programme note to *Vesalii Icones*.

After his return from America in 1964, Davies lived mainly in England in Dorset, and wrote the bulk of his music (some twenty works out of thirty between 1967 and 1974) for the Fires of London ensemble (formerly the Pierrot Players), which he directs. In recent years, his works have considerably benefited from his collaboration with people eminent in spheres of artistic activity other than music: Randolph Stow wrote the poems for the *Eight Songs for a Mad King* and *Miss Donnithorne's Maggott*;

William Louther created the dances for *Vesalii Icones*; and the actor Roy Hart the Mad King rôle. He has contributed music to two films by Ken Russell, *The Devils* and *The Boyfriend*, while Russell has sponsored two recordings of his music and was to have directed the production of *Taverner*, but this latter project did not materialise.

In 1971 Davies began to visit regularly the Orkney island of Hoy, where he has recently restored a tiny croft house near the remote settlement of Rackwick. His recent music, composed on Hoy, has had more and more to do with Orkney: *From Stone to Thorn* (1971) was the first of many settings of the Orkney poet George Mackay Brown, the *Hymn to St Magnus* (1972) celebrates the local saint, while the orchestral songs *Stone Litany: Runes from a House of the Dead* (1973) is a luminous evocation of the sound world of the islands. Davies as a nature composer would have seemed rather improbable in 1968 or 1969, bumper years for foxtrots and sleazy 'Victorian' hymns, but the special feeling he has for Orkney and its history is obviously already of great importance in his musical development and will doubtless result in many more Orkney compositions.

Two Welsh Composers: Alun Hoddinott and William Mathias

MICHAEL OLIVER

Alun Hoddinott (born in 1929) and William Mathias (born in 1934) have much in common besides their nationality. Both studied initially in Wales and subsequently with a distinguished 'conservative' composer in London. Both are now professors of music, at University Colleges at opposite ends of the principality. Both have written prolifically, often to commission from local organisations. Yet the description 'academic composer' fits neither and their musical styles are as different as their birthplaces: Hoddinott comes from Bargoed, close to the blighted landscapes of the South Wales coalfield; Mathias from Whitland in rural Carmarthenshire, a short walk from Dylan Thomas's Laugharne. Their music shares no characteristic that can be isolated and identified as Welsh. Both, of course, have written (generally in response to commissions) music with some local reference or with a text drawn from a Welsh writer. But a set of *Welsh Dances* (Hoddinott) or a cantata on the subject of *St Teilo* (Mathias) does not alter the fact that both are Welsh *composers* rather than *Welsh* composers.

Hoddinott was educated at the University College of South Wales (where he is now head of the Department of Music) and also studied privately with Arthur Benjamin. His Op. 1, the String Trio, dates from his twentieth year but was preceded by a very large corpus of juvenile compositions which he has withheld from publication. His early maturity must owe much to the self-tuition of these rejected works; certainly his earliest works are already remarkably assured and, although obviously owing a debt to Walton and others, already very personal. The First Symphony, Op. 7 (1955) is uncharacteristic only in its length (it is fully ten minutes longer than any of its successors). But its vehemence of expression—the composer uses such words as 'gloomy' and 'brutal' to describe it—is already typical of his later work. It is also worth noticing that he chose symphonic form as a vehicle for this early expression of deep, even violent emotion. He
86

seems always to have felt the need for firm structures to contain the explosive (and potentially disruptive) contrasts of his music, but he has also recognised the need for ancient forms to be modified if they are not to be burst asunder by their uncomfortable new contents. The core of his voluminous catalogue of compositions is a continuing sequence of works that adapt the classical symphony, concerto and sonata to the requirements of his language.

This language, ever since the First Symphony, has been strongly chromatic, though never strictly serial and never abandoning tonal reference. The tonal bonds, however, are sufficiently weakened to provide another impetus to the search for new forms, while surviving, vestigially, in Hoddinott's skilful use of the sense of key to heighten drama, to tauten suspense or to release tension.

His is music of strong contrast, often violent or strident, and of powerful energy and drama. It is music of disturbing upheavals and of strenuous emotional crises. It is also music of vivid colour: Hoddinott uses instruments brilliantly with, in his orchestral work, an exceptional dynamic and chromatic range. If the typical Hoddinott mood might be characterised as a grim and brooding melancholy disturbed by wrathful or hectic incursions, the typical Hoddinott sound would be dark in colour, low of pitch and firm of pulse. His use of rhythm is also characteristic, and is one of the reasons for his music's approachability: his quick movements often have a powerful impetus and he uses rhythmic motives to aid in the unification of a composition.

Towards his many commissions his attitude has proved thoroughly professional. He accepts them as challenges and responds sympathetically to the problems of the instrument or ensemble for which he is writing. His commissioned works form a series of distinguished solutions to problems that many composers might have treated as chores. There follows a discussion of certain characteristic works of Hoddinott, all of them currently available on gramophone recordings (he has been exceptionally well served by the record companies), with the aim of setting them in the context of his work as a whole.

The Second Piano Concerto, Op. 21 (1960) uses a normal-sized orchestra (its predecessor made incisive use of a wind band). The first movement is fairly gentle and restrained in character, built over a rhythmically swaying phrase; its form is also simple, the latter half a varied restatement of the former. Hoddinott's romantic vein is well illustrated by the slow movement, whose emotional weight is carried by the lyrical, occasionally impassioned string writing. The orchestra brings the movement to its climax, the soloist rhapsodically observing rather than participating. This allotting of opposed roles to soloist and orchestra is frequently found in Hoddinott's concerti; it is again apparent in the finale, which alternates a spiky toccata subject (the piano, in effect, joining the orchestra with continuous growling semiquavers in its lowest register) with much more yieldingly pianistic material. The piano part throughout is grateful and idiomatic, owing much to the instrument's nineteenth-century traditions. Hoddinott's contribution to piano literature has been fairly extensive (three concerti and six sonatas so far).

The piano's range is much further extended in such a work as the Sixth Piano Sonata (1972). The sonata's opus number (Op. 78 No. 3) indicates, by the way, that Hoddinott's catalogue of works is still more extensive than a mere reckoning-up of opus numbers would suggest. The arresting opening of the sonata, a craggy fortissimo chord-pattern, punctuates a movement of predominantly linear cast. It is a relatively simple ternary structure, but the second (and final) movement is a more developed and characteristic example of Hoddinott's formal ingenuity. It is a toccata-rondo with two episodes and an extended coda. The repetitions of the rondo subject, however, are extensively varied, harmonically and contrapuntally, and the coda's reference to the first movement is neither literal nor a nod to 'cyclic form'; the opening music is now seen from the distance traversed in the interim.

Both the works discussed so far are short and provide limited opportunity for textural contrast (the concerto by deferring to the solo part, the sonata by reason of the limitations of a single instrument). In symphonies, however, Hoddinott's liking for the widest ranges of colour and mood demands an uncommonly strong formal framework. His usual technique is to devise an ingenious but basically simple scheme, within which is a microstructure based on a formidable command of the minutiae of the composer's craft: imitation, variation, disguised repetition, etc. Among such techniques Hoddinott has made especial use of quasi-serial procedures (retrogression and inversion and—an especial favourite of his— their logical extension, palindrome). The Third Symphony, Op. 61 (1968) shows this armoury of resource at full stretch.

The work is in two bipartite movements, each half-movement reflecting its counterpart in the pattern AB:BA. The material established in the powerful and impressive opening adagio, however, is germinal to the work as a whole, and the inter-relationships between the sections are thus much more complex than such a simple summary implies. Each of the four sections, too, has its own carefully devised plan, so that within the subsections musical events are perceived both as elements in the immediate argument and as links to the larger structure. All the seemingly disparate ideas set out in the opening adagio have their function within that structure: a repeated low B flat (about which the entire work rotates); an iambic rhythm (used later almost thematically); a dark string phrase incorporating a forbidding low trill (phrase and trill are important); an expressive motif on high violins (at the root of much of the last section) and a few bars of slow march rhythm (taken up in the quick march of section 3). These elements are briefly developed before the scherzo and trio that forms the second part of the movement. The scherzo itself is brilliantly scored and rhythmically active, with stepwise phrases emerging and coalescing into a menacing horn theme. The trio further develops the iambic rhythm and the scherzo's 'repetition' is extensively varied. The counterpart of the scherzo is the allegro that begins the second movement. This is also ternary: quasi-fugal march music surrounding a horn theme that is clearly related to the scherzo and the opening of the first movement. The test of Hoddinott's formal plan is the final adagio. It is a calmer, more linear reflection of the opening, with tranquil 'recapitulations' of music from the two quick sections. When the music reaches an almost Sibelian theme (again a horn solo) and a magical, brooding final cadence, there is a distinct feeling that they have been 'earned'.

Hoddinott's use of the horn in this symphony suggests an especial affection for it and this is amply confirmed in his Horn Concerto, Op. 65 (1969) which may be taken as representative of his numerous concerti for instruments other than the piano (there are others for clarinet, oboe, harp, violin, viola and organ, as well as shorter concertante pieces for horn and cello). The fine cantilena of the opening is perfectly attuned to the instrument's character (and the addition of a solitary bell to the horn timbre was a brilliant stroke of intuition). Passion and brooding are left to the orchestra, the horn taking a detached, gravely lyrical role. Walton's First Symphony is more than once recalled in the central scherzo; again, the soloist's broad phrases are often distinct in character from the scurrying of the orchestra. The cadenza which forms the

89

finale further develops the soloist's sober lyricism; had Hoddinott discovered the instrument's latent incisiveness the concerto might not seem unbalanced by this quiet conclusion—a rare example of Hoddinott's sympathy for an instrument leading him into an uncharacteristic monochrome.

The Sinfoniettas (there are four so far) are successful examples of brief and pithy unification of contrasts. The Third Sinfonietta, Op. 71 (1970) is a fine example of this. Its opening movement is in what might be termed 'condensed sonata form': two highly dissimilar ideas are juxtaposed and then combined, the first returning (altered by the conflict) after a climax. An even more economical version of the same process appears in the second movement; the simplicity of the structure gives the climax (complete with major chord) a fine solemn grandeur. Both these are recalled in the scherzo-like finale to demonstrate the underlying links between the material of all three movements.

It is possible, however, to overemphasise the formal ingenuity of Hoddinott's large-scale structures. The most successful of them also show how far sheer imaginative force can unify a work. The orchestral piece *The Sun, the Great Luminary of the Universe*, Op. 76 (1970) is a musical parallel to a frightening passage from James Joyce, an hypnotic vision of the last judgment expressed in language of biblical intensity. The dynamic range of the piece is vast: from the most hushed of whispers to a colossal fortissimo. The range of character is still wider: quiet recollections of Bach; whirling, frenzied strings; apocalyptic fanfares; grinding dissonance. But the work has a fierce continuity of vision which would give it a satisfying if inexplicable unity even were the purely thematic interlinkings absent.

Hoddinott's most successful large-scale work to date, the Fifth Symphony, Op. 81 (1973), relies at least as much on such imaginative impetus as it does on its characteristically ingenious groundplan. It is again in two movements, the first a loose sonata rondo, the second (in the composer's phrase) a series of 'reflecting panels' in the pattern ABCCBA. The relationships between corresponding sections are inherent rather than obvious or repetitive: the two 'A' sections in the finale, for example, are a lyrical string adagio punctuated by mysterious low bells, and a highly energetic presto. The danger of unresolved juxtaposition is obvious and is not always avoided in Hoddinott's work. But when the combination of formal dexterity and imaginative urgency combine successfully

90

(as they often do) the result has a cumulative eloquence that is Hoddinott's most personal contribution to contemporary British music.

In the above light, it is curious that Hoddinott has only recently turned to that musical form above all others that calls for vividness of imagery and sharp distinction of characterisation: opera. Having now done so, however, he has spoken of his intention to concentrate on stage work, and his first contribution to the genre suggests that he was born for it. *The Beach of Falesá*, successfully premièred by the Welsh National Opera Company in 1974, contains many of the composer's characteristic traits: highly coloured orchestration (including important and dramatically evocative use of percussion); abrupt juxtaposition (here given added logic by the drama that it illustrates); and his habitual use of motivic inter-relationship. He also uses a twelve-note row as a germinative device (though the score is far from atonal). His future operas will be eagerly anticipated, but the effect of operatic experience on his symphonic thinking may be even more productive.

The music of William Mathias, who is now Professor of Music at Bangor, has little of the gritty urgency and violent expressiveness of Hoddinott. As a pupil of Lennox Berkeley, restraint was to have been expected. His music is tonal, unaffectedly melodious, often dance-based and with few harmonic asperities. It is, indeed, music that might well appeal to a wide audience, were there but opportunities to hear it at all frequently outside Wales. But it should not be assumed that his music, eager to please though it often is, lacks depth or conflict. Mathias refuses to shout and is sometimes content simply to discourse agreeably, but he often has something of moment to say, none the less. We may, in the latter half of the twentieth century, be puzzled by a composer of this kind: simplicity, paradoxically, has become difficult.

As with Hoddinott, the early works are already characteristic. In the first few opus numbers we can discover most of the seeds of his more recent work. They include an enviable melodic gift (including an ability to invent admirably self-sufficient themes that—in Vaughan Williams's phrase—'turn out to go together'); his tunes are often composed of extremely simple elements—thirds and fourths—but (enviably again) avoid the pitfalls of anonymity and blandness. He is very fond of re-using brief melodic ideas in the several sections of a large-scale work, transforming them by variation of tempo, tonality and timbre; this technique, unassumingly used, helps to give his music its often very satisfying formal logic.

Mathias has an acute sense of rhythm. Much of his music is light-footed, based on dance-measures, and makes deft use of syncopation. Perhaps, however, the most marked and most welcome characteristic of his music is its cleanliness of texture. His counterpoint is always crystal clear and he has the far from common knack of writing loud music that is not raucous. He is aided in this by his handling of the orchestra, which is highly accomplished, often calling on such instruments as celeste and piano to give light and crispness to the texture. His use of the harp is also instructive; he seldom uses it to provide the fuzzy wash of arpeggios that has so often been its fate in the past.

With such a 'conservative' musical language, the danger of derivativeness is far greater for Mathias than for Hoddinott. The shadows of Britten, Walton, Hindemith and especially Tippett are undeniable, and Bartók has been a fruitful influence once or twice. But Mathias's own personality is strong enough to overcome these; a greater danger has been his fluency and fertility of invention. There have been pages which might have been more successful had Mathias been obliged to fight for his material, had his reserve of ideas been less inexhaustible and his combinatorial skill less great. But even this danger could overwhelm only a composer whose need to compose was less than his ability to do so. And throughout Mathias's output there is music of deep feeling, great beauty and richness of incident that abundantly demonstrate a unique personal expression.

The relatively early Divertimento, Op. 7 (1958), although a lightweight work written for a student orchestra, contains examples of both accomplished craftsmanship and genuine artistic achievement. If the first movement as yet lacks a truly personal melodic substance, it has an infectious spontaneity and rhythmic liveliness that already betoken a thoroughly professional composer. Something more is demonstrated in the slow movement, which builds a finely wrought and deeply felt climax from a melody of plain outline but considerable strength. By the time of the Second Piano Concerto, Op. 13 (1961), Mathias's personal style seems fully formed (his first essay in this form, a student work, is unpublished).

The opening of the first movement is beautifully imagined, in effect a lyrical toccata: it is a quite typical Mathias sound. The strongly marked dance rhythms of the ensuing quick section may owe a minor debt to Rawsthorne, but their elegantly economical energy is another Mathias hallmark. The scherzo, too, might invite comparisons: Shostakovich is the obvious name, but in no really derivative sense. The sustained energy of the movement, fuelled by flexible time-signatures, shows Mathias working in an area already familiar from Shostakovich's concerti, but he scarcely loses by the conjunction. Again, the slow movement is the most personal; the florid writing for the soloist is luminously clear and restrainedly expressive. The whole concerto finely balances soloist against orchestra and shows a sharp ear for contrasts of texture. It is a pianist's concerto, and it is no surprise to learn that Mathias is himself a fine pianist.

Since the concerto, Mathias has become increasingly prolific and has written a great many 'occasional' and commissioned works. As in the case of Hoddinott, this makes the neat division of his music into 'periods' difficult, even if it were not too early to do so. Even so, it is surprising to find the organ Partita, Op. 19 (1962) and the String Quartet, Op. 38 (1967) so far apart in date, since both suggest Mathias using relatively monochrome resources to strengthen his style and guard against the perils of excessive fluency. The Partita uses deliberately restricted but pregnant material—a melodic phrase of widening steps and a simple dotted rhythm—to build a three-movement sonata-like structure of impressive economy and logic. Cheerfulness breaks into this sober exploration, but only a very old-fashioned church musician would object to this kind of dancing in the organ loft.

The String Quartet is a much more intense and concentrated essay; it is one of Mathias's most serious and convincing works. The language is much more obviously 'contemporary' than in most of his work, but it is post-Bartók rather than post-Schoenberg: it is still rooted in tonality, and the moving and sensitively felt coda depends on this. But the work is also an exploration of the variety that is possible within a larger unity. It embraces contrasts almost as strong (within the limits imposed by a string quartet) as any in Hoddinott, but holds them within a commandingly handled extension of sonata form.

It seems, indeed, that works for solo instrument or for small groups act as the 'workshop' in which Mathias develops the

D

93

techniques that are later applied to his larger pieces. In some ways, the splendid First Piano Sonata, Op. 23 (1963) might be regarded as a chamber symphony for piano alone, of which the Concerto for Orchestra, Op. 27 (1964) is the full-scale orchestral counterpart (the two works do not, of course, have material in common). The first movement of the sonata is on a larger scale than clock-time would indicate. It is a very rich movement, prodigal of ideas, but firm of structure. The piano writing is brilliant but far from derivative and the delicate filigree of the coda (related to the rushing staccato repeated notes earlier) is another example of a sound that could have been composed by no-one else. The slow movement contains turbulent conflicts, primarily between a heavy chordal melody and a more ornate sequence of phrases, rich in ornament, but again the resolution is convincing. The last movement is lighter in weight and agreeably witty, but builds considerable power from its dancing toccata figures. The Concerto for Orchestra, a symphony in all but name, is a fully mature and characteristic work, using sonata form for the first of its three movements. The slow movement in particular is typical of Mathias: richly romantic, apparently leisured though in fact tightly controlled, and with deep feeling building a climax from fertile development of the plaintive oboe music heard at the beginning. It will be noticed that trills are often used as expressive elements in Mathias's more deeply felt passages.

The First Symphony, Op. 31 (1966) is so characteristic a work that more detailed discussion may be useful. Unabashedly in C major, the resourceful and energetic first movement neatly adapts sonata form: the first subject group, of strongly rhythmic material, is fully developed before the second group appears. This is dominated by a lyrical cello theme, punctuated by ornamental phrases for high woodwind and celeste—another characteristic Mathias sound. The ensuing working-out clearly demonstrates close kinships between the principal ideas, but never becomes academic: the buoyant energy is well maintained throughout. After such a lively allegro, it is a little surprising to find a scherzo in second place—a true scherzo, with very crisp rhythm and incisive use of percussion, the forward impulse being especially evident in the hammered-out string phrases and rapid drumming of the middle section. But the slow movement, the longest and finest of the four, explains this: it is another of Mathias's relaxed and rhapsodic adagios. Its formal logic becomes clear as it proceeds, the beautiful opening (quiet string chords decorated by piano figures, a lyrical oboe solo with ornaments from the celeste) flowering on its first repetition into a trill-bedecked theme of great beauty and freshness of feeling. The movement also incorporates a folk-like meandering tune involving dotted rhythm and a slightly faster idea for high woodwind, sparkling with glockenspiel traceries. All three are combined ultimately in an ecstatic, multi-tiered singing texture that recalls Tippett. The same name springs to mind in connection with the finale, but here it is made clear that it is less an influence than a common emotional quality that we are dealing with: a common awareness of a Celtic ancestry, perhaps. The finale is a highly ingenious sonata rondo. After an introduction of fanfares and bell-like motives in the strings, the rondo subject, a driving moto perpetuo, is heard. On each of its repetitions it is accompanied by 'new' material: a trumpet cantilena; running woodwind figures added to the trumpet; and a noble, vigorous chorale. There are close relationships between these and the episodes that separate the returns of the rondo: agile woodwind music closely connected with the moto perpetuo and fanfares that link the opening of the movement to the chorale. The movement as a whole is a splendidly cumulative structure of great skill and excitement.

The areas mentioned so far have been further developed in a by now extensive catalogue of works. The First Symphony seems to have marked the point at which Mathias came to terms with his own facility, and from that point there is no longer a distinction between the 'private', disciplined instrumental pieces and the larger, 'public' works. He has been able, in fact, to accomplish a daunting and difficult task: the construction of taut, economical and 'composerly' structures which deploy great technical resource while using an accessible, 'popular' language. The surface simplicity covers, but should not hide from the listener, a formidable command of argument, cross-reference and thematic distillation. This is evident even in such an agreeable piece of light music as the Sinfonietta, Op. 34 (1966) in which every element, from the jaunty first allegro theme and the charmingly awkward Anglo-Caribbean blues of the slow movement to the energetic dances of the finale, has a common origin. Mathias, in fact, has never been one to give short measure of his skill to light music. The *Dance Overture*, Op. 16 (1961) is a Welsh *Portsmouth Point*, and the *Invocation and Dance* that followed it (Op. 17) has lyrical substance as well as joviality. Orchestras despairing of the dearth of good

95

modern light music could do much worse than investigate these pieces and their companions.

Mathias's choral music has been little heard outside Wales. It is improbable that such pieces as *St Teilo*, Op. 21 and *Culhwch and Olwen*, Op. 32 are unexportable, if one considers the success that *Ave Rex*, Op. 45 has had with choral societies. The latter is a sequence of carols that may be performed separately, with either orchestra or organ. It is a pity that the hearty 'Sir Christëmas' has been taken up by choirs at the expense of the exquisite 'There is No Rose of Such Virtue', its beautiful cantilena answered by twining two-part responses. And the second carol, 'Alleluya, a New Work is Come on Hand', a choral toccata in the manner of Vaughan Williams, suggests that an investigation of Mathias's other choral music would be profitable.

Mathias is an unfashionable phenomenon and is usually dismissed as a traditionalist. It would be a pity, however, if this easy classification were to prevail over a composer whose natural voice is a lyrical, tonal one, but whose debt to tradition does not lead him into derivativeness. That his voice is a personal one (however unassertively expressed) is obvious in several of the works discussed above and in such highly contrasted pieces as the beautiful Harp Concerto, Op. 50 (1970)—a work of great poetry and quiet eloquence—or the vital and forceful Third Piano Concerto, Op. 40 (1968). Above all, his use of tradition is fresh and renovative; he is a composer who may be dismissed as 'irrelevant to the problems of modern music' only by those to whom music has become an arid study instead of a source of pleasure.

Nicholas Maw

ARNOLD WHITTALL

Until the mid-Fifties, serialism had remained unexplored in Britain, save by rarely played pioneers like Lutyens and Searle. It was therefore likely that the twelve-note method would have more appeal for young composers than either the nationalism or neo-classicism of those elders who, it may have seemed, were clinging rather desperately to tonality and traditional forms. Nicholas Maw, born in 1935 and a student at the Royal Academy of Music, London from 1955 to 1958, never displayed the whole-hearted radicalism of his almost exact contemporaries Cardew and Maxwell Davies, yet the works of his student years demonstrate a willingness to exploit the twelve-note method as well as tonality, and ultimately he was able to forge a personal style which owes something to both disciplines. When in October 1962 Maw wrote in a review in the *Musical Times* of a certain composer's 'romantically orientated temperament backed by a keen intelligence and by a strong desire to write music rather than dogma', he was providing a definition applicable to himself. So, while the early Requiem is an extended tonal composition, the *Eight Chinese Lyrics*, written in four days in November 1956, are miniature twelve-note monodies which treat the note-order of the Basic Set with considerable freedom.

In the Sonatina for flute and piano (1957) Maw gets to grips for the first time with the issues involved in exploiting serial technique harmonically, and the result is in places rather disconcertingly neo-classical. The Sonatina is more than mock-Hindemith or mock-Stravinsky; its lyricism and wit foreshadow crucial and lasting elements in later works. Yet it displays rather than solves the stylistic problems facing a young composer with no impulse to run with the radicals. Someone as deeply involved as Maw with the musico-dramatic aspects of the romantic tradition is unlikely to produce instrumental works which meekly fill out the hallowed blueprints of classically proportioned forms, and in this respect the Sonatina is the first in a sequence of compositions

97

which make use of the principles associated with the sonata in a flexible, undogmatic way. Of particular interest is the way in which the tonal possibilities of the Basic Set are given due and appropriate recognition, to the extent that the work can be regarded as having a main tonal centre (not tonality in the traditional sense of diatonic major or minor scales) of F sharp. The first four notes of the Basic Set (P-0) are G sharp, F sharp, C sharp and B: the other three notes of the scale of F sharp major occur as the last three notes of the set, though presented enharmonically as F, E flat and B flat. Maw also makes significant use of two transpositions: P-7 (second subject of the first movement) which begins with D sharp, C sharp, G sharp and F sharp, and I-2 (main theme of the finale). The final cadence of the piece stresses the close association between P-0 and I-2, with tonic-dominant alternations of F sharp and C sharp in the bass, and a chord of fourths above which adds E sharp, A sharp, D sharp and G sharp to the harmony.

The pull of tonal gravity which can be sensed in all Maw's mature works from time to time—sometimes almost incidentally, as in the String Quartet and the Sonata for Strings and Two Horns, often more emphatically, as in the operas and *Life Studies*—is normally less the result of a hierarchic harmonic framework relating to those used by the classical and romantic masters, than the outcome of textural implications of thematic working, the direction of which, and the character of which, lead logically to certain specific stresses at appropriate points. In the later works this emphasis is likely to be more independent of both serial and diatonic considerations than it is in the Flute Sonatina. But even here the 'twelve-note tonality' indicates that Maw finds such stresses particularly useful in developing a coherent harmonic framework against which highly chromatic thematic material may evolve. A strict twelve-note technique could doubtless have been made to serve such a language but it may be that the sheer breadth of the melodic writing, which comes so naturally to Maw and which is the most memorable single aspect of his technique, has made the operation of serial patterns seem intolerably constricting and irrelevant.

Coming soon after the Sonatina, the Nocturne for mezzo-soprano and chamber orchestra, completed in June 1958, employs a more thoroughly romantic language, in which the pointed but rather short-breathed rhythmic figuration of the Sonatina yields to a melodic spontaneity, sometimes florid, sometimes eloquently economical, which may in places produce quite explicit tonal emphasis. Maw still uses techniques appropriate to a twelve-note composer, however: the second half of the orchestral introduction is the retrograde inversion of the first half, and the Epilogue is a retrograde of the whole introduction—but since these sections are centred on the note B flat, the 'serial' devices, like the ostinato textures, reinforce rather than undermine the tonal direction of the music.

The Nocturne is a continuous work in nine sections. Four settings of poems by Stephen Spender, Alun Lewis ('Compassion', which Tippett had already set in *The Heart's Assurance*), Herbert Read and W. H. Auden, are separated by substantial orchestral interludes entitled Cantilena, Sinfonia and Cadenzas, the whole work being framed by the Introduction and Epilogue. This form is not at all similar in proportions to Britten's Nocturne, also composed in 1958, where the orchestra has no independent movements. Yet the coincidence of subject inevitably raises the question of similarity. Night, as a time of human vulnerability, is one of the great recurring images in Britten's subject-matter, matching perfectly his own attachment to that most insecure of modern compositional techniques, tonality. The resonances in Maw's case are slighter: one is less conscious of night as a metaphor of menace, though this element is not excluded, than of its more straightforward romantic associations, and in particular as a time when parted lovers feel lonely. In view of the occasional tendency to stress Maw's 'expressionism' and to link him stylistically with early Schoenberg, it should be emphasised that, while nostalgia, frustration and other emotions are often more prominent than simple ecstasy in his chosen texts, the Freudian guilt of Schoenberg's *Erwartung*, the sexual dementia of Berg's *Wozzeck* and *Lulu*, even the more reticent deviations of Britten's *Peter Grimes* and *Billy Budd*, are, as yet, remote from his music, even though the capacity for tension and conflict which his style demonstrates might eventually prove an ideal vehicle for such subject-matter.

All the music so far considered was the product of Maw's student years, and it is clear that the civilised, refined qualities, which his teacher Lennox Berkeley had absorbed during his own studies with Nadia Boulanger during the late Twenties and early Thirties were by no means as antipathetic to Maw as they must have been to wilder spirits in the mid-Fifties. Nevertheless, Maw's own studies in France during 1958 and 1959 failed to provoke any enduring commitment to the neo-classical manner. Ultimately, no doubt, it was too restricted for 'a romantically orientated temperament'; Maw was developing a capacity to regard the great nineteenth-century masters as both more far-reaching in importance and more potent in influence than the neo-classicists could allow. Eventually, he was even able to describe *Le Marteau sans Maître* by Boulez as 'a twentieth-century manifestation of that dark side of nineteenth-century romanticism which found its fullest expression in Goethe's *Faust*', and to characterise Boulez himself as 'a disruptive force who at the same time has his roots firmly in a tradition'. (13) But the romanticism that has given Maw himself the greatest stimulus is that of light rather than darkness, of integration rather than of disruption; and it has been his special achievement to devise a musical style ideally appropriate in its richness and subtlety to this most positive kind of emotional expression.

The last of Maw's 'student' works was written in Paris and London during the summer and autumn of 1959. The *Six Chinese Songs* for voice and piano are not merely twelve-note, but atonal in a manner which suggests an equal desire to explore and to exorcise the melodically angular, rhythmically febrile idiom of the late-Fifties avant-garde. By their very efficiency, these songs appear to have exhausted Maw's interest in the style, for although he revised three of them in May and June 1960 his next work is the *Essay for Organ* (first version completed 1961, revised in 1963) in which serial methods are again at the service of tonal harmonic feeling and design. Compared to the Flute Sonatina, very few of the conventions of neo-classicism survive, even in the final Gigue. The florid melodic writing and elaborate rhythms of the Nocturne are further developed, in terms of ambitious and coherent forms which build impressively to the final page with its satisfying cadential acceptance of E as tonal centre.

On his return from France, Maw embarked on what is probably a fairly typical life for a young composer, even one fortunate enough to have captured the interest of a publisher. Freelance journalism and editorial work, lecturing and teaching formed the background, and often the interruption, to his composing. Nevertheless, his mature musical style was first displayed in its full richness and range in *Scenes and Arias*, for three female voices and large orchestra, commissioned by the BBC and first performed at the Proms in 1962 (as with most of Maw's pieces, revision followed performance, and the work was finally complete in 1966).

At first glance, Maw's chosen text seems distinctly unpromising for a work lasting half an hour. It is an anonymous early fourteenth-century poem in two parts, 'Lines from Love Letters'. Part One gives the man's words to his beloved, and Part Two gives her reply, both in a regular verse-pattern of French, English and Latin. Yet the text is appropriate simply because it does not narrate a sequence of events, but provides a framework for what is surely one of the most remarkable evocations of romantic love in music. The 'pre-Freudian' avoidance of all those psychological nuances which so many post-Wagnerian romantics have felt unable to by-pass is liberating rather than limiting, and in post-war British music only the final stages of Tippett's first opera, *The Midsummer Marriage*, are remotely comparable as an ecstatic celebration of emotional fulfilment. Structurally, there is ample variety in *Scenes and Arias*, but an impressive unity of idiom and material, in which often highly complex harmonic units are unerringly directed towards resolution into a diatonically ambiguous yet convincingly self-sufficient pair of chords, is the overriding reason for the work's technical as well as expressive conviction.

Scenes and Arias is not a 'music drama', even to the extent that it might have been had Maw simply used a male voice for Part One and a female for Part Two. Yet as the composer himself said later, it was 'a kind of study for opera-writing'. (214) One other work was completed in 1962, in response to a commission from the University of Southampton for their centenary celebrations. This was *Chamber Music* for oboe, clarinet, horn, bassoon and piano, an extended six-movement piece exploring structural and thematic techniques that were to achieve stronger definition later on. Then Maw was commissioned by the (then) LCC to write an opera for the opening of the Jeannetta Cochrane Theatre in London. For the next two years he was immersed in *One Man Show*.

On the strength of the Nocturne and *Scenes and Arias*, one might have expected Maw to prefer an operatic subject which, though not necessarily tragic, centred on the agonies and ecstasies of romantic love. Indeed, some of the early problems that he experienced when working on *One Man Show* were the direct result of choosing a comic subject at a time when his musical style had attained such a high degree of richness and sophistication. Maw has said that about six months' work was wasted, and a large amount of music destroyed, when 'somebody said it sounded more like Medea murdering her children than a comic opera'. (214) Would it not have been better to change the libretto at this point? A *Medea* from Maw would indeed be exciting! But that view renders scant justice to Arthur Jacobs's neat elaboration of Saki's story about the tattoo on a man's back (it turns out to consist of his name—Joe—upside-down) which briefly becomes the rage of the innovation-hungry, fashion-dominated art world, and threatens to ruin Joe's conventional but happy love-life. Story and music alike could so easily have become a ponderous sermon on the virtues of conservatism, and it is a tribute to both librettist and composer that there is no perceptible sound of grinding axes. With literate operatic comedies (especially British ones) so rare, *One Man Show*, a revised version of which was published in 1968, deserves regular revival. If, as the composer admitted, the style demanded 'a drastic paring-down of my previous musical language', this simply ensured that the many narrative scenes could move at appropriate speed: there is still ample richness, and every opportunity for expansive lyricism is taken, so that the music never seems starved of inner momentum. Of its very nature, of course, this first opera plumbs few of the emotional depths of *Scenes and Arias*, but its balance of wit and romance on a large scale displays a new dramatic range which was to be used to impressive effect in the sequence of shorter works that now ensued. Above all, *One Man Show* proved that Maw could write substantial amounts of lively music which was by no means palely neo-classical in style. It is only if we entertain the somewhat unreal belief that the composer should have immediately attempted a further intensification and expansion of the achievement of *Scenes and Arias* that *One Man Show* may disappoint. Maw's own ambivalent feelings about the enterprise may be displayed at the point where, in Act I of the opera, the motto-chords of *Scenes and Arias* are quoted as Joe reflects on the anger of his wife-to-be at his improvidence and self-indulgence. Perhaps this is self-criticism as well as self-quotation!

Maw's next major work after the opera was an ambitious move into a very different world. The single-movement form of the String Quartet (1965) is based on the 'four in one' principle: first movement, scherzo, slow movement and finale can all be detected, the main function of the 'first movement' being less to present a fully rounded design in its own right than to introduce the material for the whole work and to develop those elements of it not primarily intended for the later sections. The main respect in which the work differs from any obvious precedents is, however, the sense in which the character and treatment of the thematic material determine the form, rather than some preordained harmonic scheme. The material ranges from atonal chord sequences to unharmonised melodic statements which stress either a single pitch or several pitches that can suggest clear tonal associations. In the Quartet it is D that emerges as central in the finale section, and the emphasis in relation to the work as a whole suggests that the 'tonality' is present to contrast with prevailing atonality, thereby resolving certain tensions, but still permitting the work to return ultimately to much less explicit harmonic concerns. The beginning and end *can* be analysed in terms of D, but such an interpretation does little justice to the organic ambiguity of Maw's non-triadic harmonies. The ending is far from inconclusive, however, simply because the thematic issues, which have clear priority, have been completely and satisfyingly worked out.

Aggressive and abrupt 'resolution' onto a single note is precisely what does occur at the end of the Sinfonia for small orchestra (1966). Yet while this final F is anticipated at times throughout the work's three movements, it can barely be regarded as a 'main' tonal centre, whose ultimate 'victory' is the result of conflict, on traditional lines, between it and various subsidiary centres. Maw has described the Sinfonia as his 'most neo-classical piece', and the almost dismissive presentation of the final 'resolution' indicates his 'love/hate relationship' with those forms which in the past have employed such resolutions functionally. The form of the Sinfonia is that of extended, basically lyrical, first movement, including a scherzo; slow movement (Threnody) and finale (Theme and Variations); and the tendency of the themes to create their own points of local pitch emphasis is if anything rather more notable than in the Quartet.

In 1966 Maw also completed two song cycles, the *Six Interiors* (settings of Hardy for high voice and guitar) and *The Voice of Love* to poems by Peter Porter. Probably the most memorable Hardy settings ever made are Britten's *Winter Words*, in which the concentrated melancholia of many of the poems is matched by music of inspired simplicity. Maw's natural style is more complex, yet he controls it well, especially in the sombre 'In Tenebris' with its shivering, wintry pedal A, and in the superficially more placid 'At Tea', a chilling little anecdote about a happy wife who is unaware that 'the visiting lady' was her husband's first love. The eight poems in *The Voice of Love*, in which a woman recalls her love affair with the man she eventually married, are based on the seventeenth-century Osborne Letters. The only direct quotation from the letters used by Porter—'Shall we ever be so happy?' —indicates emotion recollected in tranquillity rather than anguished nostalgia, and Maw beautifully shapes the narrative and reflective elements of the cycle, whose opening music returns transformed at the end with perceptible emphasis on the note E.

In 1967 a Bath Festival commission gave Maw the opportunity to continue his exploration of single-movement instrumental structures, and to perfect a design which, while even more remote from traditional proportions than that of the String Quartet, still provides the three essential stages in the coherent presentation of thematic material: statement, development, restatement. The lyric and dramatic contrasts of the Sonata for Strings and Two Horns are especially striking, and any suspicion of arbitrary episodic construction that a visual inspection of the score may arouse is banished aurally by an overriding sense of proportion, balance and clarity. The thematic issues are resolved, and to this extent the typical harmonic ambiguity of the final bars does not leave the listener feeling deprived of some necessary commitment to a single centre on the composer's part, for the thematic premises do not provide for ultimate tonal centrality. Over the whole Sonata there hangs that magical, richly romantic atmosphere which was to pervade Maw's second opera, *The Rising of the Moon*, but it is a romanticism into which considerable energy and drama can be functionally integrated.

Critics of the artistic status quo might find it easy to ridicule the idea of a composer in residence at one of the senior British universities writing a romantic comedy for Glyndebourne. It may well be true that if he had been the recipient of a generous state stipend Maw would not have chosen to attach himself to Trinity College, Cambridge, from 1966 to 1970, nor to write a second comic opera. But any composer who has to make his own way owes it to himself to accept the best offers he can, and Maw was understandably attracted by the opportunity to profit from the experiences of his first opera.

I learnt a tremendous amount about dramatic timing from *One Man Show*. I got it wrong there, but I think I've learnt what it means now. It is something you can only learn by experience: no matter how many operas you know by other people, you have to learn how it works in your own music. In the nineteenth century it was possible to write a dozen operas before getting it right—Verdi did! Nowadays it's much harder, because you only get about three chances. (224)

Maw said that it took two years to find the right subject for what he describes as 'essentially a singer's opera', but his librettist Beverley Cross came up with the basic idea of a conflict 'between the inhabitants of a small deserted town in County Mayo and the English county regiment that occupies the town' (224); the date is 1895. It is safe to predict that no Anglo-Irish subject could have been given comic connotations a few years after Maw and Cross began work on *The Rising of the Moon*, but in fact one of the notable features of the story is the extent to which caricature is controlled, at least as far as the basic situation is concerned. Since English and Irish are both shown to be similarly absurd and fallible, political issues can be kept safely at a distance, as indeed can religious ones. Possibly less successful is the characterisation of the romance between Beaumont, the new young officer with a taste for music, botany and watercolours, and Cathleen, the Irish girl who falls in love with him. Their feelings are simply given too little space to blossom, and in this sense they become the victims of the plot, which needs to move rapidly if all the necessary events are to be included. If the romance of Cathleen and Beaumont were no more central to the plot than that of Fenton and Nanetta in Verdi's *Falstaff*—Maw's own favourite operatic comedy—it would matter less. But in a *romantic* comedy the claims of the two elements can get in each other's way. As Maw rightly says, 'the trouble with comedy is that it must move fast': romance needs more time, so the balance is delicate and very difficult to get right. Nevertheless, Maw is particularly successful in the large amounts of energetic, eventful music which is always of interest for musical reasons, as well as being dramatically apt. Fortunately, too, the best act is the last, with a superbly impressive range from the liveliest and largest of comic ensembles to the tenderest and most passionate love music.

Perhaps a more serious subject would require a tauter musical substructure. Yet the musical language demonstrates Maw's unfailing sense of the subtle shades of tension possible when harmony is in a constant but never aimless state of motion between tonal and atonal. Pure triads hardly ever occur, save in the military music, but the movement towards specific tonal areas, notably D flat and A flat in Act III, is finely calculated to achieve the maximum expressive effect with the minimum of conventional diatonic procedure. This is truly allusive music, and in places, like the final exit of Frau von Zastrow (Figure 386), it is also truly magical, and as moving as anything in modern British music. And for all its 'anti-*Tristan*' ending, with the lovers accepting separation (and staying alive), the moments of passion in this last act have an epic quality which indicates that grander dramatic subjects might one day prove irresistible.

The Rising of the Moon received its world première at Glyndebourne on 19 July 1970, and was revived the following season. In 1973 Maw produced an orchestral work called *Concert Music* which derives from the opera (it is not a suite, being in one continuous movement). The sequence is not strictly chronological—Frau von Zastrow's 'exit' music precedes Atalanta's delightful Waltz Song from Act II—but *Concert Music* begins and ends as the opera itself begins and ends, and provides a most attractive digest of some of its best moments.

Maw's activities since the completion of *The Rising of the Moon* are best discussed in terms of 'work in progress', since several important works have yet to take on their definitive form. The *Serenade* is another composition for small orchestra—flute, two each of oboes, bassoons and horns, and strings—which, like the Sinfonia, employs a multi-movement design, even though both the atmosphere and instrumentation link it just as strongly to the Sonata for Strings and Two Horns. The unselfconscious richness of the thematic writing is particularly evident in the central Notturno, and here too the tendency to centre tonally on E is most striking. The outer movements—at least in the original version of the work composed for the English Chamber Orchestra's tour of the Far East in 1973 —are called Pastorale and Capriccio, and both display that inventive approach to essentially traditional designs which has been characteristic of all Maw's earlier instrumental writing.

Maw's next major work, *Life Studies* for fifteen solo strings, is a significant departure in this specifically structural respect. In the first version, performed by the Academy of St Martin's at the 1973 Cheltenham Festival, there were seven separate movements, the order of which could be varied in performance, subject to the fact that the first two were linked together. Among other changes since the première, Maw has combined the original Nos. 1 and 2 into a single study, and is writing a new No. 2. A substantial new movement (No. 8) has also been added, with a link at the end of No. 7, to allow 7 and 8 to be played as a pair. The practice of allowing the performers some freedom of choice in the order and number of movements to be played on any given occasion was first used by Maw in *Chamber Music*, though in that case the basic 'frame' of first movement and finale was fixed. As its layout indicates, *Life Studies* contains moments of considerable complexity, but most striking of all are the concentrated dramatic power and the intense lyricism, which is perhaps most remarkably employed in the unaccompanied melody for violins towards the end of No. 8. Local tonal focus plays a considerable part, even admitting the use of a key signature in one section, but there is no question of a single centre being given any overriding supremacy, or of the kind of conflict between centres which other modern composers have used as a substitute for the functional relationships of the past.

Both *Life Studies* and the still more recent *Personae* for piano, the first two of which were performed in August 1973, indicate that even if Maw's structures come to display less dependence on the proportions and sequence of events found in the traditional tonal forms, he is unlikely to lose that essentially romantic concern with thematic process which is his most important link with the past. Meanwhile, with a major work for large orchestra nearing completion, and plans for a third opera well advanced, Maw is entering a phase of his career in which expansive dramatic designs are likely to achieve even broader definition and more fully elaborated expression than in what we shall probably come to regard as his early music.

Richard Rodney Bennett

CHRISTOPHER PALMER and LEWIS FOREMAN

The late Sir Noël Coward once surmised that he owed his success as a writer of popular songs to the fact that he came of a generation that took its light music seriously. Few present-day 'serious' musicians take their light music seriously. If they did the distinction traditionally drawn between 'serious' and 'non-serious' music would to a large extent be devoid of meaning. As it is, incidental music written for a film is automatically put into the 'non-serious' category, whereas if a basically similar music be written for a ballet it suddenly becomes 'serious'. The music of pop-songs and musicals, except for the few cult-figures who have won themselves the dubious distinction of academic approbation (Keller's Gershwin, Mellers's Beatles and now Rifkin's Joplin), appears to stand on an even lower pedestal of respectability. This may be readily gathered from the fact that whereas a daily paper's music critic will unquestionably be sent to cover the umpteenth revival of *Trial by Jury* or *The Merry Widow* (the kind of light music to which, the Establishment has decreed, no critical stigma need be attached) any important new musical or revue is automatically assigned to the drama critic. He, as likely as not, has no specifically musical knowledge (why should he?) and is therefore ill-equipped to pass judgment on it from the musical point of view for better or for worse. This is, alas, a critical malaise for which no ready-made cure is likely to be found; all the more reason, therefore, both for drawing attention to the fact that it does exist, and for rejoicing with exceeding great joy at the occasional advent of a composer who has emerged unscathed from the complex and insidious processes of socio-cultural brainwashing and indoctrination that produce it. Richard Rodney Bennett is a 'serious' composer who takes his light music seriously.

Bennett was born in 1936 at Broadstairs, Kent. He won a scholarship to the Royal Academy of Music in 1953, where he studied with Lennox Berkeley and Howard Ferguson. In 1957 a further scholarship awarded by the French Government enabled him to study with Pierre Boulez in Paris for two years. He has developed into one of Britain's most prolific and successful composers. His works include three full-length operas; two symphonies; concerti for horn, oboe, piano and viola; a choral work, *Epithalamion,* to a text by a favourite poet, Herrick; four string quartets and other chamber works including the four *Commedia* pieces; instrumental and vocal works, educational music. The range of his achievements is impressive. His 'serious' music has been well covered and appraised in the musical press. Less note has been taken of Bennett's jazz, and even less of his popular music arrangements and film scores. Yet through the latter Bennett has probably reached his greatest public, albeit an unconscious one. For the cinema is the one place where a lay audience may be exposed to 'serious' music without being aware of it, and the part played by film music in conditioning the musical tastes and responsiveness of whole generations is enormously important; it could form the basis of a fascinating musico-sociological study in itself.

Bennett was the most spectacular rising star on the British musical scene in the Fifties. Almost as soon as he had arrived at the Royal Academy his works started appearing in concert programmes, and even at that stage of his career they were very far from being juvenilia. For example, writing about his early quartets, composed in his mid-teens, Donald Mitchell commented in the *Musical Times* (November 1954):

[In the Second Quartet] . . . the slow introduction to his last movement (so much more impressive than the work's actual *Lento*) disclosed a real sensitivity and a fine feeling for quartet texture.

And of the Third Quartet, written when the composer was seventeen (*Musical Times,* March 1955):

Mr Bennett has long shown exceptional promise and his new quartet shows real achievement. A concise first movement, *Lento appassionato,* offered striking thematic material strikingly developed and extended—these were moments of real inspiration—and a sardonic, grotesque *Allegretto scherzando* proved to be a genuine character piece . . . The whole piece, however, displayed a very convincing and personal use of the twelve-note method.

It is this convincing and personal use of the twelve-tone method that has characterised Bennett's 'serious' music. In his handling of

109

voices, too, he has a sensitive and natural feel. From the early *Nocturnall Upon St Lucie's Day* ('Cantata No. 2') for mezzo-soprano and percussion to his most recent opera, *Victory*, he has always found writing for voices sympathetic and this has obviously been of importance in his jazz works too. In all his works his sense of drama is evident. This is even reflected in the instrumental music, of which the *Commedia I–IV* are the most recent and best examples. *Commedia I*, which is for six players (*players* not instrumentalists) was commissioned for the Oxford Bach Festival in 1972. At the beginning of the score the following note appears:

Commedia I was suggested by the characters of traditional Italian and French comedy; though there is no 'plot' the instruments represent those characters (except in the ensembles) as follows: flute—Columbine; bass clarinet—Pantaloon; alto saxophone—Harlequin; trumpet—Punchinella; cello—Pierrot.

This approach to apparently abstract instrumental composition has coloured Bennett's concerti as well. He has commented (in a record sleeve note):

I am naturally concerned with exploring the possibilities offered by the solo instrument, but more particularly I am stimulated by the idea of a dramatic confrontation inherent in a concertante work. I think of this series of works as monodramas rather than simply as abstract instrumental compositions.

In these concerti Bennett's use of the orchestra, and his scoring in general, is generally light and colourful. Even in his most Bergian work—the *Aubade* that he composed in memory of the conductor John Hollingsworth—the characteristic use of particularly instrumental strands running through the texture, especially that of the horn emerging from a dense orchestral texture, goes a long way towards creating the work's muted passion that is its appeal.

Bennett has written remarkably few major orchestral works, the Nocturnes for Chamber Orchestra and the rather lightweight *Suite Française* being the only ones other than the *Aubade* before he wrote his symphonies. His Piano Concerto of 1968 is a typical example of his style. It is bland and faceless, indeed the lack of strongly recognisable characteristics of its composer must count against its success—it is not lovable music. It is a large-scale, four-movement work. In the first movement the skilful and finely spun piano line contrasts with the largely muted strings and a variety of other instrumental lines—the music is basically three blocks of textures moving against each other. The aggressive second (*Presto*) movement is certainly most effective, and owners of the recording may be tempted to play this movement on its own. The work as a whole has very considerable surface appeal but in the last analysis fails to stick in the memory or offer any individual musical experience. The work must be counted as one of its composer's most skilful essays, but when compared with his film and jazz scores, one cannot help but feel that real Bennett may be found in the latter.

The First Symphony dates from the autumn of 1965 and is in three movements, and the Second (in one movement) from the summer of 1967. The conception of a stage work extends even to Bennett's approach to the symphony. As Stanley Sadie points out in a record sleeve note: 'Bennett admits the influence in the [First] Symphony of a comic opera element, linked in mood with the lighter music of the "play within a play" section in Act 2 of *The Mines of Sulphur* . . .'

Bennett's operatic achievement is strangely less impressive than one feels it ought to be. After a powerful one-acter (*The Ledge*), two three-act tragedies (*The Mines of Sulphur* and *Victory*), a full-length comedy (*A Penny for a Song*) and a children's opera (*All the King's Men*), one feels that it is in the last that the composer has been most successful. It is significant that Bennett has juxtaposed deliberately contrasted styles in two of his operas—the play-within-a-play in *Mines of Sulphur*, and the contrasted elements representing the Hotel, the Island paradise and the 'Ladies' Orchestra' in *Victory*. Bennett's genius for pastiche that has been revealed in his film music is well demonstrated in his use of the popular music of the 1880s (and in particular a popular musical of the time, *The Geisha*) when writing the Ladies' Orchestra music.

Bennett calls all his resources of inventive freshness and economy into play in *All the King's Men* (1968). The libretto, by Beverley Cross, is based on an incident that actually occurred in 1643, at the time of the Civil War in England. The music is distinguished both by the terseness of its characterisation and by the expertise of its pastiches. The noble and fearless bearing of the Roundheads, the jaunty arrogance of the Royalists, the twittering fluffiness of the Queen and her retinue, the bumbling pedantry of Dr Chillingworth: all are found musical equivalents in deft and telling strokes, and the pathos of the drummer-boy's solo with which the opera ends—and the music is quite free of archness or affected simplicity

111

—is particularly treasurable. Nor is this the only moment of genuine beauty and emotion. The lullaby for Queen Henrietta is a Dowland pastiche, but the music it makes is so moving and so infinitely tender that the imitation is barely distinguishable from the prototype. This applies as much to Beverley Cross's poem as to the music: both catch the fragrance, courtliness and innocently amorous atmosphere to perfection. The setting is exquisitely wrought, each verse gaining something in contrapuntal elaboration until the climax which weaves an ornate tapestry of gliding, intersecting lines. Then a gradual elimination of texture and sonority until a solo string quartet sinks back into the night whence it arose. At the other end of the emotional spectrum from this sweet and haunting elegy is the splendid work-song of the Royalists —another pastiche, but this time the bias is distinctly Latin-American with a syncopated rumba lilt and a colourful array of exotic percussion instruments and rhythms. Bennett gains a powerfully cumulative effect by the simple but drastic expedient of shifting up a semi-tone for each new verse; his procedure in the later chorus of rejoicing (quoting the original text of the old nursery-rhyme) is rather more sophisticated in that at the climax the tune is taken simultaneously in augmentation by the chorus, in diminution by the accompaniment. But here as elsewhere Bennett wears his learning lightly.

Bennett's exceptional versatility lies at the root of his successes in the popular musical media. He has a remarkable capacity for absorption and imitation of widely disparate styles; the stuff of his musical thought is not a stubborn, but a soft and ductile substance, ready to be moulded by his imagination into whatever forms it is necessary for it to assume. In the case of his film music it has indeed assumed a multiplicity of forms. He has never suffered from the delusion that film people want him for the sound of his 'serious' music, although there have been occasions when the latter has been put to good use in an intrafilmic context. Film people like him because his versatility enables him to produce music that combines seriousness of purpose with immediacy of popular appeal, and because, from the purely technical viewpoint, he is ideal. Bennett works quickly, accurately and with unimpeachable professionalism, and has to boot a genuine love of and interest in the work. He has said that he learnt more from composing film scores than from three years' study at the Royal Academy, and that he still finds the discipline stimulating.

Bennett composed his first film score while still a student at the invitation of John Hollingsworth; the film was called *The World Assured* (1956) and was a quasi-documentary study and history of insurance. Since then he has scored over thirty-five films at the average rate of two per year. The range of music therein encompassed varies enormously, for he has always striven to isolate a different nuance of language and colour for each new film subject he has tackled. Bennett adheres strictly to the procedure he has found best suited to his creative temperament. He is never moved to compose either by script or by rushes. He relies absolutely on the fine cut to galvanise his machinery into action— for in his quest for musical differentiation between subjects he habitually ransacks his films for some detail to seize upon, some recurrent or pervasive feature of visual or even aural texture that he can translate into a characterful musical image, thereby giving each score its own individual consistency of tone and temper. In Joseph Losey's *Secret Ceremony* (1968) this came from the (rather Ravelian) preoccupation with clocks, musical boxes and other kindred gadgets in the house where the action was set. In the same director's *Figures in a Landscape* (1969) the chirruping of grasshoppers and other continuous natural sounds provided the clue. The mystical quality of *Voices* (1973) suggested the suppression of all sharp and strident sonorities in favour of multi-divided strings and harps. For *Billion Dollar Brain* (1967), with its fantasy-violence, hysteria and general larger-than-lifeness, the vertiginous Ondes Martenot (supported by a complement of three pianos, harps, percussion and eleven brass which gave the overall sound a suitably metallic, abrasive edge) proved a perfect fit.

Detailed examination must here be restricted to three of Bennett's biggest and best scores, for two of which (*Far from the Madding Crowd* and *Nicholas and Alexandra*) he won Academy Award nominations. In *Far from the Madding Crowd* (1967) the composer took as his *point de départ* the film's inevitable and necessary insistence on the pathetic fallacy, the inextricable intertwining of nature—landscapes, the countryside, the play of the elements— with character (Bennett often seems to react more strongly to places than to personalities). Human passions merge with the texture of the Wessex country scene and move to the rhythm of the seasons, and so Bennett has recourse to the folksongs and dances of

113

the West of England, but with a difference. Being out of sympathy with the English 'pastoral school' and determined on no account to confect what Patrick Hadley used to term 'bogal' (i.e. bogus modal) music, he avoids the intermediary of the English folklorist-symphonists and returns to these tunes *in status quo*, allowing their natural contours to suggest the simplest of modal melodies and harmonies to him. He simulates the idiom with complete plausibility. For much of the time he restricts himself to the kind of chamber music ensemble to which he has often been drawn in his film work: harp, string quartet, a few solo winds. The result is a score of crystal purity and great lyric transparency. For much of the time the music exists literally as background, as musical scenery; elsewhere vocal renderings of 'Bushes and Briars', 'The Tinker's Song', 'I Sowed the Seeds of Love' and 'The Bold Grenadier' serve as a kind of abstract commentary on the action (the words bearing some symbolic relevance to what is happening on the screen) in a manner much favoured by present-day directors. On the rare occasions when Bennett employs the full symphony orchestra (as in the storm-scene) he knows how to adapt his borrowed themes to his own purposes, which are very different from Vaughan Williams's; here 'The Tinker's Song' is not in any way 'symphonically' integrated, rather does it stand out as the most prominent landmark, the emotional cynosure as it were, in a terrain couched basically in terms of the composer's own musical language.

Folk-music also plays an important part in the score for *Nicholas and Alexandra* (1971) but in a quite different way. The film is an intimate portrait of the Russian royal family in the years immediately preceding the Revolution, and culminates in their assassination at the hands of the Bolsheviks. Initially the music eases us into the world of monarchist comfort and complacency. Bennett's two main themes—the one epic in quality, the other lyrical—are Slav-romantic in style and beautifully tinctured with Russian folksong as filtered through Stravinsky and earlier Nationalists; and both help to encircle the early scenes with an aura of nostalgia and unreality. A magnificent peal of horns announces the Romanov tercentenary; but tension is adumbrated in such details as the fragile, again rather Ravelian waltz for the princesses. But as the clouds gather and the atmosphere becomes progressively darker and more electrically charged, so the musical textures become more fragmentary and elliptical, the harmony more acrid and dissonant, the general colouring more expressionistic. By the time the storm eventually does break (the scenes of Rasputin's death and the revolt of the militia on behalf of the starving populace) Bennett is writing in something which approaches and even ventures beyond his own concert idiom. So too in the scenes of merrymaking in the snow at Tobolsk, when the full orchestra periodically swoops down upon the 'onstage' accordions, injecting a note of hysteria and fanaticism which presages the fate of the Imperial Family at the hands of the approaching Reds. This of course also serves to throw those episodes still scored in the 'Old Style' into great and often moving relief, as for instance when the Czar and his family prepare for their enforced exile and the music imparts a tragic air of emotion-filled finality. This is one of the few film scores in which the music's development keeps pace on its own terms with that of the drama.

In *Lady Caroline Lamb* (1972) Bennett contrives to find an ingenious aural complement for the fundamental conflict—one central to the film's argument—between 'classical' self-discipline and 'romantic' self-indulgence. The composer's approach is clearly defined by the director, Robert Bolt, in notes written for the soundtrack album:

Romantic music at its best invokes and deepens our emotions, at its worst invokes and cheapens them. Classical music at its best invokes emotion but contains it, at its worst is merely polite. I thought at first to have a classical theme for William Lamb, a romantic one for Caroline. But Richard Rodney Bennett pointed out that this would pull the story into its component parts instead of binding it together. He also told me that the tale I had told was a thoroughly romantic one, and only its framing and background were classical . . .

And in its 'framing and background' the score is classical too— the main theme has a Bachian cut, the harpsichord is used liberally, likewise conventions of Bachian figuration; but the essential stuff of the music—its harmony, texture, emotional 'feel'—is all uncompromisingly romantic. Bennett works the clever stylistic trick of projecting a personalised emotion into a stylised or archaic musical mould, grafting the subjective onto the objective. The dichotomy is epitomised in the choice of instruments for the main theme—when associated with William and Caroline it is generally given to the oboe, all clarity, poise and formality; but for *Byron* and Caroline it is passed to the husky, sensuous viola. Its final transformation, as Caroline meets her lonely death in her garden on a raging stormswept night, is thrilling: for here the full resources of the big romantic orchestra are unleashed for the first time to serve as a final definitive comment on the tragedy.

Bennett had the happy idea of re-working the score in the form of a self-contained orchestral piece with concertante viola under the title of *Elegy for Caroline Lamb*: a kind of contemporary paraphrase on the Byronic *Harold in Italy* concept. All the familiar episodes in the score are here shown in a fresh perspective: the stately dance for Caroline's and William's honeymoon diversions with its enchantingly wide-ranging melodic leaps, the burlesque march accompanying Byron's arrival for Wellington's ball, the spiralling string *agitato* for Caroline's ride through the forest on her way to Dover (not used in the final print) and the duet for harp and harpsichord, also from the honeymoon scene by the brook. There are affectionate reminders of a great English viola concerto very dear to Bennett's heart, and highly appropriate they are. Did not Walton once describe himself as 'a classical composer with a strong feeling for lyricism'—with a strong romantic bias?

Bennett's feeling for popular music dates back to the days of his youth when he was an ardent admirer of that arch-exponent of syncopated pianism, Billy Mayerl. He was also much influenced by Lambert and Walton, both composers who veered to a greater or lesser extent in the direction of pop idioms. Lambert in particular: not only was he the first English critic of note to foster serious appreciation of jazz, but his entire attitude to light music and pop was at variance with that of the typical gentleman-musician of the day. Bennett's approach is undoubtedly in some degree a reflection of Lambert's. Bennett has made many arrangements of American and English popular songs, mainly from the period bounded roughly by the late Twenties and early Fifties: among them Gershwin transcriptions for the King's Singers; Rodgers, Porter and Weill arrangements for Eartha Kitt, one of a number of singers for whom he has acted as accompanist; and a Coward anthology for the 1970 Aldeburgh Festival. Those which come closest to personal statements on Bennett's part are often those that possess a strong blues undercurrent: Gershwin's 'The Half of it Dearie Blues', in which (as in 'Our Love is Here to Stay') he marvellously exploits the six-voice close-harmony blend which the King's Singers have developed to a high pitch of virtuosity; Tadd Dameron's 'If They Could See Me Now'; Berlin's 'Supper-time'; Porter's 'Love for Sale'. The Coward anthology well illustrates Bennett's rare ability to 'identify' with the popular music of yesteryear. He frequently reharmonises Coward's melodies, but never gratuitously or in a spirit of oneupmanship; rather does he do it out of a feeling of kinship with the music and a desire to make it creatively his own in a manner profoundly conditioned by his in-depth training as a jazz pianist. In fact, Coward's own harmonisations often do his melodies scant justice (he was not a schooled musician), and Bennett's reharmonisations might more properly be termed 'realisations' inasmuch as each one enlarges or refines upon the emotional implications of the lyric. Thus he adds a touch of Ravelian spice to 'You and I Were Dancing', enhances the nostalgia of 'This is a Changing World', and in his beautiful transformation of 'Sigh No More' reveals himself as great a romantic at heart as any of the Grand Old Men of popular song whose cause he has espoused, and a master harmonist into the bargain. Again the blues pieces touch a particularly responsive nerve. 'Twentieth Century Blues' perhaps for the first time in its life sounds like a real raw-boned Negro blues, not a papier-mâché imitation. The nocturnal 'City' acquires an Ellingtonian sultriness and four-in-the-morning feeling; and 'World Weary' is charged with the same authentically Negroid burden of urban nostalgia. The final climactic chorus of 'Mad about the Boy' is raised to a higher power of almost Arlen-like intensity.

In Bennett's jazz works *per se* the voice of Cleo Laine has been a powerful inspirational factor. For although in 1963–64 he wrote a thirty-minute instrumental ballet in jazz—*Jazz Calendar*—his main interest in jazz has always been predominantly vocal. He has written: 'I believe that for a composer an understanding of the vocal flexibility and of the wide range of timbre used by the most creative jazz singers of the recent past can suggest many new possibilities.' In the case of Cleo Laine—to whom both *Soliloquy* and *Jazz Pastoral* are dedicated—Bennett's imagination was fired by what he described as 'her huge variety of vocal colour, faultless intelligence, musicality and great ability to project her material'. The first piece is a kind of extended dramatic *scena*, the second a song-cycle, both forms borrowed from the classical repertoire. Instrumental jazz has often sought to broaden its vistas in this way, but jazz vocalists in relation thereto have been poorly catered for. Bennett has here succeeded in repairing the deficiency.

117

Soliloquy (1966) is one of his finest works in any medium. Scored for an accompaniment of two saxophones, two brass, piano, bass and drums, it is elaborately constructed. Each of its sections is concerned with some aspect of a broken love-affair and so arranged as to form a logical musical and emotional sequence. The plan is this: (A) Introduction—Fury. (B) Blues-aria I—Sudden sense of loss. (C) Recit.—Dull ache. (D) Slow March—Nostalgic flashback to the sunshine days. (E) Recit.—Dull ache. (F) Fast Waltz—Assault of common sense. (G) Recit.—Dull ache. (H) Blues-aria II—Resignation and acceptance.

The Introduction—the ejection of the unwanted lover—is declaimed to a fury of ad lib drums, and there are other breaks for solo instruments in the fast jazz waltz (F) which is the main focus of contrast. The retrospective (D) over a syncopated pedal-point beautifully evokes the two lovers walking hand in hand 'along the towpath of the dry canal, all summer long . . .'. Bennett's substitution in the finale of a poignant slow ballad for the expected recapitulation of B is surely a masterstroke.

Jazz Pastoral (1969) is a longer piece than *Soliloquy* and is scored for a considerably larger jazz ensemble. It is a setting of six poems from Herrick's *Hesperides*, one of the few times that jazz has been mated with Elizabethan English; and it is a measure of Bennett's achievement that, working as he is in a medium evolved in an utterly alien emotional environment, he seems never beset by emotional disparity between words and music. Once again he gives careful attention to matters of balance. In tempo and texture Nos. 1 ('Introduction') and 6 ('To Daffadills') are akin one to another. No. 2 ('To Primroses') grows naturally out of the fresh, limber tone of No. 1. Nos. 3 and 5 are slow and pensive, but No. 4 by contrast is a fast jazz waltz carrying some melodic reminiscence of No. 3. The two slow movements ('To the Willow-tree' and 'To Musique') must rank among the loveliest music composed in jazz, by Bennett or anyone else. Both have an almost Delian rapture and sensuous glow with melodic lines of classical purity and symmetry. Interestingly, Bennett interprets the final poem in his cycle, 'To Daffadills', quite differently from Delius. Delius's treatment is elegiac and autumnal whereas Bennett's is for the most part playful and fleet with some scat passages for the singer. He seems to be pointing to the objective fact of the flowers' brief quick life rather than to the human tragedy in symbolic terms. The latter is merely hinted at—highly effectively—in the few bars of coda in which the harmony comes to a complete standstill and the voice gradually slows down and dies away: rather as if the onlooker, suddenly looking about him, had discovered that his favourite flower had gone the way of all flesh.

No account of Bennett's art would be complete without further mention of his children's music. At the one end of the scale lie the piano suite *A Week of Birthdays* (1961) and the two 1966 song-cycles for unison voices and piano *The Aviary* and *The Insect World* (these also exist collectively in the form of *Suite for Small Orchestra*); at the other, a setting for (school) chorus and orchestra of Andrew Marvell's *The Bermudas* (1971) and *All the King's Men*. Much in these pieces, both stylistically and technically, stems from Britten, but in the lovingly written insect and bird songs there is also discernible a particular neatness, unclutteredness and epigrammatic precision arguably Gallic in spirit (it may possibly reflect something of the influence of Bennett's teacher, Lennox Berkeley). Ravel's name has been invoked on a number of occasions during the course of this essay. When matching music to the motions of the great express in his score for the film of the Agatha Christie thriller *Murder on the Orient Express* (1974) Bennett took his cue from *La Valse*, not *Pacific 231*. And the composer of the *Histoires Naturelles* and *L'Enfant et les Sortilèges* would surely have admired *The Aviary* and *The Insect World*; in fact one of the most attractive in the latter series is 'Clock-a-clay' (John Clare), one of Bennett's many Ravelian waltzes. Whilst both song-cycles are tailored technically to the limitations of children, there is nothing musically 'childish' about them. Rather are they full of clever illustrative detail (the moaning of the wind in 'Clock-a-clay', the millwheel's sound in 'The Widow Bird') and many are pointed by wit ('The Fly'), poetry ('Glow-worms') and eloquence ('The Early Nightingale').

In his children's music, certainly in his film music, and in fact in all his music intended for popular consumption, Bennett continues to prove the truth of the old Horatian maxim which holds that in matters of art intrinsic merit is not incompatible with accessibility and utility. Bennett is one of the leading British musical exponents of the *dulce et utile*.

David Blake

MALCOLM MacDONALD

> To have gathered from the air a live tradition. . . .
> This is not vanity.
> Here error is all in the not done. . . .
> Ezra Pound, *Canto LXXXI*

Until the first performance of *Lumina*, his large-scale choral work on the *Cantos* of Ezra Pound, it was still possible to regard David Blake as a minor figure in contemporary British music, despite the contrary evidence of such a tough-minded score as his Chamber Symphony (1966). But *Lumina* is a masterpiece, one of the most impressive British works of recent years, and Blake's subsequent music has amply confirmed the position it established for him as one of the outstanding composers of his generation, a generation that includes such figures as Harrison Birtwistle, Peter Maxwell Davies, Alexander Goehr and Hugh Wood. Blake has some general affinities with these composers—the first group to assimilate the achievements of the Second Viennese School as an integral part of their cultural heritage. But he has had to wait much longer for recognition, partly because he was a fairly late starter (he has suppressed all he wrote before 1960) and his career has so far kept him out of the ambiguous limelight of the London musical scene. Nor does his output impress by sheer bulk: he acknowledges so far only eighteen works. Moreover (perhaps this is the biggest drawback of all) his music has neither the gimmick appeal of the avant-garde, nor does it court by mere tunefulness the over-easy popularity of some more conservative styles. Instead, he produces complex, deeply-felt, demanding works whose rich rewards and profound but unsensational strengths depend on his formidable craftsmanship and the creative sustenance he draws from the central traditions of the Second (and the First!) Viennese School.

Blake went to Cambridge to read music in 1957, after two years' national service in Hong Kong (during which he learned Chinese, an accomplishment that must have given him an insight into certain aspects of Pound's *Cantos* that remain opaque to other readers). On the strength of the pieces—now withdrawn—that he wrote in Cambridge, he was awarded in 1960 a Mendelssohn

Scholarship to study composition abroad. He was thus enabled to take a unique step for a British composer of his generation, and one that was clearly crucial to his musical and intellectual development. He went to East Berlin, to study with Hanns Eisler.

The impact of Eisler's teaching and personality was immense. As one of Schoenberg's most gifted pupils, and perhaps the most distinguished (certainly the most fertile) of Bertolt Brecht's musical collaborators, he represented, and partly reconciled, two vital and apparently antithetical movements in twentieth-century music. His mastery of the twelve-note medium was manifested in many compositions from *Palmström* (1924) onwards, and his passionate musicality emerges just as unmistakably in the tunefulness, harmonic originality and mass-appeal of his multitudinous Marxist works—the marches, workers' choruses, film scores, theatre music, cabaret numbers and songs that range from the famous *Einheitsfrontlied* to *Lob des Kommunismus*. He was both a master-craftsman and an uncompromising believer in music's *social* function, whose soberingly anti-romantic credo was that one should write 'what is necessary, and that changes from week to week'. And like other great teachers—like Busoni, like Schoenberg—his influence was as much moral as technical. David Blake's verdict on his studies with Eisler implicitly acknowledges this moral force: 'He did his best to change me from a dilettante to a composer.'

Eisler, in short, decisively shaped Blake's musical conscience, impelling his thought along paths into which it was already turning. Blake has not, however, tried to apply Eisler's populist-revolutionary style in his own music: that would be futile in the very different social context of contemporary Britain. His work, rather, has more obvious links with Schoenberg, though the Schoenbergian influence is refracted by stylistic affinities with Eisler's 'art music': there is a similar freedom in adapting serial principles, a similar disinclination to avoid the 'softer' intervals of thirds and sixths, or unequivocal suggestions of tonality.

These features are already apparent in the two pieces Blake wrote during his 1960–61 sojourn in East Berlin. The *Variations* for piano is not serial, and if its theme is faintly reminiscent of the Minuet from Schoenberg's Piano Suite, the piano writing has a wiry toughness more characteristic of Eisler. Despite its relative simplicity, this is still a curiously impressive little work; it establishes its composer's quality almost by understatement, with a distinct sense of power held in reserve. In the First String Quartet, the power is more apparent. Eisler, according to Blake, 'queried the social need for string quartets, although he respected my desire to write one as a compositional exercise'. But an exercise is the last thing the Quartet sounds like. It is a biggish work, abrim with rhythmic energy and splendid melodic ideas, in four movements. The finest is the finale, an organically-developing series of twenty-one short variations on a theme derived from elements of the other three. The exalted precedent for this device is the *Litanei* movement of Schoenberg's Second Quartet; and Blake seems to pay a further, maybe unconscious homage in one of his variations, where his spacing of the textures and shaping of muted-string figurations strongly recall a passage in Schoenberg's own finale, *Entrückung*—that significant moment when the 'air from other planets' began to blow through modern music. In a wry coda, the work ends where it began, abruptly encountering the first movement's scampering opening theme instead of the big gesture towards which the variations seemed to have been leading.

Blake returned to England in July 1961. There followed two years' schoolteaching, whose chief creative by-product was a schools' musical of outrageous tunefulness, *It's a Small War*, a witty and affectionate pastiche of popular styles. Blake's main target seems to be Thirties Hollywood musicals, but there is also a march in the Weill/Eisler mould, and a pop-song that could be a take-off of Lennon and McCartney—except that it was written *before* the Beatles' rise to fame.

In 1963 Blake was awarded a Granada Arts Fellowship at the new University of York; when the Music Department was established the following year he became a lecturer, and has taught there ever since. This has laid him open to the easy charge of 'academicism'. But Blake has maintained his artistic independence within York's institutional framework, and is in no sense cut off from the 'real' world; nor has he felt the need, apparently experienced by some other composers there, to create a coterie of disciples. He finds York, simply, a base for teaching activities, and a useful point of contact with practical music-making (he conducts the University Orchestras).

Blake was rather slow to follow up the success of the First Quartet: his first two years in York saw only the composition of three short choral pieces. Each of them is impressive, deeply-felt, and extends Blake's range—notably 'October', the second of the

Three Choruses to Poems by Robert Frost (1964), of which the extremely beautiful vocal colouring perhaps reflects the influence of Messiaen's *Cinq Rechants*. But one also senses that he may have been experiencing problems that he really needed to solve on a larger scale: that there were elements in his music that needed to be released from the thickets of stylistic consistency. When invited, for instance, to contribute to Oxford University Press's anthology *Carols of Today*, he responded, after some hesitation, with *On Christmas Day*, an eight-part setting of a by no means simple poem by Thomas Traherne, which is the longest, the least carol-like, and by far the most difficult piece in the collection. Though one applauds the determination not to compromise, one wonders if in this case it was not partly self-defeating. *On Christmas Day* is a fine work, but remains one of the toughest nuts in Blake's output. By contrast, in the *Four Songs of Ben Jonson* (1965) a more relaxed attitude is already discernible.

It is debatable how far these problems, if problems they were, stemmed from a difficulty in identifying the Eislerian 'what is necessary' with his own compositional needs. In a broadcast talk about his Chamber Symphony (in the course of which he characterised his style as 'thematic, densely contrapuntal, non-tonal') Blake put that issue bluntly:

Sometimes . . . when [I'm] composing at my desk . . . a youth passes by in the street . . . with a transistor radio emitting cracklings and sounds barely recognisable as music—sounds which satisfy some deep-rooted, semi-conscious need which might equally well be satisfied by alcohol, drugs, religion, or in later life gardening and car-cleaning. Certainly what I am working on is of monumental irrelevance to him and just about 98% of the population . . .

He then confessed that the question 'did not occupy him at all' when he wrote the symphony. But one might still suggest that it did, obliquely. For he has also said that 'a drop-out composer counts for nothing'; and the composer, especially, who allows his problems to force him into silence is the biggest 'irrelevance' of all. Blake does not seek soft options in music or thought. While he continues to grapple with the essentials of his art, and thus his means of communication, he still remains 'relevant' whenever anyone is willing to listen.

So when he was commissioned to write a work for the 1966 York Festival, Blake found he needed to write a 'complex, contrapuntal' piece on a fairly large scale; in which, one surmises, he could really work through the stylistic issues raised by the choral works. The result was the three-movement Symphony for Chamber Orchestra, which fully vindicates the early promise of the First Quartet. It is partly a homage to Eisler, who had died in 1962, and a twelve-note theme from Eisler's own Chamber Symphony appears in the outer movements—fragmentarily in the finale, complete at the climax of the first. The first movement (actually written last) is a set of variations—a form of which Blake, like Eisler, seems particularly fond, and which is closely allied to the basic concepts of serialism. In this case the twenty-three variations on the opening solo horn theme are grouped to produce a sonata-like *Allegro deciso* movement with a *Comodo* introduction. The scherzo, subtitled 'Bagatelles', deftly intercuts and super-imposes three distinct but related musics, respectively airy, brusque and romantic, for different instrumental groups; and it culminates in an Eislerian irony—a chorale-apotheosis that is gently mocked by a scherzando accompaniment, before the movement skitters off into silence. The finale (written first) is explicitly titled 'Sonata', and is the most substantial movement. It combines the requirements of a serious slow movement with the kind of dramatic thematic and textural contrasts inherent in sonata style; works up to the symphony's biggest climax; and ends with an implicitly heroic, marchlike transformation of the first subject which blows up into a surging multiple ostinato—a typical Blake device—for full forces. Not an easy work to listen to: it is 'complex and contrapuntal' indeed, its cragginess maybe more a result of its motivic density than its lack of tonal anchorage (there is, in fact, a perceptible pull to A, which even the final eleven-note chord cannot quite conceal). But, by the same token, the rewards for the patient listener are considerable, and the underlying expressive urge communicates strongly even at a first hearing. It remains one of Blake's finest achievements to date.

Three fine vocal works followed the Chamber Symphony, all testifying in different ways to an increased fluency in Blake's music. The cantata for soprano and piano *Beata l'Alma* (1966), to a text by Herbert Read, is one of his most attractive works, despite its strictly serial method and comparatively spare textures, and shows a quickening interest in colouristic resources—most obviously in those passages where the pianist plays *pizzicato* on the strings of the piano. The solo part is remarkable for its rhythmic fluidity, which adapts very flexibly to the natural speech-patterns

124

of the text. This is also true of *The Almanack* (1968), a set of three choruses with strongly tonal leanings, to words by the York poet John Hatfield; and of *What is the Cause* (1967), a tough, declamatory setting of a characteristically sombre and disturbing sonnet by Fulke Greville. Blake is not the kind of vocal composer who ransacks the anthologies for pleasing lyrics. He says he has never set a text he has not believed in (at least at the time of composition), and his preference, characteristically, is for poems of dialectical strength that face up—whether in light or serious vein—to the problems and paradoxes of life, free of the wishful thinking that pretends there are any easy answers.

This is most strikingly illustrated in the text of the magnificent *Lumina* for soprano, baritone, chorus and large orchestra, composed in 1968–69 and first performed at the 1970 Leeds Triennial Festival. (Blake's long-term devotion to Ezra Pound's *Cantos*, with their Confucian stress on seeing clearly things as they are, on right definition and acting not by dogma but through self-knowledge, makes it unlikely that, despite his strongly-held left-wing principles, he should ever accept for himself the clannish but blinkered Maoism that has engulfed a section of the British avant-garde.) In seeking to distil from Pound's gigantic linguistic ideogram of human experience the basis of a one-hour cantata, Blake has avoided the danger of merely summarising its multifarious contents into nothingness, and the meaningless alternative of taking the more obviously 'poetic' passages out of context. Instead, he has pursued the guiding theme implicit in his title, *Lumina*. On the cover of the published vocal score this appears alongside the Chinese Ming ideogram, signifying 'bright, clear, intelligent, to understand, cleanse, illustrate': for Pound, the 'total light process' active in human existence. It is opposed to the forces of evil, of confusion, of the cheapening of humanity, whose most significant manifestation in Pound is *usura*—usury, with the all-embracing connotations of the consumer society, profit motive, and lust for power.

Blake thus groups his chosen texts allusively around one of the most fundamental of the many polarities explored by the *Cantos*, and responds to it with music of magisterial intensity. For all the strengths of his earlier scores, none of them fully prepares us for the sheer triumphant power of *Lumina*. It is, in every sense, his biggest work: its large size and forces are functions of its encyclopaedic nature, its exuberant variety, colour, and pressure of inspiration—

E

and its effect in performance can be overwhelming. Its moods range from lush sweetness to furious violence, and like the *Cantos* themselves it is full of dramatic stylistic juxtapositions. Harmonically these extend from a particularly rich serial method (the *lumina* and *usura* forces, and the compound figure of Pound/Odysseus as narrator and actor, are associated respectively with three related note-rows), through much freely chromatic music, to passages with unequivocal tonal implications. The textural range is equally wide, from full chorus (singing or *parlando*) and full orchestra, to soloists with chamber-musical accompaniments; from simple melody and accompaniment all the way up to twelve-note chords and Ivesian multi-textural collage.

The three parts of *Lumina* roughly correspond to three of the main structural divisions of Pound's poem. The first, centred around the multi-level 'overture' of the first thirty cantos, opens with a big orchestral prelude, itself divided into two parts. It starts with a depiction of Odysseus's descent into the Underworld (Canto I). After a momentary appearance of the chordal motif most often associated with the 'light process', the baritone sings a line from Dante's *Inferno*, 'I came to a place devoid of light', which forms a transition to the second half of the prelude, Pound's vision (Cantos XIV–XV) of Hell—or rather, of the usury-dominated society *as* Hell. It takes the form of a violent exposition of material based on the '*usura*' series. Writing in the *Musical Times* before the first performance, Blake regretted that the 'magnificent obscenity' with which Pound flays usury in these cantos had precluded a choral setting, but in the event his orchestral 'transcription' of the passage is ample reward: a raging, cacophonous, yet tightly-controlled outburst of a blistering fury unparalleled in Blake's music. Its excoriating vehemence is almost shocking, and remains in the mind to qualify the later events; but it is also a vast extension of Blake's expressive range which suddenly makes us realise that *Lumina* stands head and shoulders above his previous work. It also makes us wonder what inner fires the earlier scores' more civilised surfaces concealed.

Light floods back in the main portion of Part I, a setting for baritone, chorus and orchestra of much of Canto XVII—which is a brilliant fusion, all brightness and movement, of landscape, waterscape, and the clearly-seen world of forms in nature, classical mythology, and renaissance Venice. Appropriately the music is fast-moving, its textures swiftly-changing, soloist and chorus alternating in narration and comment against a dazzling orchestral background. No-one need question Blake's powers as an orchestral composer: his timbres shine and flash. Part I closes with the lines 'In the gloom the gold/gathers the light about it' and a vast quiet agglomerative twelve-note chord that slowly dissolves to reveal the same timpani-roll E on which the work began.

In Part II, lines from Canto XIII—Confucius's vision of humane order (solo baritone with a 'Chinese' ensemble of alto flute, cor anglais, clarinet, horn, mandoline and string quintet)—are poised against an indictment of *usura* from Canto XLV (development of the Hell material for orchestra and speaking chorus). Then follows a rapt, contemplative setting (for soprano, chorus and orchestra) of Canto XLIX, the still central point of Pound's design, evoking the autumnal calm of a Chinese landscape. This culminates in a translation of the ancient Chinese 'Sun-up Song': 'Sun up; work/ sun down; to rest'; then percussion alone introduces the exultant opening of Canto LI: 'SHINES/in the mind of heaven God/who made it/more than the sun/in our eye', with which Part II ends.

Part III opens with a trilling twelve-note string chord nearly six octaves deep, and draws its texts exclusively from the semi-autobiographical Pisan Cantos written by Pound in prison camp. As they draw upon themes from earlier cantos with added point and urgency, so does Blake recapitulate and develop music from previous sections. Soprano and baritone comment on the outrages of imprisonment and capital punishment, contrasted with the healing and life-giving power of cool rain (Canto LXXXIII). The tensions implicit here precipitate the climax of the work: a splendidly wrathful choral setting of the famous conclusion to Canto LXXXI: 'Pull down thy vanity, it is not man/made courage, or made order, or made grace, . . . Learn of the green world what can be thy place.' Then at the end there is consolation —the words quoted at the head of this chapter, the simple tag 'Amo ergo sum', and finally the benedictory closing lines of the Pisan sequence: 'If the hoar frost grip they tent/Thou wilt give thanks when night is spent'. The music here is that of the 'Sun-up Song', now revealed as a firm, serene E major.

It is not an easy text, true. But its basic message is cogent: the acknowledgement of evil, the moral imperatives of natural order and clear thinking, the solace of useful work, of beauty in the real world—even of art. And by *his* art Blake has proclaimed it with such force that few indeed can listen unmoved. If listeners are then sent off to the complete *Cantos*—probably *in toto* the least-read major poem of the century—that, in Blake's view, will be all to the good. For the strength of *Lumina*, as of very few works of recent years, is partly an educative, and thus perhaps even a moral, civilising one. It is, without doubt, an achievement of the first order. Regrettably, at the time of writing there have been only two performances.

One important stimulus in writing *Lumina*, Blake found, was the idea

of metamorphosis. Together with Homer and Dante, Ovid is one of Pound's crucial sources and the concept of transformation is derived from the poet's basic technique of cross-reference, repetition, reminiscence and the juxtaposition of violently contrasting subject matter and language. This inevitably suggested a musical leitmotif technique, with variation techniques as a musical equivalent to the element of metamorphosis.

His next work, the exuberant *Metamorphoses* for orchestra (1970–71), is therefore closely related to the classical mythological vision in *Lumina*, Part I. In its colour and vitality this is one of the most engaging orchestral compositions of the past few years, and though it plays continuously it practically amounts to a four-movement symphony. The outer movements, 'Hymn' and 'Dithyramb', are inspired by the Homeric Hymns. The former is grave and incantatory, growing out of a glowing four-horn harmony; the latter is an exciting, dance-like finale, frankly Dionysiac in character. They enclose two 'Metamorphosis' movements after Ovid: a pell-mell scherzo (Actaeon changed into a stag), and a slow movement (Echo and Narcissus) in which some of the most ravishing string writing in modern British music, its textures saturated with 'tonal' thirds, is punctuated by florid cadenzas for clarinet and two violas. The work is especially rich in Blakeian multiple-ostinato patterns, including an extraordinary example in 'Metamorphosis I' for muted brass in eleven parts. The orchestration has, in fact, all the brilliance that Blake demonstrated in *Lumina*: the work could be an instant success at the Proms.

Metamorphoses was followed by the Nonet for wind instruments (1971), a grittier work which shows the Schoenbergian in Blake is as strong as ever; then in 1972 he wrote, for John Shirley-Quirk,

The Bones of Chuang Tzu, a cantata for baritone and piano on Arthur Waley's translation of a poem by Chang Heng. As in the earlier *Beata l'Alma,* Blake makes use here of unusual piano sonorities. The poem is a dialogue between a traveller-narrator and the spirit of the man whose bones he finds at the roadside, and Blake wished to distinguish the protagonists by entirely different sound-worlds. The traveller's music, therefore, is highly chromatic, agitated and swift-moving; but that of the passionless spirit is almost diatonic, static, sparse-textured and impersonal, with certain piano notes 'prepared' to create eerie, percussive timbres reminiscent of distant gongs and bells. It is a strikingly effective device: so much so that, although Blake subsequently made a version—including gong—for voice and chamber orchestra, he wonders if the prepared piano does not still create the more evocative sound.

The different musics of *The Bones of Chuang Tzu* underline the inclusiveness of Blake's attitude to harmony, and especially to tonal reference. His actual period of strict twelve-note composition was very brief: he has said that he no longer wants to deprive himself of the expressive resources of tonality, and although his language continues freely chromatic and influenced by serialism, the general effect in recent works is covertly tonal, if not too often key-centred.

In *Scenes* for solo cello, commissioned by Moray Welsh and first performed by him in 1972, Blake's handling of germinal motifs (particularly the opening one of three notes separated by a semitone and tritone, which invades the music from all angles) clearly derives from serial procedures. But *Scenes* is, in fact, the most tonal in effect of his recent works: the general sound sometimes uncannily echoes Shostakovich—especially in the first of the three interconnected movements, a melancholy, introspective soliloquy undercut by a snarling *sul ponticello* tritone. The second movement is a kind of dance-scene, an almost surrealistic throwback (in tango and waltz tempi) to the Twenties, with satirical quotations from *Die Zauberflöte* as well as popular music of the time. The finale is a set of free, indeed capricious, variations, in which the snarling tritone reappears. So, in the coda, do other motifs from the previous movements, and here, in Blake's words, 'a sort of Transfiguration takes place'. Some of the work's bizarre juxtapositions are prompted by a literary, programmatic element (which Blake is now chary of revealing as he has lost sympathy

with the novel in question!). In fact the 'programme' is not vital—
its influence has simply added a *frisson* of fantasy to an already
satisfying musical design. The full range of cello technique is
explored (save that the instrument is never scraped or beaten,
only played) in this valuable addition to the limited solo repertoire.

A commission from the Music Theatre Ensemble gave rise to
one of Blake's loveliest scores: *In Praise of Krishna* (1972–73), a
cycle of seven love songs from the Bengali for soprano, flute, clarinet,
bass clarinet, horn, harp and four solo strings. The sensuality of
the poems brought forth music of warm, exotic lyricism: Blake
wanted to write a sensuously beautiful piece, and certainly
succeeded. The fifth song, for instance ('O my friend, my sorrow is
unending'), with its mournful alto flute obbligato, compares
favourably with, of all things, one of Delius's best (and similarly
scored) *Songs of Sunset*. Aptly, the flautist has a prominent role
throughout the cycle: Krishna was the flute-playing god. Harmonically speaking, *In Praise of Krishna* drips with honeyed tonal
references, especially in the fourth song ('Let the earth of my body
be mixed with the earth my beloved walks on'), whose triadic
basis is insistently stressed; and in the last where, after a triumphant
welcome to the returning lover, the soprano ends in an ecstatic
vocalise while the accompaniment evanesces on a clear, tranquil
E major.

Lest it be thought that, with *Krishna*, Blake has turned decadent,
his most recently completed work, the Second String Quartet
(1973), proves to be as tough and closely argued as one could
wish, in the best traditions of the Bartók and Schoenberg quartets
whose sound-worlds are so close to its own. It has a curious but
convincing two-movement design. The first, much the larger of
the two, is perhaps the finest set of variations Blake has yet written.
Not just the main theme, but the whole complex of its counterpoints and subsidiary motifs, is subjected to far-reaching developments in large-scale variations of widely contrasting character.
Moreover each variation is 'interrupted' by a snatch of unfamiliar
music which proves to be a distorted anticipation of the next, so
that the whole design is very closely meshed together. In the latter
half of the movement, the tempo and excitement steadily mount
until the music arrives at Blake's first use of a limited aleatoricism.
Each instrument plays, three times, its own complex, unbarred
part, uncoordinated with the others—producing a kind of mobile

in sound as this, the most extreme transformation of the material and also the densest passage motivically, is seen in constantly shifting perspective. It is significant that, unlike so many other instances of such techniques, the general pulse and sense of forward movement are never lost. Nor is it introduced for mere effect—it is the logical outcome of the variations' increasing freedom and accumulating tension. Finally a rushing *allegro impetuoso* coda brings the movement to a fierce conclusion, taking off in the last bars into the alarm-siren whine of an upward-swooping glissando.

The short *Lento molto* finale begins in assuaging calm, with a hushed, somewhat chorale-like music, and a tender cello melody. Tonal reference, not particularly apparent in the first movement, is again strong. But the calm persists until it begins to seem ghostly and strained, the music's muted, whispering textures bottling up fresh tension. A brief *fortissimo* outburst leads to a more impassioned return of the opening music, and then the movement ebbs away in an unsettling coda which the ear tends to interpret as a 'tragic' G minor. Around an insistent, minatory inner pedal E flat from the first violin, the other instruments move to an ambiguous cadence; with the last chord the E flat cuts off, and the second violin's lowest G is left rasping on alone, *sempre f*, like the blast of a distant drill. A bleak, enigmatic ending; but its very problematic effect is fresh evidence of Blake's realism, his awareness of the lack of easy answers in music as in life.

It is a sense that will doubtless stand him in good stead now he has embarked on his largest work since *Lumina*: an opera commissioned for the English National Opera, on the subject of the black Haitian general who led a successful anti-colonial revolution during the Napoleonic wars and so established the world's first black republic. Blake's *Toussaint l'Ouverture* will certainly not be one of those modern British operas whose historical settings in exotic climates are a function of their remoteness from hard reality. The subject raises sharp issues of colour, sex and politics (not least in the misuse of revolution—Haiti has had a succession of more or less corrupt president-dictators right up to the present day) and Anthony Ward's libretto faces them squarely. If there is any British composer who can translate them into musical terms that will challenge *and* entertain, it is surely David Blake.

As Pound's Confucius says: 'Anyone can run to excesses,/It is easy to shoot past the mark,/It is hard to stand firm in the middle'.

But Blake has stood firm; his music assimilates, consolidates and extends the best elements of Western musical tradition; and with the prospect of *Toussaint* and the Violin Concerto commissioned for the Proms, we may confidently expect that his finest music is yet to come.

David Bedford

CAROLYN STOKOE

To the original and influential musical language and ideas that have emerged in the work of young British composers in the last decade and a half, David Bedford (born in 1937) has made a valuable contribution not only in terms of musical quality, but also in his attitudes towards music, and his involvement in areas of composition that have been generally neglected in this country.

Bedford's total rejection of the esoteric or occult sets his work apart from those many contemporaries whose approach he considers over-intellectual. He feels free to use any available source that will provide the sound he wants, and finds in pop music both sounds and attitudes that are lacking in the world of serious music. Some of his pieces combine standard orchestral instruments with electric guitars, beat drums, and other instruments usually associated with pop music, resulting in hybrid ensembles which have extensive sonorous and stylistic possibilities. For example *Star's End*, commissioned by the Royal Philharmonic Orchestra, is scored for symphony orchestra, electric guitar, electric bass guitar and drums, and features the pop musicians both as soloists and as members of the orchestra. This is still a fairly novel concept, and in widening the music spectrum may also weaken the barriers that intrude between good pop and serious music.

After studying at the Royal Academy of Music under Lennox Berkeley, Bedford spent a year in Italy, working part of the time with Luigi Nono and the rest in the Milan Electronic Studios. Both experiences would seem to have had a strong influence on his music, although he has not up till now used pure electronic sounds in any of his pieces. Under Nono he spent some time experimenting with tone colours, extracting all the sonorities and textures possible from groups of instruments and their various combinations, and the timbral sensitivity he now possesses is one of the most outstanding features of his scores. He is concerned more with the sounds his music makes than with specific technical processes or

133

even musical argument, and his essentially simple style provides a flexible and direct means of communicating his musical ideas.

Bedford's formal structures are as clearly divined by the ear as by the eye, and in the majority of works are basically sectional. He discarded strict serial techniques in the early Sixties, and has tended more recently to build his material around selected chords. These are flexible enough to provide a wide range of sounds, being largely unrestricted as to register, and are used as motivic and intervallic cells. In the case of vocal pieces, Bedford to a large extent allows the text to generate the musical structure, and his skill in this respect is evident in a work such as *That White and Radiant Legend* (1966). Here, Kenneth Patchen's text clearly dictates the sectional character of the setting, in which each section presents a new combination of sounds and attacks. The scoring is for soprano, flute, oboe, clarinet, bassoon, violin, viola, cello and double bass, with the addition of a reader who is heard in the latter part of the work recounting the tale of a gory and surrealistic murder. In the original text this mock-gothic narrative repeatedly interrupts the main flow of words; Bedford exaggerates the opposition of incongruous elements by interrupting a sung text with a spoken one, and contrasting the sustained and expressive accompaniment of the former with the reader's sinister and expressionistic background of scrapings, rattlings, harmonics and glissandi. The work is balanced and consolidated by a central instrumental interlude, which concentrates the most important musical ideas into a powerful and climactic section of considerable density and rising dynamic violence.

That White and Radiant Legend is typical of Bedford's outstanding imaginative response to a text, which is heightened by the special rapport he feels with the work of the American poet Kenneth Patchen. The fluency and originality of his vocal music in many cases transcends its text, and even lists of names, as in *Some Stars Above Magnitude 2.9*, have formed the basis of distinctive settings. Patchen's work in particular suggests to him a complementary world of sound, consisting as it does of sentiments and ideas similar to those that motivate Bedford himself.

Bedford's treatment of the voice is technically inventive without incurring distortion of its natural qualities, and his choral writing is particularly rich in its range of moods and colours and its technical assurance. This is amply demonstrated in *Star Clusters, Nebulae and Places in Devon*, which he composed in 1971, and which now exists in two versions. The first is for two eight-part choirs and orchestra, while the second replaces the orchestra with brass: horns, trumpets, trombones and tuba. The juxtaposition of the two lists of names that form the text arises from an idea based on astronomical phenomena: the distance that separates the earth from some of the visible star clusters and nebulae is so vast that the light which set out from them at the time when Bronze Age settlements existed in Devon is only just reaching us now, three-and-a-half thousand light-years later. Thus Choir I sings the names of star clusters and nebulae taken from various astronomical catalogues, and Choir II sings the names of places in Devon.

The text operates in two distinct ways: first, it supplies wide phonetic variety ('The Great Lagoon Nebula in Sagittarius', 'Drizzlecombe', 'Belstone Corner'), and secondly the interrelation-ship of the names creates unity and atmosphere without having to involve specific meaning. As the piece proceeds, syllables of the names become split up among the voice parts of each choir, so that all syllables of a completed name may be sounding together. Choral density is created by staggering points of attack throughout each choir, sometimes in notated canon, but elsewhere by allowing each singer a free choice as to his or her point of entry within a set time limit. At one stage in the piece Bedford divides each of the sixteen parts into six, making a total of ninety-six independent lines, and each one has a notated glissando at a different moment. This continues through to a point of climax on a pianissimo twelve-note chord, which then merges into octave C. The passage is short and deceptively simple in construction, but as is so often the case with Bedford's music, overwhelming in terms of sound.

Instrumental textures are similarly impressive, and frequently contrived by the constant regrouping, rephrasing and inversion of small repeated note groups. Spaced or canonic entries are common, and Bedford displays his characteristic flair in handling tone colours and instrumental effects, the latter particularly during the 'Imitation Game'. Here, groups of singers are asked to imitate sounds they have heard made by the instruments. The sounds are changed periodically, and are passed on by imitation from one group to another like an uproarious version of Chinese Whispers. The brass score at this point includes effects such as *wawa*-muted notes, flutter-tonguing and glissandi (sometimes combined), in addition to legato and staccato note groups at all pitch areas within the tuba to trumpet range. Eventually, the instrumentalists are asked to imitate the singers' imitations, so that the sounds become even more wildly distorted. Quite apart from being very funny, the game produces spontaneously exciting sounds and brings the singers and players into the closest possible aural contact.

This work reveals an accomplished and resourceful handling of choral and brass sonorities and employs constantly fluctuating colours and textures. These include passages where the brass players use their mouthpieces only, and where the instrumental sound becomes totally opaque by means of reiterated and un-synchronised attacks on all twelve notes of the scale. The choirs occasionally have a traditional sound, for example at mass entry points and during their more sustained and slow-moving passages, while elsewhere they perform *bocca chiusa* glissandi, or sing 'tremolo' through a brass flutter-tongue section by patting their chests rapidly with their hands. One of the most successful aspects of the work is that it achieves a controlled synthesis of the traditional and the new in choral writing, and accommodates a wide variety of styles and techniques without any aural incongruity. This is perhaps due in part to its sectional structure, which allows highly flexible relationships to exist between the material of successive sections.

Star Clusters, Nebulae and Places in Devon is also interesting in that it incorporates both metric notation and Bedford's own form of space-time notation, which he devised during the early Sixties. He now uses the latter system in writing a large proportion of his music, but is not averse to using traditional notation, or graphics, if he feels this would convey the required sound to the performer in the clearest possible way. He sometimes employs two different methods simultaneously, as on occasions in *Star Clusters* and *Some Stars Above Magnitude 2.9*. In the latter work the perpetuum mobile vocal line is barred to a time signature throughout, while the piano accompaniment is initially much more free.

Bedford worked out his space-time notation in 1963, when he found that conventional metric divisions were creating more problems than were necessary for the satisfactory performance of his music. The calculation of the more intricate note values in his *Piece for Mo* was demanding protracted rehearsal time, and was also inhibiting the performers' instrumental fluency. Bedford realised that dispensing with rhythmic values and allowing players to place notes according to their visual spacing on the page would result in equally acceptable interpretations, and performances

136

could become more spontaneous and relaxed. The first of his pieces to incorporate this notation was the setting of two poems by Kenneth Patchen for twenty-four-part choir, in 1963, followed by *Music for Albion Moonlight* in which he used it exclusively. He aims to produce the clearest visual representation of the intended sounds, and has reduced the elements of notation to a flexible minimum. His music is written on normal staves and divided into 'bars' the durations of which are given in seconds. Arrows placed above the stave indicate signals or downbeats from the conductor, so that the ensemble coincides at these points even if their inter-mediate timings have been slightly different.

Bedford uses two basic types of notes: black spots, which indi-cate short staccato sounds, and open notes (which may be joined like quavers) whose duration is determined by the length of a horizontal line in relation to the timing of the bar. When joined together these notes are played legato. Other special vocal or instrumental effects are frequent, but vary from one piece to another. *Come In Here Child* (1968), for soprano and amplified piano, is unusual in that it involves the pianist in the reading of an additional five-line stave which indicates the volume settings of his amplifier. The top line of this stave is thickened to indicate full volume, the middle line to direct that the sound from the piano and that from the loudspeaker at the back of the hall should be equal, and the bottom line to indicate that the sound from the loudspeaker should be barely audible to the pianist. Zigzag lines through the stave mean that the volume is to be turned rapidly up and down. Towards the end of the piece, the pianist creates new sounds by manipulating milk bottles on the amplified piano strings. The extra actions the pianist has to perform in this piece are made feasible by the clarity and spacing of the keyboard writing, which nevertheless explores a wide range of contrasting textures. The most telling effects are frequently simple in conception, such as the calculated succession of individual notes which highlights the acoustic properties of their varying registers. The tremolando effects and sustained chords used extensively in *Come In Here Child* are developed further in Bedford's *Piano Piece 2*, written in the same year, but in general texture the setting shows more resemblance to his *Piano Piece 1*, dating from 1966. Kenneth Patchen's poignant text is sensitively expressed by the widely-spaced soprano line, which like the piano part condenses a spacious musical character into a deceptively short piece.

137

Although Bedford's notation is basically determinate, it can also be extended to encompass material of a freer nature, and he has experimented in various directions with elements of improvisation. Quite a number of pieces contain short sections which may be chosen at random by the performer, or repeated as often as necessary until a signal is given to stop. More extensive aleatoric processes occur in works such as *A Dream of the Seven Lost Stars* (1965), which has a fully composed SSATBB chorus part but an orchestral accompaniment that varies in its parts and in its structure according to chance elements. The orchestra's material is similar in construction to that of the choir, but each player has the choice of three lines of music whenever he is called upon to play. Except in a single instance, he may begin anywhere along the chosen line and then continue with another until the signal is given to stop. There are two conductors: the orchestral conductor determines the order of instrumental sections (and thus timbre-mixtures) by means of a system of lights, and also controls the interpolation of optional instrumental interludes, while the choral conductor has the power to terminate these interludes whenever he chooses by bringing the choir back in. Thus although the piece is firmly controlled in its overall shape, the success of any performance hangs heavily on the rapport between the two conductors, and on the sensitivity of the orchestral conductor in responding to the vocal sounds he accompanies.

One of Bedford's most extensively improvisational works is *The Garden of Love* (1970), though again the chance elements operate within a tightly organised structure. It is scored for a mixed instrumental quintet of flute, clarinet, horn, trumpet and double bass, and a pop group consisting of two electric guitars, organ, saxophone and drums. The score also calls for 'six beautiful girls for dancing and turning pages'. The pop group double on Indian bird warblers and a Swanee whistle (for which Bedford writes with delightful ingenuity), and except for the organist, they play most of the time from semi-determinate notation of various kinds. The quintet has a wider range of notations, from graphics to the normal stave with time signatures, and including space-time notation on both three and five lines.

The two groups of sonorities are so manipulated as to create numerous different musical relationships, though the improvisational character of the piece dominates the atmosphere throughout. Six Imitation Games are included in the score, each one for an independent combination of instruments, until in Number Six they all play their individual games simultaneously. Then follows a massive improvisational climax involving the whole ensemble.

This is primarily music to be enjoyed, by performers and audience alike, and indeed the audience is invited to join the dancing girls for the concluding bars, when the pop group performs 'The Garden of Love' (a Blake setting) in informal 'club' style. It is not the only piece by Bedford to involve audience participation: *With 100 Kazoos* requires one hundred members of the audience to interpret a picture, using kazoos, but the work's 1972 première had to be cancelled because of the organisers' objections to this particular section.

One influence on Bedford's wide-ranging and imaginative style has certainly been his teaching experience with children. He has composed several pieces for use in schools, including *It's Easier Than It Looks* for recorders, *Wide, Wide in the Rose's Side* and *Some Bright Stars for Queen's College* for voices and instruments, *Whitefield Music 1* and *2*, and *An Exciting New Game for Children of All Ages*. Of these, the last two take the form of musical games which can be played successfully even by those pupils who have had no musical training. The players simply move around a board, either stepwise or by throwing a dice, and perform the musical activity indicated at each stage. A good performance of any of these pieces demands considerable aural concentration, and an awareness of the corporate sound of the group as well as of the individual activities within it. This is an aspect of music teaching which tends to be badly neglected; children are generally given too little scope for making creative decisions or applying positive self-criticism, though their ability to do so is obvious by the way they tackle scores such as these.

There is little stylistic distinction between Bedford's school and adult music, and indeed *Whitefield Music 1* is outstanding at any level. His development of space-time notation means that he can avoid writing down to children, and his efforts as a teacher to make his ideas as simple and direct as possible have affected his entire output. It is also conceivable that Bedford's constant experimentation with new sound-sources and effects has its basis in the teaching situation, as for example his use of milk bottles in *Whitefield Music 1*, and later in *Come In Here Child*, *Piano Piece 2* and *Variations on a Rhythm of Mike Oldfield* (1973).

The visual impact of Bedford's scores is highly appropriate to

139

the sound-structures they represent, which themselves seem to possess a strong 'visual' quality. His sectional structures tend to be built up of almost tangible sound blocks, some relatively static while others present fluctuating textures and tone colours, or explode into polychromatic violence. The pattern of his compositional development has always evaded definition, however, and successive scores may follow apparently unrelated paths within a basic stylistic framework. Certain characteristic details recur in many pieces, such as the tendency to begin and end with simple or fragmentary figurations, isolated notes, or quiet sustained chords. The opening bars of *Piece for Mo* and *Music for Albion Moonlight* are made immediately evocative by narrow glissandi which move slowly around a unison note, while the latter work, like *A Dream of the Seven Lost Stars*, closes with vocal humming in a disintegrating or fragmentary texture. Most of Bedford's works avoid a definite ending; they either die away to inaudibility, or are suddenly curtailed in the course of repeated figurations. His orchestral and instrumental pieces, including among others *Trona* (1967), *Gastrula* (1968), *The Sword of Orion* (1970) and *Star's End* (1974), tend to explore specific areas of sound production or instrumental activity, and while not always as compelling as his vocal music, they develop these ideas with skill and imagination.

The smaller-scale instrumental works include two quintets, piano music, and pieces for electric and acoustic guitars. Bedford himself is a keyboard player, but the technical familiarity and assurance of his guitar music is considerable, and is no doubt due in some measure to his close association with pop musicians as composer, arranger and performer. *18 Bricks Left on April 21st* for two electric guitars was written in 1967, and is an extended conversation between the two players, exploiting the idiosyncratic potential possessed by the electrical equipment. Near the end of the piece, the players are given five minutes in which to improvise, the only conditions being that all sounds must be produced entirely through various types of electrical feedback, and that the whole five minutes should be extremely loud. In *You Asked For It*, a six-minute solo written two years later for Timothy Walker, the range of sounds is again very great but this time the timbral variations have to be made on the guitar itself. These include several different ways of striking the strings and the wood, as well as moving between all playing positions from bridge to fingerboard. At one point in the piece the player is asked to damp the strings with paper to produce a flat, non-resonant quality through a section of rapid staccato notes and chords, and elsewhere to make the wood squeal with his finger or hand. A teaspoon bounced on the strings is also surprisingly effective, both in playing individual notes and also rebounding to create a tremolo effect with chords. This is a virtuosic piece, rich in contrasts and textural inventiveness, in which Bedford explores the full range of the instrument from its mellow bass notes up to the highest possible harmonics.

The second half of the Sixties was a productive period for Bedford; in addition to these and other instrumental pieces he also composed some substantial vocal works, including *Music for Albion Moonlight* and *The Tentacles of the Dark Nebula*. *Music for Albion Moonlight* (1965) is a particularly colourful score, containing many of Bedford's most idiomatic techniques. It is an impressive setting of four poems by Kenneth Patchen, which are separated in the work by three short instrumental interludes. The scoring is for soprano, flute, clarinet, violin, cello, alto-melodica and piano. The soprano dominates the ensemble with an expansive vocal line, heightening the impact of her words with several different kinds of delivery: humming, whispering, speaking, shouting, and toneless or dead-toned singing in addition to normal vibrato. During the first poem she also screams the word 'hell' into the open piano, with a chilling downward glissando which is amplified by the resonance of the strings.

The settings run a wide emotional gamut, from outbursts of extreme violence and aggression, as in the third poem, to the kind of calm tranquillity found in the last, where the somnolent vocal line is thrown into relief by delicate instrumental interjections: 'And the earth takes it softly in natural love/Exactly as we take each other and go to sleep.' Changes of mood also occur rapidly from moment to moment within each poem, and call up many fascinating instrumental responses. There is a characteristically frequent use of flutter-tongue, harmonics and glissandi, and the players also perform finger-trills on the wood of the stringed instruments and piano, and on the keys of the woodwinds. The second poem, leading up to the expressionistic second interlude, is especially rich in colourful sounds; for example the passage where all players produce, staccato and fff, 'what they consider to be the ugliest noise possible on their instrument', while the soprano

141

says viciously 'They wanted to murder the thing within the house/
I saw my own face with the knives above it.' Earlier, the players
bang the wood and casing of their instruments with bows and
mouthpieces: grotesque sounds underlining grotesque images.
Many different sounds are coaxed from the piano by using the
keyboard, the pedals, the wood and the strings, and even other
instruments playing into it. Bedford has also devised a 'cluster
stick', which is a T-shaped wooden and rubber-edged stick used
directly on the piano strings to strike them or damp their tone.

The performers are given some degree of practical and inter-
pretational freedom in the course of the piece, most obviously near
the beginning when they are asked to interpret the word 'Sklitter'
without the aid of any other notation. The word is an imaginary
one, but evokes associations such as 'slide', 'skelter' and 'glitter'
which shape the character of the improvisation. Notwithstanding
certain chance elements the work is meticulously composed, and
the constant opposition of sustained chords with brittle staccato
groups (frequently of a quasi-ostinato nature) is finely manipulated
and controlled. Textures vary from sparse austerity to the extreme
density of large static sound-complexes, and there are long
passages where points of colour are interpolated in rapid succession
by individual instruments. These studies in sonority recall the
work Bedford did in Italy, particularly the section that begins
'Cities blackened . . .', where voice and instruments engage in
shifting timbral combinations all on the note A.

The eloquence and vision of his writing have become increasingly
familiar in Bedford's vocal music, and is equally in evidence in the
very different setting he composed for tenor and string orchestra
in 1969, which he called *The Tentacles of the Dark Nebula*. As is
obvious from the titles and generating ideas of many of Bedford's
pieces he is fascinated by astronomy and science fiction, and this
is one of the factors that drew him to set the Arthur C. Clarke short
story entitled 'Transience', from the collection *The Other Side of
the Sky*. In its prophetic account of the history of mankind the text
is divided into three different episodes, and Bedford accentuates
this structure by interpolating two short instrumental interludes
between them. Literary elements common to each scene (the
beach, the child, the incoming tide, etc.) are given musical counter-
parts which recur in varied or developed form each time they
appear. In the first scene a Neanderthal boy comes to a beach
which has never before borne the imprint of a human foot; in the

second a boy is on the beach in our own time, with a town nearby and many people round about. The final section is set in the future, when a child plays on the beach for the last time. The Dark Nebula has now rendered the earth uninhabitable, and the entire human race is emigrating to another planet:

The beach lay waiting for the end. It was alone now as it had been in the beginning. Only the waves would move, and but for a little while, upon its golden sands. For man had come and gone.

The string writing is ideally suited to these images; it is quiet and understated, with little vibrato but extensive use of mutes. The instrumental interludes are designed to contrast with the character of the vocal sections, in which orchestral sounds complement the shadings of the text, within a prevailing unity of mood. A striking feature of the score is its almost constant use of glissandi which are frequently placed above dark, threatening sounds from the lowest bass strings. Quarter-tones and strings slightly out of tune intensify the pitch instability created by the glissandi, and contribute to a pervading sense of desolation. Only in the instrumental interludes is this effect relieved by static pitch levels. The vocal line is predominantly lyrical and melismatic and carries the greater weight of direct expression, though it blends with the middle instrumental registers during its less animated passages. Pitch extremes are common throughout the piece, with violins placed at the uppermost limits of their range and double basses at the bottom of theirs. The spread is accentuated when chords are compiled additively from bass to treble, and held fixed while their various component pitches are subjected to renewed attacks.

It is in works like these that Bedford's distinctive musical personality is most fully revealed, hinging as it does on his acute sensitivity to language and atmosphere. The importance of the words themselves varies with the context; their function in *The Tentacles of the Dark Nebula* is naturally more specific than in, for example, the *Two Poems for Chorus*, where only a few key words of the text, dissolving into scattered phonetic sounds, emerge from a wash of vocal colour. Bedford maintains no rigid compositional aesthetic, and the flexibility with which he adapts his style to transfigure each new text or idea undermines the comparisons frequently made between his own music and that of the Polish avant-garde. It can be said that he shares with them an overriding

143

concern with the sheer impact of sound, manipulating his material in broad contrasting blocks of colour and intensity, but the range and variety of his music evades superficial analogies and stems from generating forces which are wholly individual.

Two Traditionalists: Kenneth Leighton and John McCabe

HAROLD TRUSCOTT

Both Kenneth Leighton and John McCabe, different though each is from the other, are accurately described as traditionalists, provided the word 'tradition' is understood to mean just what it does mean, and not something else—convention—with which it is all too often confused. A tradition is a system of thought or behaviour, or a means of expression, which is alive, and which has proved its usefulness and adaptability to the understanding and needs of people at large, while retaining its fundamental principles. For instance, a language is a tradition: it is alive, it is constantly adaptable, and it retains its fundamental principles, battered though these may often be, as the noble adagio tune is battered but retains its shape and nature unbowed in the first movement of Nielsen's Fifth Symphony. But a tradition, or, more correctly, the use of a tradition, can in particular instances be allowed to lapse into a convention; it can, in other words, become something dead, because there is no impetus to keep it alive; it is a copy without a vital spark, and it will then simply retain the outer shape of its original. It will become a fossil.

In the lively sense of my definition the two subjects of this essay are true traditionalists. Just as Benjamin Britten and Edmund Rubbra, two composers who could not be further apart in outlook and expression, are equally traditionalists. The significant thing is that, in an age in which composers have veered away from or violently repudiated the symphonic style or anything for which the symphony stands, these two are producing such works—and works which are really symphonic, and are not merely using a title or description. That title here covers and accurately suggests a significant reality.

Leighton, the elder of the two by ten years, was born in Wakefield in 1929, and had a cathedral chorister's upbringing. This could not fail to leave its mark on his musical mind and, thus, on his music; and on his music as a whole, not only his church music, although differences between categories are fairly strongly marked in his work. However, a merging of categories is suggested by his own statement, in a lecture entitled 'The Composer Today' given at Manchester University in 1972, that 'the main achievement of twentieth-century church music has been to break down the barriers between sacred and secular'. Leighton has not always brought off the intermingling of style that this 'barrier-breaking' implies; in fact, it appears to be a case of one-way traffic at the most. As one examines his music it seems that the church music has at times influenced his secular music, but that the secular remains apart, giving little or nothing back to the church music.

In an interview with Robin Fulton, printed in the *New Edinburgh Review*, in February 1970, Leighton said that up to the time he went to Italy in 1951 to study with Petrassi his musical background was narrowly British and his idols were Vaughan Williams, Walton and Britten. This is interesting, for in those I have been able to study of the works written prior to that Italian period there is to my mind no trace of influence from any one of these three English composers. But there is something else. Leighton has also said that in the Fifties—that is, presumably, as a result of his study in Italy—the most obvious influences on his music were those of Bartók, Hindemith and, to a lesser extent, Dallapiccola. Nowhere in his music is there much to remind one of Bartók, even in the most subtle manner, and nothing at all of Dallapiccola, unless it was very quickly absorbed. But of Hindemith there are strong traces, not only in music written in the Fifties, but in works composed during the preceding years when, he has said, his musical outlook was narrowly British. The two Sonatinas for piano, composed in 1946, and especially the First Piano Sonata of 1948, show an evocative Hindemithian texture of harmony and polyphonic movement, but the feeling they express is at times just as redolent of an English composer not among Leighton's chosen three. This is John Ireland. The combination of these two produced a highly interesting style, with quite a personality; it persisted for some time, deepening as it went.

The mixture proved to be very fruitful. True, the German gradually ousted the Englishman, and disappeared himself, as an obvious force, as soon as the influence had been absorbed. But its effect, though not its personal mark, can be heard now definitely in Leighton's own language, so that unless it had been traced from its beginning its origin would never be suspected, nor its standing as authentic Leightonism questioned, in works written as late as

146

1970: the Concerto for organ, timpani and strings, Op. 58, a masterpiece, and the *Second Dance Suite* for orchestra, Op. 59.

But this influence had a basic musical outlook to feed upon; an ingrained way of thinking that I assume is natural to the composer, since it is in evidence, no matter how imperfectly, even at the outset. This way of thinking is not trendy, not avant-garde; nor is it gimmicky. Leighton is very little affected by current trends, except to note that they are there and, possibly, avoid those that would stifle him. He has occasionally used a serial technique, but it has never been anything but a convenience at the time, and its use never obtrudes itself but merely serves to strengthen the growth and intensity of his personal sound in the particular case. Kenneth Leighton has had, too, a distinguished academic career, which he is still pursuing—he is Professor of Music at Edinburgh University—but he is no more an academic composer than he is avant-garde. To say something intelligible, and this is his concern, one must have a suitable means, or what I have called an ingrained, natural way of thinking. His can be divided into two main parts: counterpoint and symphonic thought.

This shows strongly in most departments of his work, even in the church music. Almost anywhere one looks in this music, designed though most of it is for liturgical use in the Church of England, one finds a symphonic build to the music, even in an unaccompanied motet like the superb *God's Grandeur*. It is a vocal symphonism, and shows itself in the gradual mixed growth of chordal and linear styles. In such a piece it remains vocal and the symphonic approach never comes near suggesting actual symphonic writing, any more than one can imagine the symphonic build of the *Kyrie* and *Sanctus* from Bruckner's E minor *Mass* forming parts of one of his symphonies, however much they feature certain aspects of his symphonic writing. But the Leighton motet style does lend facets to his symphonic writing proper, while taking little or nothing back. On the other hand, larger-scaled works, such as the *Second Service* and *Crucifixus Pro Nobis*, with its beautiful final unaccompanied hymn, 'Drop, Drop, Slow Tears', each show, in varying degree, a symphonic growth in the organ part which, while integrating with the vocal and choral writing, almost pursues a life of its own. This is especially true of the *Second Service*. On a varying scale this feature runs almost throughout Leighton's most important body of church music, and up to very recently had found its most extensive, though not its most succinct,

147

expression in the outstanding Sinfonia Sacra *The Light Invisible*, set to words taken variously from Jeremiah IV, Lamentations I, Psalm CXXX and T. S. Eliot's *The Rock*. With its beautifully timed climaxes, its fluid lines and deep, moving sonorities, this work, which solved most but not all of the problems it raised, pinpoints two other things prominent and important throughout Leighton's work as a whole.

The first is tonality. Leighton's style, growing from Hindemithian roots (and Hindemith significantly goes back to that major influence on so much twentieth-century music, Reger) uses a great deal of chromaticism, sometimes producing a sound not unlike that of the German composer Karl Marx. Now chromaticism, especially if, like Leighton's, it is structural and not primarily emotional, so far from disrupting tonality, will only the more effectively affirm a fundamental tonal centre. This is a fact that the majority of serialists, including Schoenberg in a fair amount of his music, both serial and overtly tonal, have not grasped. Whether or not Leighton realises this fact consciously I do not know, but his music does, unerringly; there are no mistakes in that. In a manner not in the least obvious nor particularly redolent of the past (not that it would matter a jot if it were) he is fundamentally a tonal thinker, and, I imagine, will remain so.

The second characteristic of his work is that, in an age when in so much contemporary music what is grandly termed melody is so, even at its best, no more than a child's school essay can be called great literature, Leighton is an outstanding, I would almost say a great, melodist. And if anyone asks for proof of the quality of his melodic writing, his consistent contrapuntal mastery is sufficient. Only an outstanding melodist can produce counterpoint that *sounds* like counterpoint and not like thorns crackling under a pot.

Leighton is a splendid pianist, and a fine interpreter of his own music. It is no surprise, therefore, that he has recourse to the piano at intervals, or that this instrument carries some of his key works. In 1956 he won the Busoni prize at Bolzano with his *Fantasia Contrappuntistica*, subtitled 'Homage to Bach'. This work I firmly believe is the composer's first undoubted masterpiece. It is both a creation and a genuine re-creation, as much so as Hindemith's *Ludus Tonalis* or, to go further back, Franck's *Prelude, Choral and Fugue*. The balance of the structure, from the *Adagio* opening, through the *Toccata*, the magnificent *Choral* and the two beautifully constructed fugues, is near perfect. But also one finds the Leighton-absorbed Hindemith legacy in many of the rhythms and the free, athletic linear movement of the music, deeply expressive but with strong sinewy muscles, all now Leighton's own, expressed with a command of keyboard technique that is novel and exciting, virtuosic but always used to further the musical content.

With this work I will couple another, much later, piano piece: *Conflicts*, a fantasy on two themes, Op. 51, composed in 1967. This, too, I believe belongs to the masterpiece class. In some ways it picks up threads from the *Fantasia Contrappuntistica*, to use them in a very different way. The basis of the whole is the opening theme, set low down on the keyboard, on rising dissonant intervals against descending concordant ones, and the strands that grow from and climb and intertwine about it. The work is a sort of set of variations, and growth is the keyword, inevitable from the start to the finish. It is one of Leighton's mellowest works, making strongly lyrical music out of apparently intractable intervals. There is one peculiarity, however. In its *Prestissimo* 6/8 section is the only echo of Walton I have found anywhere in Leighton's music; not an influence (it comes too late for that) but a reference, probably quite coincidental, to an actual Walton piece; not a very well-known one, either. It is the little piece of ballet music Walton wrote for the film *Escape Me Never*, of about 1935 vintage, which starred Elizabeth Bergner.

In the Sixties Leighton's symphonic thought flowered in such works as the Second and Third Piano Concertos, the Concerto for string orchestra and the First Symphony, to be followed in the Seventies by the Concerto for organ, timpani and strings and the Second Symphony (*Sinfonia Mistica*), for soprano solo, chorus and orchestra. Leaving aside the last-named, which I have not heard, these works show almost every facet of Leighton's great talent at its best, in some of the finest and most alive symphonic writing in this century. There is only one lack: almost always where it is not sadly beautiful his symphonic music is nervously energetic, rather like a thoroughbred horse, and grimly earnest. One longs for a sense of humour. I except the middle movement of the Concerto for strings, which displays a crookedly humorous, perhaps rather rueful, smile; and the brilliant fugue in the finale must also be mentioned, again with the great broad melody binding elements together at times.

149

Among other things, the First Symphony and the Second and Third Piano Concertos show Leighton as a composer handling the contemporary orchestra of symphonic strength with ease, and with complete certainty as to what he wants it to help him say. So, too, does John McCabe. But there is a fundamental and interesting difference in how they do this, which does much to highlight the manner of thinking of each composer. In Leighton's case, much is determined by his basic contrapuntal outlook, for because of this his works, large-scale as well as small, always have strongly individual themes or melodic· lines, and one gets the impression that he starts by thinking the music he wants to write, and having done so, begins to think of the particular colour that will best express that music. I do not mean, obviously, that in the case of an orchestral work, for instance, he has no ideas of instrumentation in his mind as he shapes the music, but that, mainly, such things are left until the music is completed—in a black and white state. With McCabe, on the other hand, although his compositions are as individual and varied as are Leighton's, the starting-point, I feel sure, is instrumental colour, sonority. The medium, in other words, *is* the work; it is from this that the ideas spread and germinate the music. The result is not impressionism, but a definite symphonism.

The opening of McCabe's Second Symphony is an excellent illustration of the point. The work begins with three flutes and a harp. The harp and second flute sustain C an octave apart, the first flute has a figure using a minor second to D flat, the third flute simultaneously a similar figure moving down a major second to B flat; these intervals oscillate for a few bars, and then the three flutes drop by four chords and a clarinet sustains an E and wriggles a mordent, the bass clarinet runs down a scale to a low F and a long tremolando string chord, fragments of rhythm, a very rhythmic figure on horns, and a figure of a rising second on a bassoon. Now, this is like no Leighton beginning that I know; but neither is it like any symphonic opening by any other composer. No big theme; bits of rhythm, a figure of seconds. And one may add that not even Sibelius, in spite of all that has been misguidedly written about his methods, ever wrote anything like this. In spite of what is not there, what *is* is very positive. Something has been set going, and it knows exactly where it is going. All that I have described makes up the theme, especially the particular sound-colours. It may never recur precisely like this, but one will recognise the origin of whatever comes from it. It opens out, too. Fresh figures come, speeded up, but using the seconds; but most important, the colour flashes about, and always one gets the impression that the colour begets the idea. The thought is continuous—and, what is also interesting, for such static-looking music, music not using any of the normal means of conveying a sense of speed, the pace is clearly felt to be rapid.

Having stressed Kenneth Leighton's addiction to contrapuntal writing, I feel that here is the basis of another distinction between these two composers. It would be an exaggeration to say that there is no counterpoint in McCabe's music, but it is true that there is, as yet, very little. He has found homophony, so far, more responsive to his needs than counterpoint. One of his earliest works is the Partita for string quartet (1960), and this is a very interesting work indeed. McCabe tells me that he thinks it is too long (it started life as the first movement only, the rest being added later), and he is inclined to apologise for it. I do not think he need. His thinking is particularly rewarding in this work for two reasons: it is one of the rare works that contain a good deal of counterpoint (some of it peculiarly Handelian) and, at the same time, a presage of the future.

John McCabe's output since 1960 has very nearly equalled that of the older composer in extent. On the other hand, he has not followed an academic career. After a short period as pianist-in-residence at Cardiff University, he decided to give most of his time to composition and performance, and still does so; a further difference from Leighton, who has continued to follow an academic career along with that of composer and pianist. McCabe's outlook is very catholic; he has no inhibitions about genuine tradition—his most admired and loved composer of all is Haydn—and is sympathetic to any fresh technique that can further music and not try to stifle everything else that is good in music. Such open-mindedness can only be beneficial, especially as it has the opposite effect in his own work, that of helping him to concentrate completely on precisely what he wants to say, and the best way to say it.

Thematically, the Partita was a considerable generator for much of McCabe's later music. It is no adverse criticism to say that the basic material of any large-scale work of his is not very much in extent; in fact, to realise the wide-ranging and diverse results he has managed to extract from these thematic odds and ends is to begin to appreciate his extraordinary creative power. Oscillating minor seconds, which grow into minor thirds and to wider angular intervals, but always with much expressive emphasis on the seconds and thirds—these things have set going many a movement, very different from its companions; and these thematic elements appear to begin with the Partita. Other things contribute also, notably certain types of rhythm. McCabe's use of percussion is highly personal and varied; and certain rhythms grow from work to work. For instance, the second variation in the *Variations on a Theme of Hartmann* (1962) is a fair-sized scherzo; it begins with a horn on soh, doh, the doh sustained for four bars. The initial soh, doh is followed by a three-fold statement of a side drum rhythm of four notes, the first three a rapid triplet. This rhythm is prominent and grows in the course of the variation, while the thematic side grows also. In the following year, John McCabe wrote the beautiful but brief First Symphony. Its middle movement, a Dance, sets off rapidly with precisely the same rhythm, again on side drum, this time two-fold in a 5/4 bar. Here, it is not only a far more integral part of the piece (the thematic ideas seem to grow from or be affected by it, and feature the seconds and thirds), but the piece itself is very different from the variation, lighter and swifter, and beautifully balances the deeply-felt opening and closing movements. These basic ideas can generate so much different music, and once the momentum of colour and figures is set going, long, sweeping tunes seem to emerge effortlessly and almost of their own volition.

The last six or seven years have seen McCabe writing fewer but deeper large-scale works. The Second Symphony of 1971 already mentioned is a case in point, an experience that takes far longer for the listener to penetrate than the immediately persuasive First. And 1967 brought one of his most penetrating works, *Aspects of Whiteness*. This setting of a passage from Melville's *Moby Dick*, a meditation on white, and what white has meant to the human race, is for chorus and piano. The free-rhythmed choral writing seems to gain an expansion of expressive power in inverse ratio to its actual astonishingly circumscribed range of pitch; but the subtlest thing in the work is the use of the piano. Its comments are always apt, but, more than this, its sound becomes in fact the whiteness which is the work's subject. Consciously or unconsciously, the composer has realised that the sound of a piano has no colour of its own, that it is, in fact, whiteness in sound. All of his piano writing, from the 1962 *Variations* to the superb *Fantasy on a Theme of Liszt*, composed in the same year as *Aspects*, uses this colour, or absence of colour, as a positive thing, and has the power at times of making the carefully placed clusters sound almost like the consonance of a common chord; but the use of the piano, in *Aspects of Whiteness* as a whole, and especially in the passage that begins the work, seems to me to be the apex in this direction—so far.

In the succeeding works there is a move towards a more contrapuntal manner of writing. The Concerto for piano and wind quintet, a work important for its bearing on McCabe's development in the Seventies, set going in 1969 a tendency to write for wind instruments in a manner rapid, chattering, and becoming menacing at times, which flowed into a masterpiece in 1970, *Notturni ed Alba*, in the instrumental section called *Phantoms*, where, it is true, there is percussion as well. This work, a setting of four Medieval Latin poems, is a symphonic song-cycle, and in addition to the vigorous and yet, at times, extremely delicate orchestral writing, has a soprano part which gradually releases more and more of the expressive power of close intervals, partly based on plainsong effect, but ranging far into the personal in its style and emotional force. As Mahler's *Das Lied von der Erde* set a new standard in vocal writing, so again, quite differently, does McCabe in this magnificent work.

Of the remaining works (and perforce regretfully leaving aside the delightful children's opera *The Lion, the Witch and the Wardrobe* and many shorter works which represent another side entirely of the composer's personality) there is space to say very little. *Voyage* (1972) is a sort of oratorio on incidents in the life of St Brendan, a profound study which seems to me to be in part a follow-up to the writing in *Notturni ed Alba*. The year 1973 saw the composition of three outstanding works: *The Castle of Arianrhod*, for horn and piano, a most unusual piece for both instruments, *Time Remembered*, a cantata for soprano and wind ensemble, developing further the wind writing already referred to, as does also the last of these three works, a ballet called *The Teachings of Don Juan*, with a baritone singing the part of the sorcerer; this is to a text by Monica Smith (who also wrote the libretto for *Voyage*). The ballet builds up, with menacing wind writing, to an awe-inspiring climax.

At the moment John McCabe seems to be riding the crest of a wave of deep creativity; at the time of writing he is at work on an orchestral piece and has plans for a number of works, including an opera, for the near future. But perhaps an indication of the measure of his range is seen by setting against the achievements I have discussed the wonderfully simple and haunting little tune he wrote as the title and end music of the television series *Sam*.

Both Kenneth Leighton and John McCabe are, it seems to me, at the height of their powers and, barring accidents, there is still much to come from them to help to keep music on a course of sanity.

John Tavener

TREVOR BRAY

John Tavener was born in London in 1944. He entered the Royal Academy of Music with a William Wallace Exhibition, studying composition with Lennox Berkeley. After leaving the Academy, he studied further with the Australian composer David Lumsdaine, and he now teaches one day a week, devoting the rest of his energies to composition.

Lassus and Victoria, Messiaen, Cage, Stockhausen and Stravinsky: these are the composers who have most influenced Tavener. The richness found in the polyphony of such Renaissance composers as the first two has strongly appealed to him. This richness is linked with a sense of timelessness, a quality he has explored in several of his works. With Messiaen's music, it is again the richness, even sweetness, that has attracted him. Also, Messiaen's use of block form—a piece is composed by juxtaposing different blocks of music—has suggested to Tavener one way of organising the large-scale form of a work. The influence of Cage and Stockhausen has not been through any of the stylistic features of the music but through other considerations. Tavener finds Cage's attitude to composing interesting; he considers Stockhausen a great stimulator of ideas. Finally, it was on hearing Stravinsky's *Canticum Sacrum* that Tavener first wanted to start composing seriously. Stravinsky's late serial style provided him with a starting point from which he could build his own musical language.

There are several different elements here and they can all be found in Tavener's music. Some seem quite incompatible with others. How, for instance, can the richness found in the polyphony of Lassus and Victoria be included in a style that has as one of its constituents a language based on Stravinsky's tough serial writing? But for Tavener, such self-conscious, analytical questions are irrelevant. He composes instinctively. Composition is not a process of carefully working out every note of his work, of working deliberately to a schedule with so much of it done each day. He does not review each passage he has written in the light of which contemporary composer has influenced him. Rather, he includes whatever material he feels is right at a particular moment. When inspiration is there, and Tavener considers that inspiration is God-given, then the right music will result. His attitude is refreshingly unselfconscious. Sometimes, he can go for months without writing a note, but inspiration always returns.

Much of Tavener's music has been composed as a response to religious themes. *The Whale* (1966), the work that first brought Tavener's name to a widespread public, is based on the Biblical story of Jonah, who stayed for three days and three nights in the belly of a whale. The text is in the Latin version of the Bible, the Vulgate. The text for *Cain and Abel* (1964), a dramatic cantata, is also taken from the Vulgate and, in addition, from the York cycle of mystery plays. One of Tavener's earliest works, his *Three Holy Sonnets* (1962) for baritone and chamber orchestra, is a setting of poems by John Donne. His most recent large-scale work to be performed, *Ultimos Ritos*, has poems by St John of the Cross for its text.

Since the late Sixties, death has been the motif that has inspired Tavener's most important works. The *Celtic Requiem* (1969) has several different layers of material taking place simultaneously. Most important of all, a group of children sing and play many children's games to do with death and courtship. These games comment on the other material taking place—relevant passages from the Requiem Mass, early Irish poems, a poem by Henry Vaughan, and the hymn 'Lead, Kindly Light'. In 1971, two short pieces were written as a response to death—*In Memoriam Igor Stravinsky* and *Responsorium in Memory of Annon Lee Silver*. Two years later came the *Requiem for Father Malachy* following the completion of *Ultimos Ritos* in 1972. In *Ultimos Ritos*, it is the mystical idea of 'dying to oneself', of the personal surrender of one's life for an absorption with God that underlies the work.

Tavener's music has a strong seriousness of purpose. It rarely lacks a genuine moral commitment. He finds it uninteresting to compose music that does not attempt to deal with the basic experiences of life. For this reason, Tavener feels that purely instrumental music is unsuitable for his purposes. Its range of suggestion is too limited. He needs a text to act as a vessel for the philosophic and religious ideas he wishes to portray. He can then clothe this text with suitable music. Above all, his meaning must be grasped, his music appreciated by others. He wants to communicate, and this does not mean communicating with an audience of highly-trained musicians like himself but with a wide audience of music-lovers. His music is immediately appealing and draws from the listener a deep personal response.

The largeness of Tavener's vision is enhanced by the static quality of much of his music. There is little sense of progression from the beginning to the end of a piece. Instead, a work is composed of a series of sections or blocks of music in which there is little change. In *The Whale*, for instance, the fourth section called 'The Storm' is all of a piece. One texture and combination of instruments is set up at the beginning of the section and continues more or less to the end. A similar treatment takes place during the seventh section, 'In the Belly'. The music alters only when the text suggests some appropriate change in the music and here Tavener always manages to compose material well suited to the different moods portrayed. The static treatment became more pronounced in subsequent works. The *Celtic Requiem* is an elaboration of the chord of E flat major, the work lasting for over twenty minutes. During 1970 Tavener completed two short works, *Nomine Jesu* and *Coplas*, both incorporated at a later date in *Ultimos Ritos*. As in the *Celtic Requiem* the basic material for *Nomine Jesu* is one chord and in *Coplas* one texture is retained for much of the time.

This static treatment is offset by considerable ingenuity in the treatment of the actual sound of the music, its timbre. For each work a different and varied combination of instrumentalists and singers is gathered together. *The Whale* is composed for double woodwind, a brass section, lower strings, chamber choir and mezzo-soprano and baritone soloists. There is a large percussion section played by eight players which includes such instruments as bongos, tom-toms, maracas, hand bells, sanctus bells and marimba and other 'percussion' instruments, a football rattle, two amplified metronomes and an amplified sheet of glass. Tavener also asks for a piano (with contact microphone), grand organ, Hammond organ and a tape recorder plus pre-recorded tape. The textures Tavener writes are varied. Clusters appear on the double basses, Hammon organ (full manual) and piano, both on the keys and on the strings with the help of a stick—clusters are built up through the orchestra by using trills on the woodwind and tremolandos on the strings. Many different melodic shapes, improvised in the

F

player's time, are played simultaneously. As a contrast, a clean, clear texture similar to those of Stravinsky's late serial style is used.

In Alium (1968) is scored for a high soprano voice, four-track tape recorder plus pre-recorded tape, piano, Hammond organ (two players), grand organ, four gongs and tam-tams, hand bells, sanctus bells, tubular bells and strings. Four loudspeakers are placed more or less at the four compass points of the hall from which come the sounds of children playing games, a piano being played, a hymn and voices singing, muttering, clicking tongues, kissing, popping and so on. Again, there is much variety in the actual sounds used and the idea of having a multiplicity of things going on at once, an idea that Tavener had attempted during certain passages in *The Whale*, is here taken further. At the beginning of the last section of *In Alium*, for instance, there is the sound of children saying prayers in Latin, French, German and English coming from the four loudspeakers—the soprano is singing her independent vocal line, with this same line reproduced in three-part canon coming from loudspeaker one—the strings have a four-part chord and the piano and grand organ have short phrases repeated ad lib.

In the *Celtic Requiem*, the small orchestral forces are divided into three groups, as are the chorus. About halfway through the first section of the work a great deal is happening at once. The first group includes a high soprano soloist, who has her own decorated melody set to a medieval Irish poem. She is accompanied by the first group of the choir holding a long E flat major chord, as are the strings. Several other singers hold sustained notes set to the first syllable of 'Requiem'. These notes are doubled by a trombone. An amplified solo male voice rhythmically chants another early Irish poem. A piano also belongs to this group and has isolated bell-sounds and arabesques. The second group consists of the relevant section of the chorus, again holding a sustained E flat major chord plus another amplified chanting solo male voice, but rhythmically independent of the male voice in the first group. Two sopranos have an independent part set to syllables of 'Aeternam'. A trumpet doubles this part. There are also bells and a gong playing. This arrangement is repeated yet again in the third group with independent material on the clarinet and electric guitar and a drone on the bagpipes. Finally, the children are singing one of their songs. The whole texture is united by the ever-present static

E flat chord. The combined effect of all these elements is monumental and the sound very rich.

This richness can be found not only in the type of sound Tavener writes but sometimes in his melodies. *In Alium* contains a good example. The text for the work includes the line by Charles Péguy, 'Hope is a little girl of no importance'. A sweetness, even banality is suggested, which Tavener underlines towards the middle of the work with a long melody hummed by the solo soprano and marked 'very sweet'. It is accompanied by muted strings, which double the melody in octaves and add gently chromatic harmonies underneath. The Hammond organ doubles the string parts, the melodic line being given the registration 'voix céleste with tremulants'. The overall effect is somewhat reminiscent of Messiaen. Tavener has composed a similar rich melody at the end of *Nomine Jesu*. The accompaniment is of a single static chord here, however.

The spatial dimension suggested in both *In Alium* and the *Celtic Requiem* is more fully explored in *Ultimos Ritos*. This work is to be performed in a church and for each of the five movements there is a different spatial grouping of the performers. In an introductory note in the score, Tavener suggests that during the second movement the twelve chanting basses should stand in a circle facing inwards under the central tower of the church. They are joined by three flutes, three trumpets and four trombones. At each of the four compass points of the church there is a timpani player. In a low gallery in the tower, six recorders sit facing the altar and in the highest gallery there are seven piccolo trumpets. During the movement, the spatial direction of the sounds—from the two galleries to the main orchestra at ground level—is used to symbolise the descent of the Eucharist. The large space needed to perform this work suggests a theatricality, an interest in the visual aspect of a work, an interest already evident in the gestures of the children's games in the *Celtic Requiem* (which Tavener has described as a 'theatre piece for children'). It is interesting to note that Tavener is now working on an opera *Sainte Thérèse* for Covent Garden. A previous attempt at opera, based on Genet's novel *Notre Dame des Fleurs* (1967), remains incomplete.

The idea of drawing a multiplicity of diverse elements together into a unified whole means that not only can Tavener add together different characteristics from his own style but also incorporate into his music the music of others. Already we have seen his use of the children's songs and 'Lead, Kindly Light' in the *Celtic Requiem*. Other instances of this technique can be found in other works. The *Introit for March 27, the Feast of St John Damascene* (1968) ends with a quotation from the opening *Kyrie* of Bach's B Minor Mass. The unfinished opera *Notre Dame des Fleurs* includes three Bach chorales. Yet another Bach quotation, again from the Mass, is found during the last movement of *Ultimos Ritos* (originally *Coplas*). The text by St John of the Cross is taken from his 'Stanzas concerning an ecstacy experienced in high contemplation'. The poem reflects on transcendental thought, 'this summit of all sense and knowing', which is bestowed by God. Just over halfway through the movement the beginning four bars of the *Crucifixus* are added to the texture. As the rest of the movement proceeds other short passages are played until at the end of the movement the last bars of the *Crucifixus* emerge from the texture and are clearly heard alone. The whole movement is, in fact, a slow elaboration of a harmonic progression used in the *Crucifixus* and the overall shape of *Ultimos Ritos* is derived from the proportions of the cross.

This technique could be criticised as gimmickry. But Tavener's unselfconscious approach should be remembered. The quotations are suggested to Tavener as he is composing; they are a spontaneous inclusion in the texture of the music. Each use of quotations must be judged in its own terms, its relevance, its ability to suggest a deeper insight not only into Tavener's own material but into the music of the quotation as well.

In *The Whale*, where Tavener also uses quotations in the form of pop songs and a church service (on a pre-recorded tape during the section called 'In the Belly'), he includes what may be called 'fantastic' elements. The work is subtitled 'A Biblical Fantasy', and it begins with a 'documentary'. The relevant article on the whale from Collins' Encyclopaedia is spoken 'by a baritone voice, off-stage in a box' or over the public address system. After the opening minute, the music gradually takes over. Another 'fantastic' element occurs in the third section of the work, 'Melodrama and Pantomime'. The text here deals with the rising of the storm sent by God as a signal to Jonah of his wrath. Suddenly, brief interjections are shouted through loud hailers, the performers being ranged around the circumference of the hall. During the fifth section, 'The Swallowing', the baritone soloist walks unobtrusively to the open piano and shouts several vowel sounds into it. A large cluster of notes is held down silently by the pianist with his forearms and the resulting sounds that emerge are picked up by a contact microphone. Here are three effects that again could be criticised as gimmickry. But the motivation for including these in the work is the same as for the quotations. They were spontaneously suggested as the work was being composed. Their effect adds to the immediacy of the impact of the work and to its richness of suggestion and symbolism. Tavener's original concept of the work had gradually expanded as the composition of the work progressed.

The various features found in Tavener's music add up to a style at once attractive yet capable of great seriousness. The overall effect of his style is not one of intransigence—his music does not hold you at bay. On the contrary, it attracts the listener towards it, inviting him to participate in the enactment of some of the profound experiences of life. It is likely that religious themes will continue to feature as a starting-point for his works. Tavener has himself admitted that he considers making music as a way of praising the Creator. On the evidence of Tavener's present substantial corpus of work, the praise will be rich indeed.

Miscellany:

JUSTIN CONNOLLY—JONATHAN HARVEY—ROGER SMALLEY—
ANTHONY PAYNE—TRISTRAM CARY—ANTHONY MILNER—
CHRISTOPHER HEADINGTON—ROBIN HOLLOWAY—DAVID ELLIS

MICHAEL OLIVER

How, on the one hand, is a young composer to find his own voice amid today's babel of musical styles, schools and dogmas? When he *has* found it, on the other hand, how is he to make it heard? The temptations to derivativeness are great, the chances of finding originality much smaller. There is no generally accepted *lingua franca*. The chances of being dismissed as *déjà-vu* or ignored as insufficiently extraordinary are daunting.

The early career of Justin Connolly (b 1933) exemplifies this difficulty. He was over thirty years old before he felt ready to add the momentous superscription 'Op. 1' to one of his manuscripts. In retrospect, the reasons for this long gestation are self-evident in the subsequent 'early' works. They combine an exhilarating technical virtuosity with considerable emotional force. The balance between these two elements must have been hard-won, and the narrow passage between the Scylla of intellectual brilliance for its own sake and the Charybdis of over-wrought emotionalism must have been hard to find.

For example, *Triad I* (1964—the first of a series of three-move-ment 'trios' so named) already demonstrates two characteristics of his music: a kaleidoscopic handling of short motives, and an interest in areas of musical contrast and tension other than those of pitch, tempo or tonality (density/rarefaction; static/dynamic; mensural/non-mensural, etc.). The scoring of *Obbligati I* (1965—also the first of a series) for thirteen instruments allows these areas to be explored more thoroughly; the slow fifth section of this work (inscribed 'in memoriam Edgard Varèse') is an indication of the weight of emotion that is carried by Connolly's remarkable technical skill. *Cinquepaces* (1965–66) for brass quintet has become his best-known work, but it is scarcely typical: the close motivic working is characteristically dazzling, but the dance-based rhythmic regularity of the three principal sections (the 'cinque-paces' themselves) provides less room for exploring the areas of contrast mentioned above. The interludes, however, do so and share with the main sections an overall structure based on imitation, repetition and variation that gives the work a satisfying unity. The eloquent tuba solo in the first interlude is comparable with the ornate and flexible oboe solo in the middle movement of *Triad III* (1966) in its neo-romantic expressiveness; the latter, indeed, might be heard as a latter-day equivalent of Warlock's *The Curlew*. The two outer movements of *Triad III* also give prominence to an oboe line, difficult but gratefully written, that weaves its way through mosaic-like textures.

Connolly's angular expressiveness and his sympathetic use of instruments are combined in the first two sets of *Poems of Wallace Stevens* (both 1967) with an equally idiomatic handling of words and of the human voice. *Poems of Wallace Stevens I* adds seven instruments to the solo soprano, colouring and illustrating the rapidly changing imagery of the poems with a parallel musical imagery, counterpointing the poet's thought at its own pace. In *Stevens II*, the reduced scoring (soprano, clarinet and piano) does not reduce the vividness; the clarinet acts as a lithe and agile double to the voice and portrays the formidable 'firecat' of the first poem with brilliantly lit intensity.

This imaginative use of words is extended in two short choral works (unaccompanied), *Prose* (1967) and *Verse* (1969), which might be regarded as the climax of Connolly's 'first phase'; they are among the most impressive choral music of recent years. The texts of both works (Browne, Drummond, Traherne) deal with the brutal transience of man's existence and with a wondering sense of his survival. Connolly's settings use his by now effortless command of technique (and a wide range of vocal 'effects') to evoke a savage picture of the world as a huntsman, its prey defenceless mankind, and to conjure up a vision of the 'shining eternity' in which his consolation lies.

Connolly's interest in a very closely argued microstructure (the series of solo or duo pieces called *Tesserae* are virtuoso explorations of this field) and in the dichotomies noise/music, order/disorder, precision/imprecision, have more recently awakened an interest in taped sounds and electronics. He has used these media less to provide otherwise unavailable timbres than to extend the range of what is musically practicable and notationally possible. In

Triad IV (1968), his earliest use of tape, the flautist dialogues with recordings of himself, most interestingly in the last movement where the disembodied instruments gradually disperse to leave the 'real' flautist with a plain version of what had previously been embellished. More searching enquiries into the potentialities of such techniques will be found in *Obbligati II* and *Stevens III*.

Whereas Connolly preferred to find his way forward in private, Jonathan Harvey (b 1939) has conducted his search in public. It would be too easy to describe his first seven or eight years of composition in terms of influences received and then discarded in favour of others. For Harvey, searching is finding, and even when most obviously re-exploring territory opened up by other composers, his view of its geography is often individual and interesting in itself.

Like Connolly, he has intense emotion to express (in his case often prompted by deep religious feeling). Like Connolly, too, he has searched for formal disciplines taut enough to canalise and intensify the expression of this emotion, but flexible enough to provide the contextual richness supplied in the past by tonal procedures.

After early works reportedly heavily in debt to Britten, Bartók and even Fauré (including a String Quartet of 1962—now withdrawn—that was sufficiently assured to win a Clements Prize) he began experimenting with serialism, especially with attempts to reconcile serial method with a range of expression that would include tonal reference. Key works of this early period include the Variations (1965) for violin and piano (wholly serial, but with pronouncedly tonal, Brittenesque overtones) and *Cantata I* (also 1965). This is a curiously gripping work, despite the apparent confusion of style thrown against style. In the first movement ('This endes night'), echoes of the more recent manifestations of the Great English Choral Tradition are disturbed by intense high string writing and by Messiaen-derived organ figuration. The second movement ('Song'), at times highly dramatic (especially in the soprano and baritone solos), and with bracingly angular choral textures, still finds room for an almost ethereal lyricism. The beautiful third movement ('Gaude Maria') juxtaposes agitated solos for string instruments with chordal passages for the choir upon which increasingly ornate melodies are festooned. The final

'Melodrama' is similarly eclectic: the language of Webern's cantatas rubs shoulders with baritone solos (spoken and sung) of great fervour; the haunting coda is unashamedly indebted to Britten, but the overall impression is of a single, uncommonly rich imagination.

Cantata I is one of a whole series of Harvey's works in which a fruitful line of development is implied (in this case the unification of disparate styles by a determined imagination) but immediately contradicted by what follows. What followed the cantata was the Symphony (1966), still an eclectic work but a remarkably assured one, with a more personal directness of expression within a convincing structural framework. In technique, too, it shows a distinct step forward in its use of quasi-tonal (nine-note) rows 'filtered-out' from the work's basic set. The extended tonality thus achieved is at the root of the powerful tensions and violent expression of the first movement. The references to Berg and Schoenberg (among others) are obvious, but used as elements in a richly allusive language. The central movement, a vivid, hurtling scherzo, acts as a 'lightning conductor' to the remarkable finale, in which highly varied elements (gamelan sounds in the highest register of the piano; expressive violin and oboe solos; Messiaen-like birdsong figures; rich string chords closer to Vaughan Williams's *Tallis Fantasia* than anything else) are built into a convincing and satisfying arch.

The symphony, too, could have become a plateau for extensive exploration, but immediately after its completion, Harvey became aware of the work of Stockhausen (with whom he studied briefly) and his subsequent works reflect this awareness. The Piano Sonata (1967—since withdrawn) was apparently a hard-line school-of-Stockhausen work, but none of his more recent music betrays the rigidity of control that was reportedly the sonata's main characteristic. Maxwell Davies was also an influence at this time, and a much more audible one in the almost frenzied expressiveness of *Cantata III* (1968) and in the elaborate permutational techniques of *Transformations of 'Love Bade Me Welcome'* (also 1968). This phase culminates in *Ludus Amoris* (*Cantata IV*—1969), a work on the largest scale commissioned for the Three Choirs Festival. Harvey's full battery of accumulated resources is combined in the service of a text dealing with the yearning of the soul for God. It is still more eclectic than *Cantata I* and uses a bewildering variety of resources and techniques. But

165

it is saved (by the skin of its teeth) from disjointedness by the compelling power of the vision that prompted it.

Harvey's more recent works show a consolidation of technique, especially the expansion of serial practice, in an attempt to provide a discipline for his characteristic breadth of reference and allusion. *On Vision* (*Cantata VI*—1971) further explores the derivation of sub-sets from a basic series which also controls the work's proportions. The result is far from arid: its intensity, indeed, is comparable to *Ludus Amoris*, but all the more direct for being under tight control. *Persephone Dream* (1972—a large-scale orchestral piece) uses permutational and filtering devices of extreme complexity, again to serve an essentially expressive, even neo-romantic end. It is, indeed, difficult to imagine this line of development being taken further; the apparently much simpler sound of *Inner Light I* (1973) for seven instruments and tape may indicate that Harvey's exploratory phase is over. It recalls Connolly in its investigation of the continuum determinacy/indeterminacy, but remains characteristic of Harvey in the exhilaration of its ultimate generation of (serial) order from disorder.

By comparison, the musical development of Roger Smalley (b 1943) has formed a remarkably purposeful straight line. There is no hint of indecision or immaturity in his *Piano Pieces I–V*, the earliest of which were written when he was nineteen. These extremely compressed pieces demonstrate a commanding control of structures in which each element is dependent on and related to every other; Boulez is already less of an influence than one thoroughly digested constituent of a style. *Piano Piece V*, the latest (1965) and longest of the set, is concerned with strict canonic procedures within an equally strict serial framework. In sound, however, it is far from 'strict'. This is partly due to Smalley's idiomatic use of the piano (he is a formidable pianist, which could almost have been inferred from the studies in sonority of the first three pieces). But it is also significant that the fifth piece was intended as a sketch for a larger composition, *2 Poems of D. H. Lawrence* (1965), a lyric, expressive work; Smalley's preoccupation with the techniques of his craft can be overstated at the expense of the purely musical ends that the techniques serve. It should be noticed in passing that the first two piano pieces were also 'recycled'—in *The Leaden Echo and the Golden Echo* (also 1965;

scored for trumpet, accordion and piano): the first example of Smalley's habit of composing in groups, successive works further exploring territory opened up by their predecessors.

Smalley's technical control was further developed in three works of fairly large scale all drawn from the same (fourteen-note) set and an associated durational series. These were the Septet (1963—in fact a nonet, since two solo voices join the instruments at the end), the String Sextet (1965) and the *Elegies* (1965—settings of Rilke for two soloists, strings, brass and bells). Lack of performances precludes a discussion of how far this triptych formed a preparation for the works that now seem to mark Smalley's maturity and that first aroused public interest in him.

Gloria Tibi Trinitas I (1965) is his first work for full orchestra and the first of a series derived from keyboard In Nomines (fantasias based on a plainchant fragment) by the Tudor composer William Blitheman. Five of Blitheman's six settings are used, but the work is in no sense a pastiche; it is, rather, a virtuoso extension of the motivic techniques present or implicit in the originals, in terms of the modern orchestra handled by a composer with the full range of serial techniques at his finger-tips. The sixth Blitheman setting is used as the basis for the still more elaborate *Missa Brevis*, in which fragments of the original are subjected to an exhaustive development by virtually every canonic, imitational and transformation technique available to the composer. Dauntingly difficult to sing (solo voices are specified for each of the sixteen parts) the work has a fervour that, in a totally different style, recalls nothing so much as the Taverner mass 'Gloria tibi, Trinitas' which was the first of all contrapuntal structures built on the In Nomine fragment.

The *Missa Brevis* itself, rather than its Blitheman 'original', is at the root of the two works that followed, *Missa Parodia I and II* (1967), the first for piano solo (a reinvestigation of the *Missa Brevis* and a partial redevelopment of its material in terms of a comprehensive piano technique), the second for piano and eight instruments.

Gloria Tibi Trinitas II (1966) is less related to this series than its title would suggest. It is based on a seventh Blitheman piece, a Te Deum, and is scored for soloists, chorus and orchestra. It incorporates a motet in strict isorhythm and is thus the most 'medieval' of Smalley's works (and his closest approach to the parallel but not really comparable preoccupations of Peter Maxwell Davies). In 1965 Smalley worked for a period with Stockhausen in Darmstadt. A predisposition towards Stockhausen is already perceptible in the early piano pieces, but the first evidence of Smalley's close identification with his music appears in *The Song of The Highest Tower* (1968). Smalley has since been closely involved with the performance of Stockhausen's music and, in his sometimes combative writings, with the propagation of his ideas. The technical contrast with the preceding works could scarcely be greater: variable 'moment form' (though within a firmly established ground plan) replaces tight formal control. A measure of improvisation is required and 'noise' elements are important. Yet the first of these might have been predicted from the numerous short sections of *Missa Parodia I*, and the second and third may have their origins in the melismata and spoken passages in the *Missa Brevis*.

The year 1968 also saw Smalley's first use of electronics. *Transformation I*, for piano with electronic modulation, may be seen as a study for the more thoroughgoing use of 'live electronics' that followed it and for which Smalley assembled his performing group 'Intermodulation'.

Pulses for 5 x 4 Players (1969) can be seen as a statement of the position he had reached by then. It uses moment form and allows a great deal of (controlled) freedom to the twenty brass players; a high proportion of the score consists of verbal or symbolic instructions; electronic modification is used. None of these factors prepares one for the work's readily approachable character. This is largely due to its extremely simple material—within each moment, each instrument plays only a single pitch (modified rhythmically or otherwise). Accessibility is also aided by the quality implied in the work's title—a pronounced and obvious rhythmic pulse (Smalley's interest in pop music has its effect here). One should also mention the quasi-imitative overlapping of the moments: at any given time, part of what the audience hears, at one level of its attention or another, consists of developments and recollections of what has already occurred.

The shortest line from *Pulses* to Smalley's current work passes, not through the compositions that immediately followed it, but through *Beat Music* (1971). Between the two, however, he had more closely investigated two areas that his development up till then had opened up: the provision of frameworks within which guided improvisation can fruitfully take place without abandoning the controlling, co-creative role of the composer (*Melody Studies*, 1970); and the related question of devising formal plans for variable moment structures (*Strata*, 1971). The fruits of these enquiries, fertilised by the implications of the all-interval chord on which *Strata* is based, are found in *Beat Music*. The basic material here is the harmonic series itself, in an attempt to establish total inter-relationship between all the constituents of a work by natural rather than (or as well as) 'artificial' means. Thus the 'micro-pulsations' which produce the phenomenon of sound are used to generate the 'macro-pulsations' of rhythm: pitch and duration become inherently related phenomena. *Beat Music* was followed by *Monody* (1972) for piano with electronic modulation. This work links the *Melody Studies* to Smalley's most recent composition at the time of writing, *Zeitebenen* (1973). Scored for four instrumental-ists (with electronic modulation) and four-track tape, this thoroughly Stockhausenesque title designates a work that seems to predict a new phase in Smalley's development. Using material from *Monody* and incorporating natural sounds on tape as well as quotations from Mao Tse Tung and the last act of *Tristan und Isolde*, it is an avowedly programmatic, even didactic piece. Formally, it also marks a departure: the remnants of moment form are seen in *Zeitebenen*'s montage of disparate elements, but the work's message seems to have taken over from purely musical processes the function of integrating the whole. Smalley's pro-gress from this unpredicted point can at present only be guessed.

Anthony Payne (b 1936) read music at Durham University, and has been known for some while as a perceptive writer and critic. As a composer, however, he is self-taught. His career was as late in starting as Connolly's. Indeed, the stylistic jungle referred to at the outset of this chapter, to which, as a reviewer, he has been more subjected than most, seems not only to have caused him difficulties in finding a personal voice, but even to have destroyed his desire to compose for some while.

The first work that he now accepts was not begun until 1965 and was not completed for seven years (although several shorter works appeared in the intervening period). The work in question, *Phoenix Mass*, is in fact so titled to commemorate 'the resurgence of creativity after a fallow period, as well as the discovery of a new manner'. If it may be regarded as Payne's first work, it is

169

one of the most assured and impressive 'Op. 1's by any composer discussed in this chapter. Its immediate coherency is due largely to a deliberately restricted choice of intervals; although those chosen avoid obvious consonances, this restraint produces textures of great clarity having slight, but telling, overtones of earlier liturgical music. It is scored for chorus, three trumpets and three trombones and is in four movements (the Credo is not set).

The Kyrie acts as an exposition of the work's resources (which include unpitched speech); the 'prayerful' interval of the falling semitone is important here. The Gloria is set in English; in this movement the brass writing becomes increasingly complex and motivic (recalling Connolly's *Cinquepaces*), often under slower-moving voices. Earlier, there are jubilant bell-like overlappings in the brass parts, and the final crescendo uses rapid speech, as of an excited crowd. The moving and passionate Sanctus (text in Latin) gives exultant, flaming figures to the voices and slower, chant-like music to the brass; these positions are then reversed. The Osanna, a fervent crescendo, leads to an extended setting of the Benedictus, the voices solemn over carolling brass. The mass ends with a bi-lingual Agnus Dei, the Latin phrases sung, the English translation spoken (and shouted) over brass fanfares. There is a quiet and beautiful ending on the words 'dona nobis pacem'.

While intermittently working on the Mass, Payne completed several smaller pieces, among them *Paraphrases and Cadenzas* (1969) for clarinet, viola and piano. The title is literal: it is based on some of the highly fruitful material used in the Mass.

Payne's individual and exciting use of voices is continued in his *Two Songs Without Words* (1970), for five male voices (including counter-tenor). The use of solo singers allows still greater flexibility and the parts are virtuoso in their requirements. The songs use a random number series to control both pitch and rhythm, only the larger structure of the second being random. The first is in 'sonata form', the first subject group being a sequence of brief, lyrically vocal solos, the second chords of varying densities. The colour values of different vowel sounds are exploited, especially in the 'second subject', but the subsequent song makes far greater use of this device, as well as various vocal 'effects'. Although each singer is called upon to produce almost instrumental ranges of tone quality, the music is always 'vocal': one is more conscious of the physical act of singing in this work and in the Mass than in much recent music for voices.

Sonatas and Ricercars (also 1970) shows a similarly sympathetic handling of instruments. It is for wind quintet and sets accompanied cadenzas for each instrument in turn as prelude, postlude and interludes to a sequence of four movements (scherzo, chorale variations, motet and quodlibet) for the complete quintet. It is a very taut and 'composerly' structure, readily incorporating both the pithy and angular polyphony of the 'motet' and the romantic horn solo with its dying fall that forms the coda.

Payne has since completed a *Paean* for solo piano (1971) and his first orchestral work, *Concerto for Orchestra*.

Tristram Cary (b 1925) stands at some distance from the other composers in this chapter in that an important proportion of his work has been in the field of pure (as opposed to 'live') electronic music. While in the Royal Navy he received training in radar and electronics (and is thus probably the only living British composer to be a Chartered Engineer). In the late Forties he began experimenting with electronic music, using primitive disc equipment, as was Schaeffer in Paris around the same time. His earliest purely electronic compositions date from the early Fifties.

A very high proportion of his extensive output has been music for the theatre, for film, for radio and television. As the composer responsible for the scores to *The Ladykillers* (1955), *Sammy Going South* (1963) and *A Christmas Carol* (1971) he is better known to the general public (though not, probably, by name) than most living composers. These scores were all for conventional instruments, but he has also contributed electronic music to documentary, cartoon and experimental films: Richard Williams's *The Little Island* (1958) owed much of its success to Cary's imaginative sound-score. His contribution to radio and television has been distinguished, involving collaboration with such writers and directors as Louis MacNeice (the almost legendary *East of the Sun and West of the Moon*), Francis Dillon, Douglas Cleverdon and Christopher Holme. His scores for the *Dr Who* television series brought electronic music to probably its widest public.

Although Cary has continued to write for conventional instruments, most of his recent concert music has been either purely electronic or has combined tape and live sounds. His *January Piece* (1967) is a short study (realised on single-track tape) in rapid and percussive sound. There is a very perceptible pulse, and the

171

sound-world inhabited by the piece is close to the virtuoso drumming of West Africa.

3, 4, 5 . . . (also 1967) is described as 'a study in limited resources' and is an example of the musical fields open to the electronic composer but not even approachable with conventional resources. It uses only the pitches 3, 4 and 5 Hz (and their multiples by 10), and the same simple 'series' also governs the durational aspect of the music. The use of space is striking (it is Cary's first concert work to use stereophony) and the sound events are easy to take in and to relate to one another within a simple but satisfying formal structure.

Birth is Life is Power is Death is God is (1968) is based on one of Cary's scores for the British pavilion at Expo '67. Some of the sound here used is 'concrete', that is pure or transformed recorded material, rather than sounds generated solely by electronic means, but the score (like most of Cary's work) is happily free of the bathroom and aircraft-coming-in-to-land clichés that have afflicted so many composers when faced with the theoretically limitless range of sound available from a sine-wave generator. The sounds of this piece, indeed, are dramatic and varied, often giving an impression of grandeur of scale.

An example of the scarcely tapped potentialities of electronic 'light music' is provided by *Music for Light* (1968), a cheerfully gaudy piece originally conceived to accompany a light-show. It is also an example of Cary's 'commercial' work interacting with his 'concert' music; in the same way, his music to Ray Bradbury's *Leviathan 99* (1968), an early and highly imaginative use of stereophonic radio, has generated a concert suite in which the full potentialities of the material and its medium are exploited.

Cary's imaginative language has grown as his command of resources has expanded. This can be heard in *Winter Song* (1969), a short but impressive study in dark, grave, slow-moving sound: the materials it uses are restricted, but used with great resource. The process continues in such works as *Narcissus* (1970—Cary's first use of live electronics, scored for flute and tape recorders) and the more recent, large-scale *Peccata Mundi*, for speaker, chorus, orchestra and four-track tape. It should be mentioned that Cary is active in educating musicians in the use of electronic resources—until recently a gravely neglected area in British musical colleges.

The music of Anthony Milner (b 1925) is often classified as conservative or traditionalist. In a sense this is accurate enough, but since the two terms are frequently regarded as synonyms for old-fashioned or reactionary, it should be said that no old-fashioned reactionary would accept Milner as an ally. His 'conservatism', if that is what it is, is based on an intimate knowledge of the techniques of pre-classical music, both as musicologist and as performer (he was associated with Tippett in performances of early choral music at Morley College, and for several years led an ensemble specialising in the then neglected chamber music and cantatas of the Baroque period). The influence of this experience is felt in his music, combined with an extreme technical ingenuity and a receptiveness to the techniques of both earlier and later periods— he is as fond of isorhythm as is Maxwell Davies and his use of quasi-serial motivic working is as virtuoso as anything in the work of Connolly. In some ways, indeed, he may be said to have joined the 'avant-garde' from the opposite direction.

His Op. 1, *Salutatio Angelica* (1948), made a great impression at its first performance in 1950. The chaste and beautiful vocal lines of this exquisite cantata may have convinced some that Milner was a younger Gerald Finzi, but in retrospect other characteristics of the work seem more relevant to his later development: an ingenious but highly satisfying use of form (a chacony, a fugue and an ostinato are framed, rondo-wise, by related ritornelli); great rhythmic flexibility (in later works manifesting itself in restlessly changing bar-lengths and two-against-three syncopations); a profound religious sensibility; and a delight in technique that is aural rather than visual—it soon became apparent that Milner wants us to *hear* his imitative and canonic devices and to share his pleasure in them. This is part of the strength of his Mass, Op. 3 (1952), a remarkably expressive and cunningly-wrought composition. The precision of its effects—the bell-like opening of the Sanctus; the athletic canons of the Gloria—give it a richness of incident out of all proportion to its dimensions—fifteen pages of score lasting a bare nine minutes.

The Oboe Quartet, Op. 4 (1953) is again brief, economical and rich in invention. The influence of Tippett is evident in the busy syncopations of the first movement, but the wiry lyricism has an individual flavour and the strong formal control of the arch-like second movement is indication enough that Milner was by then ready for larger forms.

The *City of Desolation*, Op. 7 (1955) and *Saint Francis*, Op. 8 (1956) are both short, but use fuller forces than the earlier cantata. The former is notable for the freshness and assurance of its dramatic choral writing and the vehemence and urgency of its soprano solos which refurbish the tradition in which it is evidently rooted. The latter work is more personal: the choral parts, in particular, have a rhythmic freedom and variety of texture that are a long way from the nineteenth century—closer, indeed, to the roots of the English choral tradition. The beautiful simplicity of the setting of Psalm XXIII in Op. 7 and the swaying dance-measures of the 'canticle' in Op. 8 are both examples of Milner's gift for accessible and memorable ideas; both works show a further development of his technical armoury (Op. 8 includes his first use of iso-rhythm).

The Harrowing of Hell, Op. 9 (1956) is a highly accomplished response to a well-nigh impossible brief—a setting of a lengthy and luridly dramatic text for voices alone (double choir and two soloists). A better indication of Milner's achievement by the later Fifties can be gained from the brilliance and graphic imagery of his partsong *Cast Wide the Folding Doorways of the East*, Op. 12 (1957—written for the eighty-fifth birthday of Vaughan Williams and paying that master the compliment of not imitating him at all) and by the hauntingly beautiful song-cycle *Our Lady's Hours*, Op. 13 (also 1957).

None of this, however, is much preparation for the formidable command of instrumental resources on the largest scale shown by the Variations for Orchestra, Op. 14 (1958). The medieval Advent hymn 'Es ist ein Ros' entsprungen' is here treated as a 'theme' in the conventional sense, as a note-row (it appears in retrograde, inversion and retrograde-inversion) and as a quarry of intervallic outlines. The fourteen variations are grouped as a quasi-symphonic three-movement structure. Violent contrasts (toccata, berceuse, march, scherzo) mark the first section; the second builds painfully to a savage climax; the third begins with exuberant hocketing between instruments, pauses for a slow 'intrada' and builds to a triumphant return of 'Es ist ein Ros' ' which vanishes into the distance before a coda recalling the opening pages. The structure is impressively coherent, and displays the composer's technical resources at full stretch.

Milner's most important works since the Variations (he is not a prolific composer) have been an extended dramatic oratorio

The Water and the Fire, Op. 16 (1961) and a Symphony, Op. 23 (completed in 1972, but in gestation from 1964).

The oratorio represents the fertilisation of the masterly handling of voices shown in the earlier cantatas by the formal and motivic mastery that matured in the Variations. It is a rich, complex and imaginative mystical drama, proceeding from the black despair of scene 1 (ending with an eerie orchestral depiction of 'the dark night of the soul') via the encounter with Christ in scene 2 and the beautiful soprano interlude of scene 3 to the mysterious and ecstatic ceremonial of the long final scene (*Parsifal* re-interpreted by ears that have heard *The Midsummer Marriage*). Throughout, the deep expressiveness is refined and intensified by impressive coherency and formal control.

The fascinating discipline and logic of the oratorio are applied to 'the large-scale resolution of conflicts' in the Symphony, one of the most successful of recent attempts to use the ancient form without shirking the essential disruptiveness of a wholly twentieth-century musical language. It is tonal, but its formal cohesiveness is due at least as much to Milner's structural logic, which relates each incident to the whole. Its 'lessons' may, paradoxically, be more readily learned by those who have abandoned tonality than by those who have not.

The remaining three composers in this chapter will be discussed fairly briefly. They have all been subject to the problems hinted at at the outset, but to these have been added the besetting problem of most younger British composers: the practical impossibility of obtaining performances. All three, however, have demonstrated by the handful of works that have received adequate performance that their inclusion in a chapter dealing with 'significant' figures is abundantly justified.

Christopher Headington (b 1930) has composed few works for large forces (though his Violin Concerto of 1959 is highly spoken of). Whether this is due to inclination or force of circumstances is hard to say, but the excellence of his songs suggests either an instinctive attraction to the genre or a remarkable adaptation to a *faute de mieux* reliance on it. His short song-cycle *Reflections of Summer* (1965) is an impressive revivification of the English song tradition, recognisably by a compatriot of John Ireland but with beautifully crisp, clean textures and not a single note of padding.

175

The declamatory passages in the second song, the quiet evocative-
ness of the third and above all the Auden setting that ends the
set demonstrate a major song-writing talent. The final song,
indeed, challenges comparison with Britten (who used the same
text in the *Spring Symphony*) and does not suffer by it.

Sensitivity to word and ambience is suggested by the very
different world of the *Three Poems of Rainer Maria Rilke*, whose
intimate expression, elegant line and economical piano part are
sensitively attuned to the words. The final song even manages to
quote from Mahler at the beginning and maintain the emotional
level through to a beautiful coda. The *Toccata* for piano uses
traditional pianistic resources in a fresh and personal neo-tonal
manner; some of the short choral pieces suggest a comparable
cleaning-up of another English tradition. Headington's works also
include a Piano Sonata (1956), a crisp and airy Oboe Sonatina
(1960) and another of the same year for solo flute, as well as a
string quartet and several more sets of songs.

Robin Holloway (b 1943) might be regarded as Headington's
diametric opposite: he has shown a marked bent for orchestral
music of very large scale. His Concerto for Orchestra (1969) is
said to be the first work in which he found his personal manner
(though the earlier Organ Concerto, the two Concertinos and a
Melodrama to words by Sylvia Plath were all well received). The
Concerto is a work of astonishing assurance and inventiveness, with
huge exuberance in the first movement, rich fantasy in the second
and, in the enormous last movement (it plays for over twenty
minutes), vivid imagination is controlled by impressive audible
logic. The quotations from Brahms that occur at climactic
moments (and the fact that the initial impetus for the work was a
feeling that Tippett had muffed his chances in *his* Concerto for
Orchestra) indicate a curious characteristic of this composer—a
dependence on outside musical stimuli to set the composition
process going. This is at its most obvious and fascinating in
Souvenirs de Schumann (1970), an extended and serious essay in
re-composition: a group of Schumann songs are analytically
rewritten, elegantly taking up possibilities left untouched by the
earlier composer and using his phrases as the raw material for a
wholly original work. Quotations from Wagner and Mahler are
introduced as quite natural elements of this rich sound-world.
The process is taken still further in *Liederkreis* (1971) which, in
performance, incorporates a complete hearing of Schumann's

176

Op. 24 upon which it is based. The last work in the series is *Domination of Black* (1974), in which the Wagnerian and Mahlerian connotations are vestigial. The latter work contains some of the most communicative orchestral writing of any British composer in the last few years: the hunting scherzo in particular is physically exciting in the extreme. *Evening with Angels* (1972)—'a textless song-cycle after Tennyson'—is again long, neo-romantic and splendidly laid out for orchestra. Its nine landscape-like sections cover a huge range of expression, from dark poetry to airy elusiveness, from intense feeling to satirical parody. The comprehensiveness and richly allusive quality of Holloway's language and his apparent remoteness from ideological narrowness make him a composer of whose future importance there can be little doubt.

David Ellis (b 1933), finally, is an eclectic by choice. He favours large-scale structures in which his characteristic breadth of reference is given elbow-room. In his Piano Sonata, the presence of Schumann, Debussy and of jazz piano playing are evident, but welded into an imaginative whole, in part due to the unifying use of a typical three-note rising figure that permeates the work. The startling conjunctions of style in his music have grown greater rather than less as he has developed. While the Violin Concerto (1960) inhabits a fairly consistent neo-romantic area (largely dictated by the solo instrument's character), more recent pieces such as the impressive Symphony and the broodingly intense *Elegy* rely more and more on simple thematic means to give shape to structures in which almost anything can happen. Ellis is perhaps the most distinguished of the small number of younger composers who are endeavouring to progress by deliberate inclusiveness rather than a narrow but concentrated exclusiveness. Of the importance of this endeavour there can be no doubt: music as a means of communication has reached an impasse that has affected every composer discussed in this chapter, either inhibiting their first steps or holding them back from anything but a tiny minority of the musical public. That an artist like Ellis, who has tried to break down this situation, should have encountered particular difficulty in obtaining performances of his music is ironic. But if a generally acceptable *lingua franca* is to be constructed amidst the present fragmentation of the art of music, then Ellis's work will be seen to have made a not inconsiderable contribution to that task.

Postlude—A Note on Christopher Shaw

MALCOLM MacDONALD

In January 1974 the BBC gave the first performance of Christopher Shaw's short cantata for soli, chorus and orchestra, *Peter and the Lame Man*. It was the first broadcast of a major score by a composer who has reached his fiftieth year without receiving any critical attention, and who, despite thirty years' dedicated creative work, wishes to be judged by just that one cantata and a handful of small choral pieces, only one of which has been published. Without the broadcast, it is unlikely that his existence would have been noticed in these pages: a sobering thought. For *Peter and the Lame Man* (1965–67) is a work of unusual distinction, and the choral pieces, in their different ways, are equally impressive.

Shaw's is a curious case. If this is yet another Neglected English Composer, he has acquiesced in his own neglect. He undoubtedly did suffer, at the beginning of his career, for his interest in the twelve-note method at a time when it was decidedly *not* the done thing in British music. Performance and encouragement were not forthcoming; and since fashion and reputation-building seem alien to his temperament, he appears to have accepted that, and gone on composing regardless. But seldom can the muse have had a less pliant servant. Shaw's dissatisfaction with something like nine-tenths of his output has meant the suppression, not only of the orchestral works and cantatas mentioned by David Drew in the only previous article about him (256), but also of many smaller pieces—even the *Four Poems by James Joyce*, which excited much interest at its first performance in 1956, and of his few published scores, such as the Clarinet Sonata.

Yet this is *not* the despair of a forgotten composer—it is as eloquent of his self-assurance as the music he has allowed to stand. Knowing his own strength, he knows when he has not fully exercised it. The few withdrawn scores which I have seen confirm the rectitude of Shaw's judgement, inasmuch as they lack the perfection of those he deems adequate. But they are fine works by any other standards, and better than many that find performance and

178

publication. This is presumably true of yet others he has rejected: it is said, for instance, by those who laid eyes on it, that the unfinished opera on Laclos's *Les Liaisons Dangereuses* contained much beautiful and witty music. And it seems needful to record (since it may never be said elsewhere) that the refined contrapuntal strength of the Keats *Sonnet* for tenor and clarinet (1955) and the slow movement of the Trio for clarinet, viola and piano (1953–54) represent a quite individual achievement in the British music of that period. Clearly the indifference—on both sides—which allows Shaw to pare away the inessentials of his art may not have injured *him*; but we, the listeners, have unwittingly lost something we might, if only we knew it, have wanted to preserve.

Writing in 1963, David Drew warned that to claim 'some portentous significance' for Shaw's work 'would be a poor tribute to the modesty and reticence which are among its most valuable assets'. Here, perhaps, his characterisation of the music was coloured by his knowledge of the man: Shaw's music is *not* reticent—just superbly under control. Simultaneously with Drew's article the *Musical Times* published Shaw's *A Lesson from Ecclesiastes* —possibly the finest musical supplement ever commissioned by that journal. Ten years later, it was still unperformed—a delay out of all proportion to its difficulty—and has not yet been heard in public. This five-minute anthem for chorus and organ is far more substantial than its dimensions suggest: it is a gripping musical experience of considerable emotional and intellectual force. The organ outbursts may reflect a Messiaenic influence, but the close-textured vocal polyphony is inimitably Shavian. The grim text (Ecclesiastes V, 1–7) is surely significant, especially perhaps V. 2: 'Let not thine heart be hasty to utter any thing before God. For God is in heaven, and thou upon earth: therefore let thy words be few.'

Shaw was certainly not 'hasty' with *Peter and the Lame Man*: 'I remember writing the first line for the tenor sometime in the summer of '64 and wondering if anything could be made of it and came to the conclusion that there might about the middle of '65. A snail-like pace!' That tenor line gave him a twelve-note row: like Schoenberg, Shaw clearly derives his series from melodic ideas, not *vice versa*. The Schoenberg of *Moses und Aron*, the later Stravinsky, and a third master to whom Shaw is perhaps closest in spirit—Dallapiccola—indicate the world this work inhabits, yet the music's gravity, rhythmic vitality and translucent textures define an independent sensibility. The evanescent coda, the chorus softly singing against darkly radiant harmonies in lower strings and eight solo violins, achieves a 'Stravinskian' release into time-lessness with quite un-Stravinskian luminosity.

A similar effect occurs in the recent SATB setting of Horace's Ode *To the Bandusian Spring* (1974): the gradual slowing down of a six-note ostinato (transposed and mirrored in the four voices so that each complete statement allows the rotation of all twelve notes twice) enacts Horace's proud boast of fixing for ever the cascading waters by means of his art. The more strictly Shaw adheres to twelve-note principles, the more profoundly 'tonal', in the widest sense, his music becomes. In this little chorus the harmony has the consistency of marble, matching exactly the sonorous poise of Horace's verse; yet it has warmth too, and the final cadence, so tonally suggestive, must be one of the most spine-tingling in twelve-note music.

Shaw's frequent revisions (for instance of *Peter* in 1970) stem no more from uncertainty than his suppressions: rather they bespeak a recognition that he did his best at the time of composition, but having since progressed he can now do better. It was surely in this spirit that he withdrew the short piece for speaker and orchestra *In Memoriam Jan Palach* (1969—listed among his works in the current *Who's Who in Music*) and began to use its material as part of a new and larger conception, a cantata on the same subject. At the time of writing only the first number of this new work is drafted: but that contains music of an intensity unusual even by Shaw's standards, expressed within—indeed through—a rigorous serial discipline.

The smallness of Shaw's acknowledged output requires us to temper any assessment with moderation. But, if he has developed into a composer of some mastery, the musical world at large has not lifted a finger to help him on his way; if it remains indifferent, the loss will be ours, not his. For he does possess qualities not equally present in all the composers discussed in these pages—the self-knowledge, and self-possession, of an independent creative mind.

Other Composers

There are so many composers of talent writing today that it would be impossible to represent them all at length in a one-volume study, even within the fairly strict terms of reference chosen for this book. This section contains a selection of composers who in the Editor's opinion have achieved a significant body of work, the treatment of each individual reflecting in most cases the extent of information supplied by him or her to the Editor, as well as the number of works completed.

ABBREVIATIONS

ARCO	= Associate of the Royal College of Organists	mvts	= movements
		nar	= narrator
arr	= arrangement	ob	= oboe
b	= bass	orch	= orchestra, orchestral
bar	= baritone	org	= organ
bs	= bassoon	ovt	= overture
c	= contralto	perc	= percussion
ch	= chamber	pf	= piano
chor	= chorus, choir	QEH	= Queen Elizabeth Hall
clar	= clarinet	qtet	= quartet
coll	= college	RAM	= Royal Academy of Music
conc	= concerto		
cond	= conductor	RCM	= Royal College of Music
d	= double		
db	= double bass	rdr	= recorder
dr	= drum	rec	= reciter
ens	= ensemble	RFH	= Royal Festival Hall
fest	= festival	RMCM	= Royal Manchester College of Music
fl	= flute		
GSM	= Guildhall School of Music and Drama	RSAM	= Royal Scottish Academy of Music
gtr	= guitar	s	= soprano
h	= high	SATB	= soprano, alto, tenor, bass (choir)
hp	= harp		
hpschd	= harpsichord	sch	= school
insts	= instruments	schol	= scholar, scholarship
m-s	= mezzo-soprano	son	= sonata

spkr	= speaker	tromb	= trombone
strs	= strings	U	= University
sym	= symphony	unac	= unaccompanied
t	= tenor	v	= voice
TCM	= Trinity College of	var	= variations
	Music	vla	= viola
tmpt	= trumpet	vlc	= cello
tr	= treble	vln	= violin

BARLOW, David (b 1927)

Studied Cambridge U, RCM, Nadia Boulanger. 2nd Sym (1958) prize work in Northern Composers' Guild. Composer of the Year, Newcastle Fes, 1969.

Works include: 2 syms, 2nd str trio, str qtet, str quintet; *David & Bathsheba*—one-act opera. Currently working on opera for school-children.

BLYTON, Carey (b London 1932)

Studied zoology at U Coll London for one year, then abandoned science in favour of music, working as a research assistant for the Gas Council while studying music privately. Studied TCM 1935; won Sir Granville Bantock composition prize (1954). Studied in Denmark with Jorgen Jersild (1957–8). Publisher's music editor 1958–63; since 1963 has freelanced as composer, arranger, editor and lecturer. Part-time teacher TCM, and since 1964 music editor to Faber Music, being Benjamin Britten's editor, responsible for editorial preparation from *Curlew River* onwards.

Works include: *Cinque Port* (suite in five mvts for orch), overture *The Hobbit*, *Lyrics from the Chinese* (high v & strs), *Lachrymae—In Memoriam John Dowland* (h v & strs), many song cycles, madrigals and partsongs, *Moresques* (s, fl, hp, pf); *Symphony in Yellow* (s, cl & hp); *What Then Is Love* (v, cl & pf), *In Memorian Django Reinhardt* (gtr), folksong arrs, pf music, music for films and television commercials.

BOURGEOIS, Derek (b Kingston-on-Thames 1941)

Studied Cambridge U 1959–63, RCM 1963–5; Mus D (Cantab) 1971. Taught Cranleigh Sch 1965–71, lecturer Bristol U since 1971. Jt winner BBC 'Monarchy 1000' competition 1973.

Works include: 2 syms, symphonic vars, orch fantasy *The Globe*, conc for b tuba, concertino for clar & strs, cantata *Jabberwocky*, *Symphonic Pageant*, str qtet, 2 vln sons, 2 brass quintets, son for 2 pfs. Currently working on full-length opera.

BURGON, Geoffrey (b Hambledon, Hants 1941)

Studied GSM. Works played at Edinburgh, Camden, Three Choirs and

182

Cheltenham Fests and many continental fests. Prince Pierre of Monaco award; has worked for films, TV, radio and theatre.

Works include: conc for str orch, *Alleluia Nativitas* for orch, *Gending, Cantus Alleluia, The Fire of Heaven, Magnificat, Joan of Arc* (Music Theatre), *The Golden Eternity, Think on Dreadful Domesday, Hymn to Venus, Five Sonnets of John Donne, This Endris Night.*

BURT, Francis (b London 1926)
Studied RAM 1948–51 (with Howard Ferguson) and Hochschule für Musik, Berlin 1951 (with Boris Blacher), 8 months in Rome (Mendelssohn Schol) 1954–5. Has lived in Vienna since 1956. Appointed Professor in Ordinary for composition at Hochschule für Musik und Darstellende Kunst, Vienna, 1973.

Works include: ballet *Der Golem, Fantasmagoria* for orch, *Iambics* for orch, operas *Volpone, Barnstable,* many pieces of theatre music and works for German and Austrian television.

CANNON, Philip (b Paris 1929)
Studied Dartington Hall (with Imogen Holst) and RCM (with Vaughan Williams and Gordon Jacob). Now Professor of Composition RCM.

Works include: *Songs to Delight,* concertino for pf and strs, *Fleeting Fancies, Cinq Chansons de Femme, L'Enfant S'amuse, Sonatine Champêtre, Son of God, Three Rivers,* str qtet (won Grand Prix, Critics Prize, International Chamber Music Competition, Paris 1965), *Oraison Funèbre de l'Âme Humaine, Carillon* for org, *Carillon* for hp, symphonic study *Spring, The Temple* (Three Choirs Fest 1974), *Burgundian Sym,* sym *Son of Man,* operas *Morvoren, Man from Venus, Dr Jekyll and Mr Hyde,* etc.

CARDEW and his 'school':
CARDEW, Cornelius (b Winchcombe, Glos 1936)
Chorister at Canterbury Cathedral 1943–50, studied RAM 1953–7 and at the Electronic Music Studios, Cologne 1957–8. Assistant to Karlheinz Stockhausen 1958–60 and was chiefly responsible for the realisation of Stockhausen's *Carré* for 4 choirs and orchs. Further study in Rome with Petrassi 1964–5. Since 1960 has performed, lectured and taught in Britain, Europe and USA. Has been much involved with experimental performing ensembles, organising music on the lines of a free or even random social activity (eg the AMM free improvisation group (since 1965) and especially the Scratch Orchestra, which he founded in 1969 with Michael Parsons and Howard Skempton). More recently, perhaps under the influence of the pianist John Tilbury, he has moved to a more rigid and formalised Maoist position, and, with the 'political' kernel of the original Scratch Orchestra, supports the

political line of the Communist Party of Great Britain, arranges numbers from Peking Opera and composes in a similar style.

Works include: *Autumn '60* (orch), *Octet '61* for Jasper Johns, *Treatise*, *Three Winter Potatoes* (pf), *The Great Learning*, *Piano Album*.

Apart from Brian Dennis and John White, several younger composers have been associated with, or taken their lead from, Cardew's activities, especially the Scratch Orchestra. They include:

HOBBS, Christopher (b 1950)
Studied with Cardew RAM 1967–9. Member of the Scratch Orchestra since 1969. In 1969 founded the *Experimental Music Catalogue* with the purpose of distributing unpublished new music. Works, some of which are founded on material by other composers, include *13 Word Pieces* (for various specified or unspecified performers), *Remorseless Lamb* (pf), *Fine Doomsday Piece* (after John Bull) (pf), transcription of Scriabin's *Poem of Ecstasy* (reed organs and toy pianos), *Arnold Wolf-Ferrari Orchestra Book*.

PARSONS, Michael (b Bolton 1938)
Studied Oxford and RCM 1961–2 with Peter Racine Fricker. Co-founder of the Scratch Orchestra. Lecturer at London Polytechnic 1963–9 and since 1970 at Portsmouth College of Art.

Works include: *Mindfulness of Breathing* (for low men's vs), *Mindfulness Occupied with the Body* (large chor), *Rhythm Studies* (2 pfs and drs).

SHRAPNEL, Hugh (b Birmingham 1947)
Studied RAM 1967–9 with Norman Demuth and attended Cardew's class in experimental music at Morley College. Member of the Scratch Orchestra since 1969 and also (since 1970) of the Promenade Theatre Orchestra (*see* John White); director of the Wood and Metal Band.

Works include: *Space-time Music* (for any material), *Anthology* (verbal piece for singers and instrumentalists), *Cantation 2* (for any number of pfs), *Tidal Wave* (for any number of electric orgs and other keyboard insts).

SKEMPTON, Howard (b Chester 1947)
Studied privately with Thomas Wess 1964–6 and Cardew 1967–8. Co-founder of the Scratch Orchestra.

Works include: *A Humming Song* (pf), *For Strings* (for any stringed inst(s)), *Two Highland Dances* (pf), *Twelve Piano Pieces*.

Other composers with affinities with Cardew's group include: Gavin BRYARS, Alec HILL, Michael CHANT.

CARHART, David (b 1937)
Studied RAM (with Lennox Berkeley). Early success with piano sonata at 1959 Cheltenham Fest—reached a stylistic impasse and did not write for 5 years; resumed composing 1969.

Works include: *On the Willow Boughs* (t & orch), pf conc, str qtet, vln son, pf son, *Tre Canzone* (m-s, fl, vlc, pf), *Time Passing* (m-s, pf), songs, pf pieces etc.

CHAPPLE, Brian (b London 1945)
Studied RAM (with Lennox Berkeley and Harry Isaacs); won Stewart Macpherson and Harry Farjeon prizes. Winner Gaudeamus Competition, Holland, 1972, jt winner BBC 'Monarch 1000' competition 1973.

Works include: *Scherzos* (4 pfs), *Hallelujahs* (d chor & org), *Praeludiana* (org), *Five Blake Songs*, *Bagatelle* (pf and tape), *Green and Pleasant* (ch orch), *Veni Sancte Spiritus* (d chor and org).

COLE, Bruce (b 1947)
Played with rock group, then studied RAM (with Harrison Birtwistle). Worked in West End stage and toured with mime troupe. Has formed a music theatre group with clarinettist Ian Mitchell. Now teaching in a Lutoslawski. On music staff of Lancaster U since 1973. Known as composer, pianist, painter and poet (often providing the texts for his own

Works include: *Harlequinade and Pantomimes* (music theatre), *Fenestrae Sanctae* (ch orch), *The House on Secker Street*, *Autumn Cicada* for children, *Eclogue for Cerberus*.

COWIE, Edward (b Birmingham 1943)
Studied TCM, Trent Park Training College and Southampton U. Teachers include Peter Racine Fricker, Alexander Goehr and Witold Lutoslawski. On music staff of Lancaster U since 1973. Known as composer pianist, painter, and poet (often providing the texts for his own compositions).

Works include: clar conc, *The Moon, Sea and Stars* (ten, horn and insts), *Four Orchestral Songs*, *Leighton Moss—December Notebook* (s, t, d chor and orch), ballet *Cyto-Genesis*, *Endymion Nocturnes* (h v and str qtet), *A Charm of Finches* (s & three fls), *Shinkokinshu* (s, fl, clar, pf), *Magdalena Songs* (v & pf).

DALBY, Martin (b Aberdeen 1942)
Played vla in National Youth Orch 1957–60. Schol RCM 1960–3 (studied with Herbert Howells and Frederick Riddle). Laird Scholar to Italy 1963–5 (played vla with Italian Ch Orch). BBC music producer London 1965–71. Cramb Fellow in composition Glasgow U 1971–2. Head of Music, BBC Scotland since 1972.

Works include: sym, conc *Martin Pescatore* for strs, vla conc, *The Tower of Victory* (orch), *Cancionero para una Mariposa*, *Whisper Music*, *Orpheus* (16 voices and insts), *Cantigas del Cancionero El Remanso del Pitido*, *Commedia* (clar, vln, pf, vlc), *Cantica* (s, clar, vla, pf).

DANKWORTH, John (b 1927)

Studied RAM, married to singer Cleo Laine. Conducts own jazz orch (formed 1953).

Works include (apart from many for jazz ens): *Tom Sawyer's Saturday* (spkr & orch), *Improvisations* (jazz band & sym orch written with Mátyás Seiber), *Escapade* (jazz band & orch), pf conc. Film scores include *Saturday Night and Sunday Morning, Darling, Morgan: A Suitable Case for Treatment, Accident*.

DICKINSON, Peter (b Lytham St Annes 1934)

Organ schol at Queen's College Cambridge; also studied Juilliard Sch of Mus NY. Broadcasts as organist and pianist and frequently accompanies his sister Meriel Dickinson.

Works include: *Monologue* (strs), *Transformations 'Homage to Satie'* (orch), org conc, conc for strs, perc & electronic org, ballet *Vitalitas*, *The Judas Tree* (musical drama for church prod), vln son, *Fanfares & Elegies* (3 tmpts, 3 trombs & org), *Translations* (recorder, vla da gamba & hpschd); song cycles incl *Extravaganzas, Winter Afternoons*; many choral works incl *The Dry Heart* (SATB), *Outcry* (SATB & orch); organ wks, pf works, music for children.

DODGSON, Stephen (b London 1924)

RN 1943–6, RCM 1947–9, in Italy 1950 (Octavia travelling schol). Since 1965 on staff at RCM (theory & composition). Composer of many substantial scores for BBC productions 1962–73. Frequent broadcaster on musical topics and occasional journalist.

Works include: *Te Deum, Wind Symphony*, concertino for pf & perc, *Four Poems of John Clare*, son for brass, suite for brass septet, 2 gtr concs, duo concertante, works for solo gtr.

DORWARD, David Campbell (b 1933)

Studied St Andrews U, RAM. At present music producer BBC.

Works include: symphony, wind conc, concs for vln, vla and vlc, 4 str qtets, one-act opera *Tonight Mrs Morrison*.

DRUCE, Duncan (b Nantwich, Cheshire 1939)

Studied RCM (with Antonio Brosa), King's Coll Cambridge. Lecturer at Leeds U, part-time lecturer UEA Norwich, Goldsmith's Coll London, Lancaster U, also worked as BBC music producer. During the last six years mainly professional violinist and violist. Performing member of the Fires of London and of Apollo Contemporary Music (director David Hellewell). Specialises in performance of baroque as well as modern music.

Works include: *Fantasy and Divisions on a theme of J H Schelzer* (orch), *Images from Nature* (str qtet), *The Tower of Needles* (s, chor), *Who's Doing It?* (rec, str orch, perc), vln son, pf trio, *Chiashata* (2 vlas), *Jugalbundi* (clar & vla), *A Red King's Crown* (pf), sonata (solo vla).

FERNEYHOUGH, Brian (b Coventry, Warwickshire 1943)
Studied Birmingham Sch of Music 1961–3, RAM 1966–7 (with Lennox Berkeley, Maurice Miles). Director and conductor of Royal Academy New Music Club 1967. Several months composition study with Ton de Leeuw at Amsterdam Conservatory 1968, studied composition master class of Klaus Huber at Music Academy Basle 1969–71. Fred Miller Composition Prize, Birmingham 1963, Mendelssohn Schol 1968, stipend from City of Basle 1969–71, stipend from Heinrich Strobel Foundation, Stüdwestfunk, Germany 1973–4. Since summer 1973 composition teacher Musikhochschule in Freiburg im Breisgau, Germany.

Works include: *Four Miniatures* (fl & pf), sonata for two pfs, *Epigrammes* (pf), *Colorature* (ob & pf), *Three Pieces for pf*, sonata for str qtet, *Prometheus* (6 wind insts), *Epicycle* (20 solo strs), *Missa Brevis* (12 vs a cappella), *Firecycle Beta* (2 str groups, perc & ch ens), *Sieben Sterne* (org), *Cassandra's Dream Song* (solo fl), *Time and Motion Study I* (solo clar), *Transit* (vs & ch orch), *Time and Motion Study II* (vlc & live electronics), *Time and Motion Study III* (16 vs & live electronics).

FINISSY, Michael (b London 1946)
Studied RCM (with Bernard Stevens & Humphrey Searle). Has been associated with London School of Contemporary Dance, and with dance and theatre music.

Works include: Music for Rene de Obaldia's *Jenousia*, and Aeschylus's *Agamemnon*, *Transformation of the Vampire* (sop and 9 players), *Autumnal*, *Irma Cortez*, *Le Dormeur du Val* (v, 3 keyboards and str qtet), *As When Upon A Tranced Summer Night* (3 vlc, perc & pf), *From the Revelations of St John the Divine* (sop & str), *Horrorzone* (sop & ch orch).

FORBES, Sebastian (b 1941)
Studied RAM 1958–60, King's Coll Cambridge 1960–4 (sang bass in Chapel Choir 1961–4). BBC producer, London, 1964–7, Organist Trinity Coll Cambridge 1968, Lecturer Bangor U 1968–72, Lecturer Surrey U 1972–.

Works include: *Essay* (clar & orch; 1970 Proms), symphony in 2 movements (Edinburgh Fest 1972), one-act opera *Tom Cree*, pf trio, org son, str qtet No 1, *Death's Dominion* (ten & ens), educational pieces, etc.

GERSH, Stephen (b London 1948)
Studied with Edwin Roxburgh and Martin Dalby, also on summer courses with Berio and Stockhausen. Read Classics at Cambridge 1966–8 (double first). Original research into the 6th-century Neo-Platonist philosophers, especially the Divine Hennads of Damascius. Plays pf, org, vln.

Works include: Variations and Fugue on a Theme from Gretry's '*Richard Coeur-de-Lion*' (org), over 300 passacaglias for keyboard insts, unfinished opera on *The Epic of Gilgamesh*, *Context I–XII* (12 pieces for vars solo insts), *Plein Jeu* (hp, celesta, vibraphone & bells), *Hoorah* (2 orchs and electronically amplified soloists), *Control* (3 orchs).

GILBERT, Anthony (b London 1934)
Studied Morley Coll 1959–63 and privately with Mátyás Seiber and Alexander Goehr. Currently composition tutor, RMCM.

Works include: *Sinfonia*, sym, *The Scene Machine* (a one-act entertainment), 2 pf sons, *The Incredible Flute Music*, *Spell Respell*, *Treatment of Silence* (vln & tape), *Brighton Piece* (perc & ens), *Nine or Ten Osannas*, *O'Grady Music* (cl, vlc, toy insts), st qtet, *Missa Brevis*, *Love Poems* (sop & ens).

HALL, John (b 1943)
Studied RAM (with Alan Bush), won R Harvey Löhr composition schol, Corder Memorial Prize, Charles Lucas Medal and Eric Coates Prize. In 1969 awarded Royal Philharmonic Prize for organ conc. Now teaches RAM.

Works include: *Symphonic Study* (orch), *Mexico* overture, *Little Suite*, org conc, 3 divertimentos, 2 str qtets, pf trio, str trio, horn trio, qtet (fl & str), ob son, suite for org, *Three Interludes and Toccata* (org), *Those Dancing Days are Gone* (v, str qtet, pf), pf works.

HARPER, Edward (b Taunton 1941)
Studied Christ Church Oxford and RCM (with Gordon Jacob). Lecturer in music Edinburgh U 1964–.

Works include: vln conc, pf conc, *Passacaglia* (orch), *Bartók Games* (orch), *Serenade* (ob & str), str qtet, 2 quintets for vars ens, *Lochinvar* (male v & 2 pfs).

HEDGES, Anthony (b Bicester, Oxon 1931)
Studied music at Oxford for five years, National Service in Royal
188

Signals Band as solo pianist and arranger. Professor RSAM for 5 years. Senior Lecturer Hull U 1962-. Chairman Composer's Guild of Great Britain 1971-2, joint Chairman 1972-3.

Works include: *Comedy Overture*, overture *War and Peace*, *Gloria* (unac ch), *Ayrshire Serenade*, *Epithalamium* (ch & orch), violin rhapsody, *Four Diversions* (str orch), *To Music* (ch, str orch), Psalm 104 (ch & brass band), symphony, *Five Preludes* (pf), *Four Pieces* (pf), vln & hpschd son, str qtet, piano son.

HEWITT-JONES, Tony (b 1926)

Read music at Oxford (pupil of Bernard Rose), ARCO (Limpus & Read prizes 1957). Studied July–Dec 1969 with Nadia Boulanger. Director of Mus, Dean Close Junior Sch, Cheltenham 1953-7, Assistant County Music Adviser Glos 1958-. Plays pf, org, hpschd, tymps.

Works include: *Sinfonietta* (strs), ob conc, clar con, *Seven Sea Poems* (ch & orch), Te Deum, *Rembrandt*, *The Divine Image*, *The Battle of Tewksebury*, *Edmund King & Martyr*, organ son, trio (clar, vla & pf), wind quintet.

HOBBS, Christopher, *see* CARDEW and his 'school'

HOLD, Trevor (b Northampton 1939)

Studied Nottingham U. Lecturer at Aberystwyth U, Liverpool U. Now music tutor on the staff of the extra-mural dept Leicester U. Known as a poet and has set some of his own texts.

Works include: *Rondo* (str orch), overture *My Uncle Silas*, *Calendar* (orch), *Gunpowder Plot Music* (orch), *The Unreturning Spring* (s, bar & sm orch), *For John Clare* (t & inst ens), *Early One Morning* (h v & gtr), *Landscapes* (bar & pf), *The Weathercock* (vla & pf), str qtct, *Cinquefoils* (pf qtet), *Measure for Measure* (women's voices, pf duet and perc) *Requiescat* (spkr, ch, brass sextet), *Kemp's Nine Daies Wonder* (pf solo), *The Falcon* (dramatic work for church perf), *After London* (s, bar, chor, pf & org), *Lark Rise* (ten, children's ch, ens & tape), *The Pied Piper* (an entertainment for children to perform).

HOPKINS, Bill (b 1943)

Musical education started after contact with Nono at Dartington 1960. Read music at Oxford (Rubbra, Wellesz), French Govt Schol with Messiaen and private study with Barraqué 1964-5, freelance music critic 1965-7. Now translator with occasional critical & editorial work. 2nd prize Lancaster U Vln Competition 1974.

Works include: *Two pomes* (s, tmpt, b clar, hp, vla), *Sensation* (s, tmpt, t sax, hp, vla), *Etudes en série*, 3 bks (pf), *Pendant* (vln).

G

HOWARTH, Elgar (b 1935)
Studied Manchester U & RMCM 1953–6. Professional trumpeter 1958–70. Conductor since 1970, with London Sinfonietta, and more recently Grimethorpe Colliery Band. Guest appearances with RPO, LSO, BBCSO.

Works include: variations for brass qtet, trombone conc, *Party Piece for Sir Arthur*, *Pagliaccio*, songs.

JOHNSON, Robert Sherlaw (b Sunderland 1932)
Studied Durham U, RAM and Paris. Radcliffe Music Award 1969 (for 2nd str qtet). Current work in electronic music. Known as a pianist as well as composer and expert on Messiaen on whom he has written a book (1975).

Works include: *Praises of Heaven and Earth* (s, pf & electronic tape), *Carmen Venalia* (s & ch orch), *Green Whispers of Gold* (s, pf & electronic tape), *Triptych* (fl, clar, vla, vlc, perc, pf) *Festival Mass of the Resurrection* (chor and orch), quintet (clar, vln, vla, vlc, pf), 2 pf sons, 2 str qtets, *Night Songs* (s, pf), *Where the Wild Things Are* (s & tape), *Songs of Love & Springtime* (s & pf), *Seven Short Pf Pieces*, *Asterogenesis* (pf).

JOSEPHS, Wilfred (b Newcastle upon Tyne, 1927)
Early pf lessons cut short by wartime evacuation. Studied dentistry at Newcastle U, and at same time music part-time with Arthur Milner. In 1954 awarded schol to GSM where he studied with Alfred Nieman. In 1958 went to Paris on a Leverhulme Schol, where he studied with Max Deutsch. In 1963 awarded first prize in First International Composition Competition of La Scala and City of Milan for his *Requiem*, since when has abandoned dentistry and composes full-time.

Works include: comedy-ovt *The Ants*, *Elegy* (strs), *Concerto a Dodici* (wind ens), *Conc da Camera* (vln, hpschd, strs), *Meditatio de Beornmundo* (vla & sm orch), concs for pf (2), vln, double-vln, vlc & ob, 6 syms (4 & 6 with vs), *Aeolian Dances* (orch), *Monkchester Dances* (orch), *Canzonas on a Theme of Rameau* (str orch), *Vars on a Theme of Beethoven* (orch), *Polemic* (str orch), *Saratoga* concerto, ovt *The Four Horsemen of the Apocalypse*, *Requiem*, *Protégez-moi* (children's vs & sch orch), *Mortales* (soli, adult & children's ch & orch), *Nightmusic* (v & orch), *Death of a Young Man* (bar & pf or ch orch), *A Child of the Universe* (multi-media), *King of the Coast* (musical for children), *The Nottingham Captain* (music theatre), *The Appointment* (TV opera), str quintet, *Chacony* (vln & pf), 3 str qtets, 2 vln sons, pf quintet, horn trio, son for brass quintet, solo vlc son, str trio.

KELLY, Bryan (b 1934)
Studied RCM. *Stabat Mater* given at Three Ch Fest; *Spider Monkey
Uncle King* (opera for children) at Cookham Fest.

Works include: *Sinfonia Concertante* (orch), *Stabat Mater, Conc da
Camera* (ob & strs), *Calypso Suite* (strs), *Cuban Suite, When Christ was Born*,
pf son, *Spider Monkey Uncle King*.

KNUSSEN, Oliver (b Glasgow 1952)
Studied Central Tutorial Sch for Young Musicians 1964–7, private
composition lessons with John Lambert, and with Gunther Schuller at
Tanglewood, USA 1970, '71, '73. Countess of Munster Awards 1965,
'66, '68; Peter Stuyvesant Fund 1966–8; Watney-Sargent Award
1969–70; Caird Travelling Schol 1971; Margaret Grant Memorial
Composition Prize, Tanglewood 1971. Début 1968 conducting LSO
in 1st sym, RFH, later at Carnegie Hall 1968. Composer in Residence
Florida International Fest 1969.

Works include: 3 syms (2nd for sop & orch, words Trakl & Plath),
con for orch, *Choral* (wind orch), *Masks* (solo fl), *Pooh Songs* (s & ens),
Rosary Songs (s & ens), *Océan de Terre, Puzzle Music, Ophelia Songs, Pan-
tomine* for nonet, *Fire Capriccio* (fl, str trio), *Turba* (db), *Study for Metamorphosis* (bs).

LAMBERT, John (b 1926)
Studied RAM and RCM and with Nadia Boulanger in Paris. From
1958 to 1962 resident composer at the Old Vic. Joined staff of RCM in
1963 where he runs an improvisation class. On council and executive
committee of the Society for the Promotion of New Music and also
Director of Music at St Vedast Church, Foster Lane, London.

Works include: *Formations and Transformations* (orch), *From the Nebula*
(vlc & strs), '. . . but then face to face' (v, 10 gtrs, pf, org, perc), *Five Songs
of Po-Chu-i* (bar & pf), *For A While* (s, fl (alt fl), clar, vla, db, pf, perc),
organ mass, *Orpheus cycle I* (ob & hpschd), '*Tread Softly* . . .' (4 gtrs),
Veni Creator Spiritus (2 h v & org).

LEFANU, Nicola (b 1947)
Educated Oxford U 1965–8, RCM 1968–9, summer sch studies with
Petrassi (Siena), Peter Maxwell Davies (Dartington). Cobbett Prize
1968, BBC Composers Competition 1972. Gulbenkian Dance Award,
Mendelssohn Schol, Harkness Fellowship 1973.

Works include: *The Hidden Landscape* (Prom 1973), *Antiworld* (music
theatre, Cockpit Theatre 1972), *The Last Laugh* (ballet, Young Vic
1973), variations for ob qtet, *But Stars Remaining* (s).

191

LIPKIN, Malcolm (b Liverpool 1932)
Studied piano privately with Gordon Green, then at RCM 1949–53.
Composition studies with Mátyás Seiber 1954–7.

Works include: Concs (pf, fl, 2 for vln), *Sinfonia di Roma*, *Psalm 96*
(ch & sm orch), *Mosaics* (ch orch), *Metamorphosis* (hpschd), string trio,
Four Departures (v & vln), vln son, 4 pf sons.

LORD, David (b Oxford 1944)
Studied RAM (with Richard Rodney Bennett). Particularly interested
in writing music for children to perform.

Works include: *How the Stars were Made*, *The Sea Journey*, *The World
Makers* (all for children); song cycle *The Wife of Winter*, concertino for
hpschd & strs, septet, *The History of the Flood*, ballet and film music,
TV & radio music. Currently writing orch piece for LSO, clar conc,
wind quintet.

MORGAN, David (b 1933)
Owing to family opposition did not enter RAM until 1961. Studied
composition with Alan Bush until 1965, winning 10 prizes for composi-
tion and becoming the first person to have a concert given at the
Academy consisting entirely of his own music while still a student.
Awarded British Council schol 1965 to study at Academy of Music in
Prague, staying 2 years and composing violin conc there, premièred
1967 at Dvořák Hall (first public perf in UK Jan 1974, Gruenberg &
RPO, at RFH). *Sinfonia da Requiem* played at RPO British Music public
playthrough April 1974. Several lighter works broadcast in UK.

Works include: violin conc, str qtet, gtr son, ob qtet, *Sinfonia da
Requiem*, *Partita* for orch, conc for clar & strs.

NEWSON, George (b London 1932)
Self-taught from age 14 to 23 when he won a schol to RAM. Before
that had worked in modern jazz bands and attended evening classes at
Blackheath Conservatoire of Music 1947–9 and Morley Coll 1950–3
where he was encouraged by Peter Racine Fricker and Iain Hamilton.
Studied with Nono and Maderna (1960) and Berio (1961–2). In 1967
Churchill Fellow in USA, researching into electronic music. At present
Cramb Research Fellow in Composition, Glasgow U.

Works include: *Three Interiors* (s, wind quintet, db), wind quintet,
variations for vlc, *The Night Walk* (chor & orch), *21 Days*, *Arena*
(Proms 1971), *Praise to the Air*, *Alan's Piece Again* (clar & 4-channel
tape), *Oute* (4-channel tape), *Cigactrice* (vln conc), *Third Time* (orch).

OGDON, John (b Mansfield 1937)
Studied RMCM 1953–6 (with Richard Hall & George Lloyd).
Travelling schol 1956–9. First British pianist to win Tchaikovsky Prize

(1962). Primarily known as a pianist through many appearances and recordings.

Works include: pf conc, *Theme & Variations* (pf), *Dance Suite* (pf), *5 Preludes* (pf), *Sonatina* (pf), str qtet, solo vln son, solo vlc son.

OLDHAM, Arthur (b 1926)

Studied RCM. Director of Music St Mary's Cathedral Edinburgh 1957–. Director of Scottish Festival Chorus 1965–. Chorus master of Scottish opera 1966–.

Works include: *Missa in Honorem Seti Thom. Mori, Laudes Creaturarum, Hymns for the Amusement of Children, Divertimento* (strs), *Chinese Lyrics*, songs, ch works, music for radio, TV and films.

ORTON, Richard (b Derby 1940)

Studied Birmingham School of Music and St John's College Cambridge. Postgraduate research into musical notation in the twentieth century 1965–7. Lecturer in Music at University of York 1967–. In 1968 began the York U Electronic Music Studio of which he remains Director. Live electronic performances with Hugh Davies 1967–70. Performed with group The Gentle Fire 1968–71.

Works include: *In Piam Memoriam* (solo voices SATB), *Canons and Prelude* (chamber ens & perc), *Heavensgate* (m-s, alto fl, 4 male vs), *Divisions I* (sm orch), *Divisions II* (orch), *Divisions III* (28 insts), wind quintet, *Mug Grunt* (music-theatre), *Cycle* (for 2 or 4 players), *Four Fragments of Gerard Manley Hopkins* (m-s & pf), *Ennead* (vlc & pf), works for electronics, works for pf.

PARSONS, Michael, *see* GARDEW and his 'school'

PATTERSON, Paul (b 1947)

Studied RAM 1964–8 and privately with Richard Rodney Bennett. Composer in residence to English Sinfonia 1968–9; Manson Fellow RAM 1971–. Many commissions from leading ensembles, orchs & performers. Associated with Manson Ensemble (live electronics), and London Chorale (cond Roy Wales).

Works include: *Requiem, Time Piece, Comedy for Five Winds, Fusions* (tape & orch), *Organ Trilogy, Chromascope*, conc for tmpt & horn, *Kyrie, Gloria, Jubilate.*

PERT, Morris (b Arbroath, Scotland 1947)

Studied Edinburgh U and RAM (with James Blades & Alan Bush). Leader of jazz/rock group Suntreader (originally Come to the Edge). Has worked in the modern percussion field particularly with Stomu Yamash'ta. Has worked as session musician in the major London recording studios.

Works include: *6 Dance Suites* for young instrumentalists, *3 pieces for Orch*, *Sun Dragon* (orch), *Xumbu-Ata* (orch), *Eilean Donnan* (str orch), *Messier 87* (v & ch ens), *Omega Centauri* (ch ens), son for basset-horn & pf, *Akhenaten* (3 clars), *Delphic Fragment* (fl, horn, vln, vlc & pf), *Suilven Moon* (pf) and *Andromeda Link* (vln & tape). Currently working on 1st sym for orch & tape.

PURSER, John W (b Ireland 1942)
Studied RSAM and with Michael Tippett and Hans Gál. Received diplomas in singing and vlc. Radio Eirean Carolan Prize 1963. Irish Government prize 1966 for work to commemorate Easter 1916. Caird schol (composition) 1963; RPS award 1962; Scottish Arts Council Award 1969; Glasgow Educational Trust Grant 1974.

Works include: *Opus Seven* (orch), *Intrada* (orch), *Epitaph* (orch), *Music for Small Orch*, ovt *Cydefair*, *Comedy Ovt*, march *Highlands Fabricators*, concs for vla & vlc, double conc horn & bs, opera *The Undertaker* (Edinburgh Fest 1969, Scottish Television 1970), opera *The Bell* (BBC 1974), *Prometheus* (t, chor, insts), *On An Island* (t, mv chor, pf, perc), *Magnificat and Nunc Dimittis*, str qtet, fl son, *Dances of Ilion* (clar & pf), *Five Landscapes* (words T S Eliot), *Six Sea Songs* (words John W R Purser), pf music, incidental music.

RANDS, Bernard (b Sheffield 1935)
Studied at U of Wales and lived in Italy where he studied composition with Dallapiccola, and later in conducting and composition seminars of Boulez and Maderna. Lectured at U of Wales and later studied composition with Berio. Awarded Harkness Fellowship to spend 2 years as visiting fellow Princeton U and at U of Illinois as composer in residence. Granada Fellow in Creative Arts York U 1969–70. Fellow in Creative Arts at Brasenose College Oxford and now member of music faculty at York U. Has worked in electronic music studios at Albany (New York), Berlin, Milan, Urbana and York.

Works include: *Wildtrack 1, 2 and 3* (orch, 3 also with s, m-s, nar, 16 mixed voices), *Mésalliance* (pf & orch), *Ology* (jazz orch), *Alum* (hp & orch), *Per Esempio* (youth orch), *Agenda* (youth orch), *Metalepsis* (m-s & orch), *Ballad 1* (m-s and insts), *Actions for Six* (fl, hp, 2 prc, vla, vlc), *Tableau* (insts), *Cuaderna* (str qtet), *Etendre* (solo db, insts), *Sound Pattern 1–5*, *Serena* (music-theatre), music for pf, db, hp, tromb.

RIDOUT, Alan (b 1934)
Studied RCM and privately with Michael Tippett, Peter Racine Fricker and Henk Badings. Professor of Composition at RCM since 1960, and Reader of Composition at Canterbury Cathedral Choir School 1964–.

Works include: 4 syms, *St Matthew Passion* (soli, chor & orch), *Funeral Games* (dance-mime), fl conc, one-act operas *The Gift, The Pardoner's Tale, The Creation* (soli, chor & orch), *Ferdinand* (nar & vln), much liturgical music, music for boy's choir and organ music.

ROBERTS, Jeremy Dale (b 1934)
Studied RAM (with William Alwyn and Priaulx Rainier). Lectures and teaches RCM, Morley College, Goldsmith College.

Works include: Suite for fl & strs, *Florilegium* (8 singers & ens), *Capriccio* (vln & pf), *Tombeau* (pf), *Sinfonia da Caccia* (orch), *Reconciliation* (spkr & musicians) *Eight Canzonets, Deathwatch* (conc vlc & 15 strs).

ROUTH, Francis (b Kidderminster 1927)
Studied piano and organ throughout school years. Studied Cambridge (with Boris Ord), RAM (with William Alwyn, Wesley Roberts and Arnold Richardson), later privately with Mátyás Seiber. Has been active also as writer (several books) and promoter of contemporary music. In 1963 founded the Redcliffe Concerts of British Music. Has lectured and occasionally appeared as pianist or conductor. Organist at St Philip's Church, Earls Court Road, 1961–73.

Works include: concs for vln, vlc, *Dialogue* for vln & orch, double conc for vln, vlc & orch, concert aria *Spring Night* (words by Sidney Keyes) for m-s & orch, sym, duo for vln & pf, *Dance Suite* (str qtet), *Circles* (s, clar, vla, pf), son solo vlc, pf qtet, 2 org fantasias, org sonatina, *Sacred Tetralogy* (org), works for v and pf: *A Woman Young and Old, Four Shakespeare Songs, Songs of Farewell, Songs of Lawrence Durrell, The Death of Iphigenia, Three Short Songs.*

ROXBURGH, Edwin (b Liverpool 1937)
Studied Matthay School of Music Liverpool, RCM and St John's College Cambridge, and a year in France and Italy. Professor at RCM where Director of Contemporary Music Dept 1967–. Principal of Sadler's Wells Opera 1964–7. Director 20th-Century Ensemble of London.

Works include: *Three Symphonic Metamorphoses after Ovid* (orch), ballet *The Tower, Night Music* (ch orch, s & solo perc), *Bosendorfer* (pf), *How Pleasant to Know Mr Lear* (nar & orch), *Partitoi* (vlc), *Monologue for Alan Hacker* (clar & tape), music for film *World Without End.*

SAXTON, Robert (b London 1953)
Studied with Elisabeth Lutyens 1970–. Read music at St Catharine's College, Cambridge. With 5 others formed Cambridge New Music Ensemble to perform twentieth-century music in Cambridge and outside.

Works include: *Canons & Canzonas* (s, alto fl, ob, 3 vlas), *Introductions,*

Vocal Fragments and Epilogues (s, fl & clar), *Ritornelli & Intermezzi* (pf), *La Promenade d'Automne* (s, fl, clar, perc, pf, vln, vla, vlc), *Magnificat and Nunc Dimittis, Krystallen* (fl & pf).

SHAW, Francis (b Maidenhead 1942)
Studied LCM, London U (Institute of Education); Accademia Chigi, Siena; Southampton U. Teachers for composition include Lennox Berkeley, Petrassi, Alexander Goehr.
   Works include: *Annunciation Cantata, Divertimento* (strs), children's opera *The Selfish Giant, Concert Ovt*, str trio, quintet (fl, clar, tmpt, vln, vlc), *Prologue & Scherzo* (brass quintet), song cycles: *One Goes Lightly, This Praising and Lamentation* (both b & pf), pf and org works, ballet for Ballet Rambert.

SHRAPNEL, Hugh, *see* CARDEW and his 'school'

SKEMPTON, Howard, *see* CARDEW and his 'school'

SOUSTER, Tim [Andrew James] (b 1942)
Studied with Bernard Rose and David Lumsden at Oxford 1961-5, Stockhausen and Berio at Darmstadt 1963, and Richard Rodney Bennett 1965. BBC music producer 1965-7; composer in residence King's College Cambridge 1969-71. Co-founder with Roger Smalley (qv) of performing group Intermodulation (1969) with which he plays as violist.
   Works include: *Metropolitan Games* (pf duet), *Tsuwanonodomo* (s, 3 chs, 3 orchs, pf, prepared pf & hp), *Titus Groan Music* (wind quintet & tape), *Chinese Whispers* (perc & 3 electronic synthesisers), *Triple Music II* (3 orchs), *Music for Eliot's Waste Land* (pf, electronic org, sax, 3 synthesisers), *Spectra* (vla & taped sounds of humpbacked whales), *Song of an Average City* (orch & tape).

STANDFORD, Patric (b Barnsley 1939)
Studied GSM (with Edmund Rubbra and Raymond Jones), Mendelssohn Schol 1964, studied in Italy with Malipiero and briefly in Poland with Lutoslawski. RPS prize 1963; Carl Meyer Award 1964, Aspen Fund Award 1966, Committee of Solidarity Award Skopje 1973, Premio Oscar Esola, Alicante 1974, Clements Memorial Prize 1974
   Works include: *Christus-Requiem*, 2 syms (No 2 *Il Paradiso*), vlc con, jazz suite *Autumn Grass, Saracinesco* (poem for orch), *Notte* (ch orch), *Antitheses* in memoriam Sir John Barbirolli, 3 str qtets, pf trio, pf son.

STEEL, Christopher (b 1939)
Studied RCM and Staatliche Hochschule für Musik Munich 1957-62. At present teaches music at Bradfield College.
   Works include: *The Rescue* (comic opera for The Scholars), 4 syms,

conc for ch & full orch, conc for str qtet & orch, ovt *Island*, organ conc,
Mass (soli, ch, orch—Three Choirs Fest 1968), *Jerusalem* (soli, ch,
orch), *Paradise Lost* (soli, ch, orch—Three Choirs Fest 1974), *Piping
Down the Valleys Wild* (Blake song cycle for bar & pf). Currently working
on opera.

STOKER, Richard (b Castleford, Yorks 1938)
Studied Huddersfield Music School, RAM (with Lennox Berkeley)
and in Paris with Nadia Boulanger. Professor of Composition at RAM
1962–.
    Works include: comic opera *Johnson Preserv'd*, cantata *Ecce Homo*,
Variations Passacaglia & Fugue (strs), *Little Symphony*, *Petite Suite* (orch),
overtures *Antic Hay* and *Feast of Fools*, *Permutations* (orch).

WARREN, Raymond [Henry Charles] (b Weston-super-Mare 1928)
Studied Cambridge U. Director of Music Woolverstone Hall School
1952–6, Lecturer Queen's U Belfast 1955–6, Professor of Music Queen's
U Belfast 1966–72, resident composer Ulster Orchestra 1967–71,
Professor of Music Bristol U 1972–.
    Works include: 2 syms, vln conc, 4 operas, *Passion Oratorio*, 2 str qtets,
3 song cycles, ch mus, cantatas, etc.

WEIR, Judith (b 1954)
Studied with Margaret Semple, John Tavener; electronic music at
MIT 1973: reading music at King's College Cambridge.
    Works include: *Where the Shining Trumpets Blow*, *Campanile* (winner
Scottish Composers Award 1974), *Ohime* (Park Lane Group QEH 1974).

WHELEN, Christopher (b London 1927)
Studied at Birmingham Midland Institute. Assistant cond (with
Rudolph Schwarz) Bournemouth Symphony Orch 1948–52, Musical
Director Old Vic 1952–5, assistant cond City of Birmingham SO
1955–7. Sprague Coolidge medal 1958. Orchestrated 5 musicals
including John Osborne's *Paul Slickey*.
    Works include: radio operas *The Cancelling Dark*, *Some Place of Dark-
ness* (BBC TV 1967), *Incident at Owl Creek*, *The Findings*, ballet *Cul de
Sac*, over 200 scores for films, TV, radio plays and theatre (including
30 of Shakespeare's plays). Currently working on full-scale stage opera
and new musico-dramatic work for BBC Radio.

WHETTAM, Graham Dudley (b 1927)
Works include: 4 syms (5th in preparation), clar conc, vlc, conc,
Masque of the Red Death ('Two scenes for dancing after Edgar Allan
Poe'), *Sinfonia Concertante*, *Sinfonietta Stravagante*, var for ob, bs & strs,
Suite for Youth (orch), str qtet, 2 solo vln sons, 2 ob qtets, sextet for wind

& pf, *Prelude Scherzo & Elegy* (pf), *Prelude & Scherzo Impetuoso* (pf), *Night Music* (pf), *Partita & Triptych* (org).

WHITE, John (b Berlin 1936)
Studied RCM (with Bernard Stevens), later privately with Elizabeth Lutyens. Began composing in 1956 under the impact of Messiaen's *Turangalîla* symphony. Musical Director of Western Theatre Ballet in late Fifties, Reader of Composition at RCM (his pupils include Roger Smalley and Brian Dennis) until late Sixties. Freelance tuba player and conductor of The Canterbury Tales in West End late Sixties, early Seventies. Has been leader or member of several performing groups, notably the Composers' Ensemble (1964) and the Promenade Theatre Orchestra ('PTO'), formed in 1969 with Hugh Shrapnel, Alec Hill and Christopher Hobbs and devoted to permutational, number games or 'machine' music and instruments as reed organs, toy pianos, chimes, etc.

Works include: 90 pf sons, *Night Piece* (bar & tromb), *Morgenstern Lieder* (bar & 2 tubas), *Symphony* (org & 6 tubas), *Carillons* (tromb & pf), *Cello & Tuba Machine, PT Machine, Gothic Chord Machine* (4 reed orgs), *Drinking/Hooting/Sunday Afternoon/Humming and Aahing/Chimes Machine, A Viennese Give Away.*

WILSON, Thomas (b Colorado, USA, 1927)
Studied Glasgow U. Staff tutor in music at Glasgow U 1967–. Member of Scottish Arts Council 1968–.

Works include: concerto for orch, 2 syms, *Touchstone*—portrait for orch, vars for orch, opera *The Charcoal Burner, Carmina Sacra* (h v & strs), *Sinfonietta* (brass), *Missa Pro Mundo Conturbato, Sequentiae Passionis, Te Deum, Concerto da Camera, Ritornelli per Archi, Pas de Quoi* (strs), *Sinfonia* (7 insts), vlc con. Currently working on opera.

WOOLFENDEN, Guy (b 1937)
Studied Christ's College Cambridge and GSM. Music Director Royal Shakespeare Company 1962–. Principal cond Liverpool Mozart Orchestra, Warwickshire SO, Morley College SO. Recently conducted 1st perf Richard Rodney Bennett's Viola Concerto with RPO.

Works include: 50 scores for Royal Shakespeare Co, *Divertimento* for ch orch, *What A Way to Run a Revolution* (musical), films, TV plays, etc.

YOUNG, Douglas (b 1947)
Studied composition with Anthony Milner.

Works include: *Sinfonietta, Departure* (orch), *Portrait* (orch), *Terrain* (orch), chamber concerto (pf & ens), ballet *Pasiphae, Realities* (2 vs & 6 insts), sonata for str trio, song cycle *Not Waving But Drowning, Essay* (str qtet).

Select Bibliography

The first section, arranged alphabetically, lists general guides on the techniques of new music, bibliographical tools and background articles by composers who are the subject of the text. The second section, arranged alphabetically by composer, lists critiques and descriptions of the composers and their works, the arrangement under each composer head being chronological. All the entries are numbered, and referenced correspondingly in the main text. All books are published in London unless otherwise stated.

I GENERALIA

1 BENNETT, R R: 'Technique of the Jazz Singer' *Music & Musicians* Feb 1972 pp 30–5
2 BRINDLE, R S: *The New Music*. Oxford University Press, 1974
3 BRITISH INSTITUTE OF RECORDED SOUND: *Music by British Composers of the Twentieth Century——handlist of tape recordings in the Institute's collection*. BIRS, 1967
    ('Preliminary draft')
4 CARDEW, C: *Scratch Music*. Latimer New Dimensions, 1972
5 ——: *Stockhausen Serves Imperialism*. Latimer, 1974
    ('. . . a swingeing attack on the masters of experimental music, Cage and Stockhausen. Cardew is also critical of his own earlier work in the musical avant-garde and sets out the rationale behind his new work aimed at serving the proletarian socialist revolution.'—from Cardew's own abstract published in *RILM Abstracts*)
6 COMPOSERS' GUILD: [*Catalogues of Music by Living British Composers*]:
    (a) *Chamber Music*. British Music Information Centre, 1970
    (b) *Orchestral Music*. British Music Information Centre, 1970
    (The latter is a revision of *British Orchestral Music—volume one of the Catalogue of Works by Members of the Composers' Guild of Great Britain*, 1958)
7 CURRAN, C: *Music and the BBC*. BBC, 1970
    (Originally published in *Listener* 11 June 1970)
8 DAVIES, P M: 'Composing for School Use' *Making Music* Summer 1961 pp 7–8
9 ——: 'Problems of a British Composer Today' *Listener* 8 Oct 1959 pp 563–4
10 ——: 'The Young British Composer' *Score* March 1956 pp 84–5
11 EWEN, D: *Composers of Tomorrow's Music*. NY, Dodd Mead, 1971
    (Account of avant-garde composers, but not including any British composers)

12   HEDGES, A: 'Local Radio and the Living British Composer' *Composer* Spring 1973 pp 15–16

13   MAW, N: 'Boulez and Tradition' *Musical Times* March 1962 pp 162–4

14   MELLERS, W: 'Music for Twentieth Century Children' *Musical Times* June 1964 pp 421–2

15   ——: *Twilight of the Gods—the Beatles in retrospect.* Faber, 1973

16   MITCHELL, D ed: *The New Oxford History of Music, Vol X—The Modern Age 1890–1960.* Oxford University Press, 1974

17   MOLES, A A: *Les Musiques Expérimentales.* Paris, Éditions du Cercle d'Art Contemporain, 1960

18   MURDOCH, J: *Australia's Contemporary Composers.* Melbourne, Macmillan, 1972
       (Includes chapters on 33 composers including Don Banks and Malcolm Williamson, and has a foreword by Peter Maxwell Davies.)

19   NORTHCOTT, B: 'Since Grimes—a concise survey of the British musical stage.' *Musical Newsletter* Spring 1974 pp 7–11, 21–2

20   NYMAN, M: *Experimental Music—Cage and Beyond.* Studio Vista, 1974

21   ORR, B: 'The Symphony Today' *Composer* Spring 1974 pp 11–14

22   *Patronage of the Creative Artist.* Artists Now, 1974

23   PORTER, A: 'Some New British Composers' IN *Contemporary Music in Europe, a comprehensive survey,* ed P H Lang and N Broder. NY, Schirmer, 1965; Dent, 1966; Norton (paperback edition), 1968, pp 12–21
       (Originally appeared in *Musical Quarterly* Jan 1965)

24   ROUTH, F: *Contemporary British Music.* MacDonald, 1972
       (Includes a wide variety of British composers including Peter Maxwell Davies, Iain Hamilton, Nicholas Maw, Anthony Milner, Thea Musgrave, Malcolm Williamson, Don Banks and a large Bibliography)

25   ——: *The Patronage and Presentation of Contemporary Music.* The Redcliff Concerts, 1970

26   SCHAFER, Murray: *British Composers in Interview.* Faber, 1961
       (Includes an interview with Alexander Goehr)

27   SOUSTER, T: 'Notes on Pop Music' *Tempo* Winter 1968/9 pp 2–6

28   VINTON, John ed: *Dictionary of Twentieth-Century Music.* Thames & Hudson, 1974. (Published in the USA under the title *Dictionary of Contemporary Music.* Dutton, 1973)
       (The selection of British composers is wayward but very useful entries will be found for many of the younger members of the British avant-garde, particularly the followers of Cardew)

29   WOOD, H: 'English Contemporary Music' IN *European Music in the Twentieth Century,* ed Howard Hartog. Harmondsworth, Pelican Books, 1961 pp 145–70
       (The hardback edition has a different chapter on English music by Anthony Milner)

30   'The Younger Generation' *Musical Times* March 1960 pp 145–50
       (Short articles on John Addison, Arthur Butterworth, Philip Cannon, Hugo Cole, Adrian Cruft, Stephen Dodgson, Alun Hoddinott, Bryan Kelly, Thea Musgrave, Leonard Salzedo and Graham Whettam)

II INDIVIDUAL COMPOSERS

ASTON, Peter

31 MELLERS, W: 'Peter Aston' *Musical Times* Feb 1963 p 115

BEDFORD, David

32 'A Conversation Between David Bedford and Cornelius Cardew' *Musical Times* March 1966 pp 198–202

33 DENNIS, B: 'Two Works by David Bedford' ['Two Poems' and 'The Tentacles of the Dark Nebula'] *Tempo* 1969/70 pp 29–32

34 NYMAN, M: 'Stockhausen and David Bedford' *Listener* 30 April 1970 p 593

35 BOWEN, M: 'David Bedford' *Music & Musicians* Feb 1972 pp 42–4

36 LAKE, S: 'Overture in Glass Ashtray Major' [interview] *Melody Maker* 9 March 1974 p 38

BENNETT, Richard Rodney

37 MARSTON, M: *The Serial Keyboard Music of Richard Rodney Bennett.* Unpublished PhD thesis, University of Wisconsin, 1962, 2 vols

38 MAW, N: 'Richard Rodney Bennett' *Musical Times* Feb 1962 pp 95–7

39 'A Composer of the New Generation' *Times* 15 Aug 1962 p 13

40 BRADSHAW, S: 'The Music of Richard Rodney Bennett' *Listener* 28 Feb 1963 396

41 JACOBSON, B: 'Friday's Child' *Music & Musicians* Nov 1964 p 17

42 BRADSHAW, S: 'Mines of Sulphur' *Music & Musicians* Feb 1965 pp 16–17

43 GOODWIN, N *and* BENNETT, R R: 'The Mines of Sulphur' *Opera* Feb 1965 pp 85–8

44 OSBORNE, C: 'The Mines of Sulphur' *London Magazine* May 1965 pp 75–81

45 REES, C B: 'Impressions—Richard Rodney Bennett' *Musical Events* Aug 1965 pp 9–10

46 BENNETT, R R: 'Composers' Forum—"Symphony" ' *Musical Events* Feb 1966 p 9

47 'No Fashions for Richard Rodney Bennett' *Times* 7 Feb 1966 p 5

48 WALSH, S: 'Richard Rodney Bennett's Symphony' *Tempo* Spring 1966 pp 21–2

49 BLYTH, A: 'Penny for an Opera' *Music & Musicians* Nov 1967 pp 22–3

50 GRAHAM, C: 'Introducing "A Penny for a Song" ' *Opera* Nov 1967 pp 870–3

51 GOODWIN, N: 'More English Eccentrics' ['Penny for a Song'] *Music & Musicians* Jan 1968 pp 26–7

52 KAY, Norman: 'Bennett's Piano Concerto' *Tempo* Autumn 1968 pp 17, 19

53 BRADSHAW, S: 'Richard Rodney Bennett' *Listener* 13 Feb 1969 p 217

54 MOORHOUSE, G: 'The Anatomy of an Opera' ['Victory'] *Guardian* 14 March 1970 p 9

55 BRADSHAW, S: 'Victory' *Musical Times* April 1970 pp 370–2

56 CROSS, B: 'Novel Into Libretto' *Opera* April 1970 p 286

57 DOWNES, E: 'A Man of Principle' ['Victory'] *Music & Musicians* May 1970 pp 30, 73
58 KELLER, H: 'Bennett's Victory' *Listener* 7 May 1970 pp 624–5
59 GOODWIN, N: 'Bennett's Victory' *Music & Musicians* June 1970 pp 22–4
60 STOKER, R: 'Bennett in Baltimore' *Composer* Autumn 1971 pp 1–7
61 GRIFFITHS, P: 'Bennett's Comedies' ['Commedia'] *Musical Times* Aug 1974 p 649

BIRTWISTLE, Harrison
62 HENDERSON, R: 'Harrison Birtwistle' *Musical Times* March 1964 pp 188–9
63 HENDERSON, L: 'Birtwistle at York' ['The Visions of Francesco Petrarca'] *Sunday Telegraph* 19 June 1966 p 13
64 SMALLEY, R: 'Birtwistle's Chorales' *Tempo* Spring 1967 pp 25–7
65 BLYTH, A: 'Harrison Birtwistle's New Musical Venture' *Times* 30 May 1967 p 6
66 GREENFIELD, E: ' "Punch and Judy" at Aldeburgh' *Guardian* 10 June 1968 p 6
67 CROSSE, G: 'Birtwistle's Punch and Judy' *Tempo* Summer 1968 pp 24–6
68 NYMAN, M: 'Harrison Birtwistle's "Punch and Judy" ' *Listener* 10 Oct 1968 p 481
69 SMALLEY, R: 'Birtwistle's "Nomos" ' *Tempo* Autumn 1968, pp 7–10
70 NYMAN, M: 'Two New Works by Birtwistle' *Tempo* Spring 1969 pp 47, 49–50
71 CHANAN, M: 'Birtwistle's Down by the Greenwoodside' *Tempo* Summer 1969 pp 19–21
72 NYMAN, M: 'Mr Birtwistle in One' *Music & Musicians* Sept 1969 pp 27–8
73 NYMAN, M: 'With Reference to Birtwistle's "Medusa" ' *Listener* 13 Nov 1969 p 676
74 NYMAN, M: 'Birtwistle's Rituals' *Listener* 27 Aug 1970 p 285
75 COWIE, E: 'Birtwistle's Time Piece' *Music & Musicians* June 1972 p 22
76 WOOD, H: 'Harrison Birtwistle's "Triumph of Time" *Listener* 26 July 1973 p 126

BLAKE, David
77 LARNER, G: 'David Blake' *Musical Times* April 1968 pp 329–30
78 BLAKE, D: 'Lumina 1968–69' *Musical Times* April 1970 pp 385–6

BLYTON, Carey
79 'Carey Blyton—a biographical note' *Musical Times* July 1964, pp 511–12
80 JACK, A: 'Think of a Title' *Music & Musicians* Dec 1971 pp 6–7
        (On Blyton's commercials and mood music)
81 GILARDINO, A: 'Composers and the Guitar' *Strumenti e Musica* May 1973
        (In Italian; an English translation by Christine Corlett is available from the composer)

82 HARVEY, P: 'Carey Blyton—an appreciation of his woodwind music' *Woodwind World* June 1973

83 GILLESPIE, J: 'Music for Soprano and Clarinet' [by Carey Blyton] *Woodwind World* Feb 1974

BURGON, Geoffrey

84 SIMMONS, D: 'Geoffrey Burgon—a profile' *Musical Opinion* July 1970 pp 523–4

BURT, Francis

85 MANN, W: ' "Volpone" at Stuttgart' *Opera* July 1960 pp 461–2

86 KARKOSCHKA, E: 'Erfolgreicher "Volpone" in Stuttgart' *Melos* July/ Aug 1960 pp 229–31
      (In German)

87 'A Briton's Opera in Germany' [Photographs of 'Volpone'] *Music & Musicians* Aug 1960 p 16

88 BRADSHAW, S: 'Francis Burt's "Barnstable" ' *Musica* Jan/Feb 1970 pp 42–4
      (In German)

BYRNE, Andrew

89 BUSH, Alan: 'An Introduction to the Music of Andrew Byrne' *Musical Times* July 1962 pp 456–8

CANNON, Philip

90 CANNON, P: 'A Composer Discusses His First Opera' ['Morvoren'] *Times* 30 June 1964 p 13

91 CANNON, P: 'Morvoren' *Musical Times* July 1964 pp 508–10

92 LAIDLAW, Jacqueline: 'A Cornish Opera' ['Morvoren'] *Opera* July 1964 pp 449–50

93 MYERS, Rollo: 'Philip Cannon—a fresh voice in British Music' *Musical Times* Nov 1965 pp 858–60

CARDEW, Cornelius

94 SCHONFIELD, V: 'Uncaged Music' *New Society* 13 April 1967 p 543

95 PARSONS, M: 'The Music of Cornelius Cardew' *Listener* 30 Nov 1967 pp 728–9

96 CONNOLLY, J: 'Cardew's "The Great Digest" . . .' *Tempo* Autumn 1968 pp 16–17

97 DENNIS, B: 'Cardew's "The Great Learning" ' *Musical Times* Nov 1971 pp 1066–8

98 NYMAN, M: 'Cornelius Cardew's "The Great Learning" ' *London Magazine* Dec 1971 pp 130–5

99 SOUSTER, Tim: 'The Great Learning' *Listener* 17 Aug 1972 p 218

CARY, Tristram

100 CARY, T: *Electronic Music.* Faber, 1972

COLE, Bruce

101 COLE, B: 'Two Essays in Music Theatre' *Musical Times* Jan 1972 p 38
102 POTTER, Keith: 'Bruce Cole and "Fenestrae Sanctae" ' *Tempo* Dec 1973 pp 19–22

COWIE, Edward

103 COWIE, E: 'Volcanoes' *Listener* 17 May 1973 p 659

CONNOLLY, Justin

104 PAYNE, A: 'Justin Connolly' *Musical Times* April 1971 pp 335–7

CROSSE, Gordon

105 WATERHOUSE, J C G: 'The Music of Gordon Crosse' *Musical Times* May 1965 pp 342–4
106 HENDERSON, R: 'Yeats Set By Crosse' *Music & Musicians* July 1966 pp 18, 60
107 CROSSE, Gordon: 'Purgatory' *Musical Times* July 1966 pp 588–90
108 CROSSE, G: 'A Setting of W B Yeats' *Opera* July 1966 pp 534–7
109 'A Young Composer's Achievement' *Times* 6 July 1966 p 16
110 WALSH, Stephen: 'Crosse's "Purgatory" ' *Tempo* Autumn 1966 pp 23–4
111 GREENFIELD, E: 'Gordon Crosse and "Changes" ' *Guardian* 23 Feb 1967 p 7
112 WALSH, S: 'Four Gordon Crosse Premières' *Tempo* Autumn 1968 pp 22–3, 25–6
113 KAY, N: 'Crosse's "The Grace of Tod" ' *Tempo* Autumn 1969 pp 32–4
114 CROSSE, G: 'In 2' *About the House* Aug 1969 pp 34–7
115 CROSSE, G: 'Gordon Crosse writes about his new Violin Concerto' *Listener* 29 Jan 1970 p 156
116 BOWEN, M: 'Gordon Crosse' *Music & Musicians* Dec 1971 pp 42–4, 46–8
117 FORD, C: 'Gordon Crosse' *Guardian* 3 Jan 1972 p 8
118 WALSH, S: 'The Story of Vasco' *Music & Musicians* March 1974 pp 26–8
119 COLE, H: 'The Story of Vasco' *Musical Times* March 1974 pp 205–6
120 NORTHCOTT, B: 'The Story of Vasco' *Opera* March 1974 pp 188–93
121 WALSH, S: 'Two New British Operas—Stephen Walsh talks to Alun Hoddinott and Gordon Crosse' *Listener* 14 March 1974 pp 344–5
122 ROSENTHAL, H: 'The Story of Vasco' *Opera* May 1974 pp 379–82

DALBY, Martin

123 SOUSTER, T: 'Martin Dalby' *Musical Times* April 1967 pp 321–3
124 BLYTH, A: 'Three Part Harmony' *Radio Times* 25 July 1974 p 9
124a McGUIRE, E: 'Martin Dalby's Viola Concerto' *Listener* 5 Sept 1974 pp 311–12

DANKWORTH, John

125 JEWELL, Derek: 'The Dankworths of Nether Hall' *Sunday Times Magazine* 21 Aug 1966 pp 28–31
126 DANKWORTH, J: 'Fifties Jazz and How I Took It Up' *Listener* 14 Aug 1969 p 77

DAVIES, Peter Maxwell

127 HENDERSON, R: 'Peter Maxwell Davies' *Musical Times* Oct 1961 pp 624–6

128 HENDERSON, R: 'Peter Maxwell Davies' *Music in Britain* Autumn 1963 pp 15–17

129 WATERHOUSE, J C G: 'Peter Maxwell Davies and his Public Image' *Listener* 7 May 1964 p 773

130 WATERHOUSE, J C G: 'Peter Maxwell Davies—towards an opera' *Tempo* Summer 1964 pp 18–25

131 WATERHOUSE, J C G: 'Meeting Point ["Veni Sancte Spiritus"]' *Music & Musicians* Oct 1964 pp 24–6

132 MELLERS, W: 'New Music—Peter Maxwell Davies' *New Statesman* 7 May 1965 p 736

133 PRUSLIN, S: 'Maxwell Davies's "Second Taverner Fantasia" ' *Tempo* Summer 1965 pp 2–11

134 SMALLEY, R: 'Some Recent Works of Peter Maxwell Davies' *Tempo* Spring 1968 pp 2–5

135 ANDREWES, J: 'Maxwell Davies' "The Shepherds Calendar" ' *Tempo* Winter 1968/9 pp 6–9

136 DAVIES, P M: 'Peter Maxwell Davies on Some of his Recent Work' *Listener* 23 Jan 1969 p 121

137 NORTHCOTT, B: 'Peter Maxwell Davies' *Music & Musicians* April 1969 pp 36–40, 80

138 HARVEY, Jonathan: 'Maxwell Davies's "Songs for a Mad King" ' *Tempo* Summer 1969 pp 2–6

139 CHANAN, M: 'Latent Bombast—Peter Maxwell Davies' *Listener* 28 Aug 1969 pp 288, 290

140 CHANAN, M: 'Dialectics in Peter Maxwell Davies' *Tempo* Autumn 1969 pp 12–22

141 LAWSON, P: 'Maxwell Davies's Worldes Bliss' *Tempo* Autumn 1969 pp 23–7

142 HAMILTON, D: 'Three Composers of Today' *Musical Newsletter* Jan 1971 pp 16–18

143 PRUSLIN, S: 'An Anatomy of Betrayal ["Taverner"]' *Music & Musicians* July 1972 pp 28–30

144 CHANAN, M: 'Peter Maxwell Davies' *Listener* 8 Nov 1973 pp 645–6

DICKINSON, Peter

145 NORRINGTON, R: 'Peter Dickinson' *Musical Times* Feb 1965 pp 109–10

146 DOMMETT, K: 'The Outcry of Nature' [Peter Dickinson] *Music & Musicians* May 1969 pp 26–8

FERNEYHOUGH, Brian

147 SCHWARTZ, E: 'Current Chronicle—London' [Brian Ferneyhough] *Musical Quarterly* Jan 1968 pp 97–103 [pp 97–99 on Ferneyhough]

148 SCHAAF, E: 'Das Porträt Brian Ferneyhough' *Melos* July/Aug 1973 pp 214–20
(In German)

FORBES, Sebastian

149 RADCLIFFE, P: 'Sebastian Forbes' *Musical Times* May 1969 pp 483–5

GILBERT, Anthony

150 HOPKINS, G W: 'The Music of Anthony Gilbert' *Musical Times* Oct 1968 pp 907–10
151 CONNOLLY, J: 'Cardew's "The Great Digest" and Gilbert's "Missa Brevis" ' *Tempo* Autumn 1968 pp 16–17
152 HENDERSON, R: 'Anthony Gilbert' *Music & Musicians* March 1972 pp 42–4
153 MACBETH, G: 'Anthony Gilbert's Scene Machine' *Listener* 2 March 1972 pp 284–5

GOEHR, Alexander

154 GOEHR, A: 'Sutter's Gold Opus 11' IN Triennial Musical Festival, Leeds, 1961 [Programme book], The Festival, 1961 [pp 43–7]
155 WOOD, H: 'The Music of Alexander Goehr' *Musical Times* May 1962 pp 312–14
156 WOOD, H: 'Alexander Goehr' *Listener* 28 June 1962
157 GOODWIN, N: 'Arden Must Die' *Music & Musicians* May 1967 pp 26–7
158 WARRACK, J: 'Goehr's New Opera' *Opera* May 1967 pp 369–71
159 DREW, D: 'Why Must Arden Die?' *Listener* 28 Sept 1967 pp 412–13 and 5 Oct 1967 pp 445–6
160 CHANAN, M: 'Goehr's "Romanza" ' *Tempo* Spring 1968 pp 23, 25
161 GOEHR, A: 'For My Performers ["Romanza"]' *Listener* 25 April 1968
162 SADIE, S: 'Naboth's Vineyard' [interview with Goehr] *Musical Times* July 1968 pp 625–6
163 PAYNE, A: 'Goehr's "Konzertstück" for Piano and Small Orchestra' *Tempo* Summer 1969 pp 16–17
164 NORTHCOTT, B: 'Goehr the Progressive' *Music & Musicians* Oct 1969 pp 36–8, 78
165 NYMAN, M: 'Alexander Goehr's "Naboth's Vineyard" ' *Tempo* Autumn 1968 pp 14–15
166 NORTHCOTT, B: 'Alexander Goehr's New Concerto' *Listener* 21 Jan 1971 p 90
167 FORD, C: 'Defender of the Faith' *Guardian* 15 June 1971 p 8
168 NORTHCOTT, B: 'Alexander Goehr's Triptych' *Listener* 25 Nov 1971 p 739
169 OAKES, M: 'Goehr's Piano Concerto' [interview] *Music & Musicians* June 1972 pp 20, 22
170 DAWNEY, M: 'Alexander Goehr . . .' [interview] *Composer* Winter 1972/3 pp 11–13
171 NORTHCOTT, B: '. . . most wickedlye murdered . . .' ['Arden Must Die'] *Music & Musicians* April 1974 pp 26–7
172 SHAW, C: 'Arden Must Die' *Tempo* Sept 1974 pp 42–3

HARVEY, Jonathan

173 BROWN, D: 'Jonathan Harvey' *Musical Times* Sept 1968 pp 808–10

174 HARVEY, J: 'Jonathan Harvey Writes About His "Persephone Dream"'
     Listener 11 Jan 1973 p 58
175 NORTHCOTT, B: 'Jonathan Harvey' *Music & Musicians* March 1973
     pp 34–40

HEDGES, Anthony
176 BRADBURY, E: 'Anthony Hedges' *Musical Times* Sept 1972 pp 858–61

HEWITT JONES, Tony
177 HARMSWORTH, G: 'A Note on Tony Hewitt Jones' *Musical Times*
     Dec 1966 pp 1051–2

HODDINOTT, Alun
178 LEIGHTON THOMAS, A F: 'Alun Hoddinott' *Musical Times* Oct 1955
     pp 523–5
179 HESFORD, B: 'The Piano Works of Alun Hoddinott' *Musical Opinion*
     April 1966 pp 411–13
180 KAY, N: 'Hoddinott's Variants' *Tempo* Winter 1966/7 pp 15–17
181 BOYD, M: 'The Beach of Falesá' *Musical Times* March 1974 pp 207–9
182 POWELL, C: 'Hoddinott's First Opera' *Music & Musicians* March 1974
     pp 20–1
183 WALSH, S: 'Two New British Operas—Stephen Walsh talks to Alun
     Hoddinott and Gordon Crosse' *Listener* 14 March 1974 pp 344–5

HOLLOWAY, Robin
184 BPN [ie NORTHCOTT, B]: 'A Composer . . . and his concerto' *Music
     & Musicians* Nov 1971 pp 18, 20
185 BLYTH, Alan: 'Three Part Harmony' *Radio Times* 25 July 1974 p 8
186 EAST, L: 'Domination of Black' *Music & Musicians* Aug 1974 pp 20–2
187 NORTHCOTT, B: 'Robin Holloway' *Musical Times* Aug 1974 pp 644–6
188 HEYWORTH, P: 'Finding the Path' ['Domination of Black'] *Observer*
     11 Aug 1974

HOROWITZ, Joseph
189 BRADBURY, E: 'Joseph Horowitz—a Survey' *Musical Times* April
     1970 pp 383–5

JOHNSON, Robert Sherlaw
190 ASTON, P: 'The Music of Robert Sherlaw Johnson' *Musical Times*
     March 1968 pp 229–30
191 DAWNEY, M: 'Robert Sherlaw Johnson . . .' *Composer* Autumn 1973

JONES, Tony Hewitt *see* HEWITT JONES, Tony

JOSEPHS, Wilfred
192 JACOBSON, B: 'Prize Requiem' *Music & Musicians* Feb 1964 p 27
193 JOSEPHS, W: 'Composers' Forum—Requiem Op 39' *Musical Events*
     Oct 1965 pp 8–9

194 JOSEPHS, W: 'Composers' Forum—Piano Concerto' *Musical Events* Feb 1967 p 29

195 FRENCH, Peter: 'Wilfred Josephs' *Musical Opinion* Feb 1968 p 262

196 GREENFIELD, E: 'A Composer With Teeth' *Guardian* 15 April 1970 p 8

197 JACOBSON, B: 'Composers of Importance Today—Wilfred Josephs' *Musical Newsletter* July 1971 pp 18–20

KELLY, Bryan

198 HOWES, F: 'Bryan Kelly' *Musical Times* Sept 1967 pp 801–4

LEFANU, Nicola

199 LEFANU, N: 'On Being A Young Composer' *Listener* 9 July 1970 p 56

200 LEFANU, N: 'Nicola Lefanu Discusses Her New Composition "The Hidden Landscape"' *Listener* 2 Aug 1973 p 157

201 DEVLIN, T: 'A Journey Through the Mind of Miss Lefanu' *Times* 6 Aug 1973 p 6

LEIGHTON, Kenneth

202 COCKSHOOT, J V: 'The Music of Kenneth Leighton' *Musical Times* April 1957 pp 193–6

LORD, David

203 'Music in Education' *Church Music* April 1972 p 20

MATHIAS, William

204 WALSH, S: 'The Music of William Mathias' *Musical Times* Jan 1969 pp 27–9

205 DAWNEY, M: 'William Mathias . . .' *Composer* Summer 1974 pp 19, 21, 22

McCABE, John

206 DICKINSON, Peter: 'John McCabe' *Musical Times* Aug 1965 pp 596–8

207 McCABE, J: 'Composers' Forum—Symphony No 1 ("Elegy")' *Musical Events* July 1966 p 14

208 McCABE, J: 'Composer Talking—1' *Novello Review* Spring 1967 pp 10–11

209 LARNER, G: 'The Lion, the Witch and the Wardrobe' *Musical Times* April 1969 p 372

210 COLE, H: 'Lone Ranger' *Guardian* 8 Oct 1971 p 10

MAW, Nicholas

211 BRADSHAW, S: 'Nicholas Maw' *Musical Times* Sept 1962 pp 608–10

212 PAYNE, A: 'The Music of Nicholas Maw' *Tempo* Spring 1964 pp 2–13

213 PAYNE, A: 'Composer in Search of a Language' *Music & Musicians* Aug 1964 pp 12–14

214 CROZIER, E: 'But Why a Comic Opera?' [interview] *Opera* Oct 1964 pp 658–61

215 JACOBS, A: 'Notes before an Opera' ['One Man Show'] *Musical Times* Nov 1964 pp 818–19

216 PAYNE, A: 'Nicholas Maw's "One Man Show" ' *Tempo* Winter 1964/5 pp 2–14

217 DALTON, J: 'Maw's Essay for Organ' *Musical Times* May 1965 pp 374–5

218 WALSH, S: 'Nicholas Maw's Sinfonia' *Tempo* Summer 1966 pp 16–18

219 HENDERSON, R: 'Nicholas Maw's Sonata for Two Horns and Strings' *Tempo* Autumn 1967 pp 25, 27

220 PAYNE, A: 'Elizabeth Lutyens, Nicholas Maw' *Listener* 9 Jan 1969 p 57

221 WALSH, S: 'Nicholas Maw's New Opera' *Tempo* Spring 1970 pp 2–15

222 NORTHCOTT, B: 'Nicholas Maw' *Music & Musicians* May 1970 pp 34–43, 82

223 WALSH, S: 'Maw's Irish Opera' *Opera* July 1970 pp 616–20

224 WIDDICOMBE, G: 'The Rising of the Moon' [interview] *Musical Times* July 1970 pp 700–1

225 LOVELAND, K: 'The Rising of the Moon' *Music & Musicians* Sept 1970 pp 18–19

226 WHITTALL, A: 'The Instrumental Music of Nicholas Maw—Questions of Tonality' *Tempo* Spring 1973 pp 26–33

MAXWELL DAVIES, Peter *see* DAVIES, Peter Maxwell

MILNER, Anthony

227 STEVENS, D: 'Anthony Milner's "Variations for Orchestra" ' *Musical Times* July 1959 pp 384–5

228 MILNER, A: 'The Water and the Fire' IN *The Composer's Point of View— essays on Twentieth Century Choral Music by Those Who Wrote It*, ed Robert S Hines. Norman, University of Oklahoma Press, 1963, pp 89–102

229 STEVENS, D: 'Milner's "The Water and the Fire" ' *Musical Times* Feb 1963 pp 106–7

230 BRADBURY, E: 'The Progress of Anthony Milner' *Musical Times* June 1963 pp 405–7

231 BRADBURY, E: 'The Music of Anthony Milner' *Listener* 24 Sept 1964 p 484

232 MILNER, A: 'Roman Spring' *Musical Times* Oct 1969 p 1036

233 EAST, L: 'Milner's Symphony' *Music & Musicians* Jan 1973 pp 18–19

234 MILNER, A: 'A New Symphony' *Musical Times* Jan 1973 p 30

MUSGRAVE, Thea

235 BRADSHAW, S: 'Newcomers—Musgrave and Maw' *The Chesterian* Summer 1960 pp 15–20

236 BRADSHAW, S: 'Thea Musgrave' *Musical Times* Dec 1963 pp 866–8

237 LINDSAY, M: 'The Disaster and "The Decision" ' *Opera* Nov 1967 pp 874–6

238 MUSGRAVE, T: 'The Decision' *Musical Times* Nov 1967 pp 988–91

239 BLYTH, A: 'Thea Musgrave's first full-length opera' *Times* 23 Nov 1967

240 BLYTH, A: 'Musgrave's Decision' *Music & Musicians* Dec 1967 p 38

241 MUSGRAVE, T: 'Starting Points' *Listener* 30 Jan 1969 p 153

242 PAYNE, A: 'Thea Musgrave's Clarinet Concerto' *Tempo* Spring 1969
    pp 50–1, 53
243 KAY, N: 'Thea Musgrave' *Music & Musicians* Dec 1969 pp 34–6, 40
244 KAY, N: 'Thea Musgrave's Beauty and the Beast' *Tempo* Winter 1969/
    70 pp 32–3
245 MUSGRAVE, T: 'A New Viola Concerto' *Musical Times* Aug 1973
    pp 790–1
246 WALSH, S: 'Musgrave's "The Voice of Ariadne"' *Musical Times* June
    1974 pp 465–7
247 MARK, P *and* MUSGRAVE, T: 'Musgrave's Ariadne' [interview] *Opera*
    June 1974 pp 476–81
248 ELGUERA, A: 'The Birth of Ariadne' *Listener* 13 June 1974
    (Reprinted in *About the House* Summer 1974 pp 41–3)

NEWSON, George
249 NEWSON, G: 'Electronic Odyssey' *Composer* Winter 1967/8 pp 11–14

OGDON, John
250 BLYTH, A: 'Ogdon—composer and pianist' *Music & Musicians* April
    1968 pp 22, 49
251 MACDONALD, C: 'Poet of Fire' *Records & Recordings* Dec 1971 pp 56–7

OLDHAM, Arthur
252 WILSON, C: 'Arthur Oldham' *Musical Times* Dec 1965 pp 946–8

PAYNE, Anthony
253 BRADSHAW, S: 'Anthony Payne and his Paean' *Tempo* June 1972
253a NORTHCOTT, B: 'Anthony Payne' *Musical Times* Jan 1975

RANDS, Bernard
254 SMALL, C: 'Bernard Rands' *Musical Times* Oct 1967 pp 905, 907

RIDOUT, Alan
255 DICKINSON, P: 'Alan Ridout' *Music & Musicians* Dec 1966 pp 28–30

RODNEY BENNETT, Richard *see* BENNETT, Richard Rodney

SHAW, Christopher
256 DREW, D: 'Christopher Shaw' *Musical Times* July 1963 pp 479–81

SMALLEY, Roger
257 WALSH, S: 'Roger Smalley' *Musical Times* Feb 1968 pp 131, 133
258 SOUSTER, T: 'Roger Smalley's "The Song of the Highest Tower"'
    Tempo Autumn 1968 pp 12–14
259 WALSH, S: 'Roger Smalley' *Music & Musicians* June 1969 pp 37–40
260 SMALLEY, R: ' "Pulses 5 x 4"—an introduction' *Musical Times* June
    1969 pp 597–9
261 DENNIS, B: 'Roger Smalley's "Pulses 5 x 4 Players" and "Transforma-
    tion I" for piano' *Tempo* Autumn 1969 pp 28–30

262 WALSH, S: 'Roger Smalley's "Gloria Tibi Trinitas I"' *Tempo* Winter 1969/70 pp 17–20
263 SMALLEY, R: 'Roger Smalley writes about his new "Beat Music"' *Listener* 12 Aug 1971 p 218
264 STADLEN, P: 'How Much Can Be Left to Chance' *Daily Telegraph* 24 Feb 1973 p 13
265 EMMERSON, S: 'Roger Smalley's "Zeitebenen"' *Tempo* Mar 1974

SOUSTER, Tim
266 THOMPSON, R: 'Tim Souster's Titus Groan Music' *Tempo* Summer 1969 pp 21–2
267 BRITTEN, P: 'Triple Music II' *Music & Musicians* Aug 1970 pp 22–3
268 SOUSTER, T: 'Triple Music II' *Listener* 13 Aug 1970 p 222
269 NYMAN, M: 'Song of an Average City' *Listener* 7 March 1974 p 312

STANDFORD, Patric
270 LARNER, G: 'Patric Standford' *Musical Times* March 1973 pp 253–6

STEEL, Christopher
271 GRAVES, R: 'Christopher Steel' *Musical Times* May 1966 pp 402–4

STEVENSON, Ronald
272 BUSH, A: 'Ronald Stevenson's "Passacaglia"' *Composer* Autumn 1964 pp 17–18
273 WALSH, S: 'Long Distance Loneliness ["Passacaglia"]' *Daily Telegraph* 25 June 1966
274 WILSON, C: [Ronald Stevenson] IN HIS *On Music* Pan Books 1967 pp 178–9
275 SCOTT-SUTHERLAND, C: 'The Music of Ronald Stevenson' *Music Review* May 1965 pp 118–28
276 DAWES, F: 'An Eighty Minute Movement' *Musical Times* June 1968
277 ORGA, A: 'Ronald Stevenson' *Music & Musicians* Oct 1968 pp 26–32
278 ORGA, A: 'The Piano Music of Ronald Stevenson' *Musical Opinion* March 1969
279 STEVENSON, R: 'Ronald Stevenson Writes about his Passacaglia on DSCH' *Listener* 9 Oct 1969 p 494
280 STEVENSON, R: 'Composers' Anthology—3: Ronald Stevenson' *Recorded Sound* April/July 1971 pp 747–54
281 'Ronald Stevenson Recordings' *Recorded Sound* April/July 1971 pp 755–7
282 RIMMER, F: [Ronald Stevenson] IN HIS *A History of Scottish Music*. BBC, 1973 pp 80–1

STOKER, Richard
283 STOKER, R: 'Composers' Forum—"Ecce Homo"' *Musical Events* March 1966 pp 12–13
284 STOKER, R: 'Proverbs Op 19' *Musical Events* Nov 1966 p 25
285 STOKER, R: 'Composers' Forum—"Johnson Preserved"' *Musical Events* June 1967 p 13

286 BROPHY, E: 'Dr Johnson Operatically "Preserv'd" ' *Opera* July 1967 pp 543-6

287 TOWNSEND, R: 'Richard Stoker' *Musical Times* May 1968 pp 424-6

TAVENER, John

288 TAVENER, J: 'Cain and Abel' *Musical Times* Oct 1966 p 867

289 PAYNE, A: 'John Tavener's "In Alium" . . .' *Tempo* Autumn 1968 pp 19-22

290 TAVENER, J: ' "Celtic Requiem"—an introduction' *Musical Times* July 1969 pp 736-7

291 DENNIS, B: 'John Tavener's "Celtic Requiem" ' *Tempo* Autumn 1969 pp 31-2

292 GREENFIELD, E: 'The Man Who Set Genet To Music' *Guardian* 28 Aug 1969 p 8

293 FORD, C: 'The Man Who Set Genet to Music' *Guardian* 16 Oct 1970 p 10

294 GRIFFITHS, P: 'Tavener and "Ultimos Ritos" ' *Musical Times* June 1974 pp 468-9, 471

295 COOPER, M: 'Sensational Scale of Tavener Work ["Ultimos Ritos"]' *Daily Telegraph* 24 June 1974

296 COLE, H: 'Tavener's Church Spectacular' *Listener* 4 July 1974 p 21

WARREN, Raymond

297 RAMSEY, B: 'Raymond Warren' *Musical Times* Aug 1964 pp 578-9

298 ACTON, C: 'The Music of Raymond Warren' *Musical Times* Oct 1969 pp 1031-3

WHETTAM, Graham

299 GARDNER, John: 'Sinfonietta Stravagante' *Listener* 3 Aug 1967 p 157

WHITE, John

300 DENNIS, B: 'The Music of John White' *Musical Times* May 1971 pp 435-7

WILSON, Thomas

301 'Touchstone—portrait for large orchestra' *Musical Times* Aug 1967 pp 697-8

WOOD, Hugh

302 WOOD, H: 'Hugh Wood on his own Work' *Listener* 29 Oct 1970 p 605

303 KAY, N: 'Work[s] by Hugh Wood . . .' *Tempo* Winter 1969/70 pp 33-4 (Cello Concerto & work by Iain Hamilton)

304 BLACK, L: 'Hugh Wood's Violin Concerto' *Listener* 11 Oct 1973 p 493

305 BLACK, L: 'The Music of Hugh Wood' *Musical Times* May 1971 pp 435-7

YOUNG, Douglas

306 LARNER, G: 'Douglas Young' *Musical Times* Aug 1973 pp 787-90

307 YOUNG, D: 'Three Regions from "Terrain"— . . . fifteen minutes of a work in progress' *Listener* 21 Feb 1974 pp 249-50

Sources of the Music

Publishers' names are slightly abbreviated—for example Faber Music as Faber, Oxford University Press as OUP—and they are listed in alphabetical order except that any publisher having the majority of a composer's work is listed first, out of sequence. When a brochure or list of works devoted to a given composer is available, the source from which it is available is identified by an asterisk. The works of composers who do not have publishers are available from the British Music Information Centre (BMIC—10 Stratford Place, London W1), from the Scottish Music Archive (SMA—7 Lillybank Gardens, Glasgow), or from the composer, as indicated.

David BARLOW	Novello; BMIC
David BEDFORD	Universal
Richard Rodney BENNETT	Mills Music; Universal
Harrison BIRTWISTLE	Universal
David BLAKE	Novello; OUP; Schott
Carey BLYTON	Ascherberg; Belwin-Mills; Boosey & Hawkes; Curwen; Faber; Mills Music; New Wind Music Co.; Novello; Thames; BMIC*; Frazer-Kemp Management Ltd (commercial commissions)*; Composer*
Derek BOURGEOIS	OUP; Composer (c/o BMIC)
Geoffrey BURGON	Chester*; Chappell; Stainer & Bell
Francis BURT	Universal; Bärenreiter; Bote und Bock
Philip CANNON	Novello*; California Press; Editions Francaise de Musique; Kronos Press; Composer*
Cornelius CARDEW	Universal; Gallery Upstairs Press; Hinrichsen
David CARHART	Composer (54D Cornwall Gardens, London SW7)
Tristram CARY	Galliard; Novello
Brian CHAPPLE	Chester*
Bruce COLE	Boosey & Hawkes; Yorke Edition
Justin CONNOLLY	OUP; Schott
Edward COWIE	Chester*
Gordon CROSSE	OUP*
Martin DALBY	Boosey & Hawkes; Chappell; Chester; Lengnick; Novello; Ricordi; Yorke Edition; SMA
John DANKWORTH	OUP; Schott
Peter Maxwell DAVIES	Boosey & Hawkes*; Schott

Peter DICKINSON	Novello*
Stephen DODGSON	Chappell*; Chester; Eschig; Novello; OUP; Ricordi
David DORWARD	Curwen; Galliard; Hinrichsen; OUP; SMA
Duncan DRUCE	Composer (Ann's Cottage, Ramsden, Oxford)
David ELLIS	Composer (c/o BBC)
Brian FERNEYHOUGH	Peters; Composer
Michael FINISSY	International*
Sebastian FORBES	Associated Board; Chappell; Chester; Novello; OUP; SMA
Stephen GERSCH	Composer
Alexander GOEHR	Schott*
Anthony GILBERT	Schott*
John HALL	Chappell*
Edward HARPER	Composer (c/o Edinburgh University)
Jonathan HARVEY	Novello*; Schott
Christopher HEADINGTON	Chappell; Chester; Faber; Francis, Day & Hunter; Weinberger
Anthony HEDGES	Chappell*; Novello; Universal
Tony HEWITT-JONES	Boosey & Hawkes; Lengnick; Novello
Alun HODDINOTT	OUP*; Mills; Novello
Trevor HOLD	Composer*; Chappell; Stainer & Bell; Thames Publishing; Universal; University of Wales Press
Robin HOLLOWAY	OUP
Bill HOPKINS	Schott; Universal
Elgar HOWARTH	Chester; Novello
Robert Sherlaw JOHNSON	Faber; Novello; OUP
Wilfred JOSEPHS	Boosey & Hawkes; Chester; Galliard; Novello; OUP; Presser*; Composer
Bryan KELLY	Chappell; Novello; OUP
Oliver KNUSSEN	Schirmer*; International; Chappell
John LAMBERT	Chappell*
Nicola LEFANU	Novello
Kenneth LEIGHTON	Lengnick; Novello
Malcolm LIPKIN	Chester*; Novello
David LORD	Chappell; Chester; Faber; OUP; Universal
William MATHIAS	OUP*
Nicholas MAW	Boosey & Hawkes; Chester; Novello; OUP
John McCABE	British & Continental; Novello*; OUP
Anthony MILNER	Novello; OUP; Universal
David MORGAN	Chandos Music; Mozart Edition
Thea MUSGRAVE	Chester*
George NEWSON	Schott; Universal
John OGDON	Ascherberg; International
Arthur OLDHAM	Boosey & Hawkes; Faber
Paul PATTERSON	Weinberger
Anthony PAYNE	Chester*
Maurice PERT	OUP; SMA

John PURSER	Composer*; SMA
Bernard RANDS	Universal*
Alan RIDOUT	Chappell*
Jeremy Dale ROBERTS	Composer
Francis ROUTH	Composer*; Boosey & Hawkes; Lengnick; BMIC
Edwin ROXBURGH	United*
Robert SAXTON	Chester*
Christopher SHAW	Novello; Composer
Francis SHAW	Chester*
Howard SKEMPTON	Faber
Roger SMALLEY	Faber; Novello
Tim SOUSTER	Galliard*
Patric STANDFORD	Novello*; Lengnick; Schirmer; Stainer & Bell; Thames
Christopher STEEL	Novello
Ronald STEVENSON	Boosey & Hawkes; Novello; OUP; Schott; Composer*
Richard STOKER	Hinrichsen*; Leeds*; Boosey & Hawkes; Breitkopf; Chappell
John TAVENER	Chester*
Judith WEIR	Composer (Hill House, Mount Park Road, Harrow-on-the-Hill)
Christopher WHELEN	Composer
Graham WHETTAM	Leeds Music*; Boosey & Hawkes; Chappell
John WHITE	Leduc
Thomas WILSON	Chappell*; Bayley & Ferguson; International; Novello
Hugh WOOD	Universal
Guy WOOLFENDEN	Gamut Publications
Douglas YOUNG	Faber

Discography

All records are 12" stereo LPs unless marked: 7"; 10"; EP = 7" extended play; m = mono; q = quadraphonic; car = cartridge; cas = cassette. All are currently available unless marked: * = deleted; † not yet issued; [   ] = American issue. Some DGG issues may only still be available as imports from Germany. Ger = German record. Argo numbers in the USA are the same as in the UK. For key to abbreviations used see page 181.

See also Addenda, pages 236-7

BEDFORD, David

Among Us
  K Ayers (voc & inst)/orch   HARVEST: SHUL 800
Come in Here Child (s & amplified pf)
  J Manning (s)   [MAINSTREAM: MS 5001
                                                                  (car M85001;
                                                                   cas M 5501)]

18 Bricks Left on April 21 (for two
  electric gtrs)
  M Warner/G Taylor (gtrs)   TRANSATLANTIC: TRA 271/B
It's Easier than It Looks
  D Bedford (rdrs & alto-melodicas)   DANDELION: 2310 165*
Mood
  Coxhill Bedford Duo   DANDELION: 2058 214*
Music for Albion Moonlight (for s &
  ch ens)
  J Manning(s)/Members of the
    BBC SO/Carewe   ARGO: ZRG 638
Nurse's Song With Elephants
  Omega Players (gtrs)/Biberian, with
    M Oldfield (b gtr)/& female voc   DANDELION: 2310 165*
[Two] *Poems for Chorus* (*The Great Bird*
  and *O Now the Drenched Land Wakes*)
  Hamburg N W German Radio
    Chorus/Franz   DGG: DG 137004
                                                                  (car 87-004;
                                                                   cas 921-023)
                                                              (IN Set 104988-93)*

Pretty Little Girl
  (pt 1) Coxhill Bedford Duo   DANDELION: 2485 021*
  —— (pts 1 & 2)   POLYDOR: 2001 253*
216

Sad and Lonely Faces (Patchen)

D Bedford (inst)/K Ayers (voc)	DANDELION:	2310 165*

Some Bright Stars for Queen's College

Girls of Queen's College, Harley Street (voc)/acc 'plastic pipe twirlers'	DANDELION:	2310 165*

Star's End

M Oldfield (gtr & b gtr)/C Cutler (drums)/RPO/Handley	VIRGIN:	V 2020

The Tentacles of the Dark Nebula

P Pears (t)/London Sinfonietta/ Bedford	DECCA:	HEAD 3

Trona

Sebastian Bell Ens	DANDELION:	2310 165*

You Asked For It

Timothy Walker (gtr)	L'OISEAU LYRE:	DSLO 3

BENNETT, Richard Rodney

(A number of arrangements and separate issues of themes from various films have not been listed)

All the King's Men (opera)

M Flaxman/P Male/T Gaunt/ B Tucker/A Stafford/C Greenstreet/ S Cornwall/Trinity School Croydon Ch & Orch/Squibb	ABBEY:	XMS 703

The Aviary

Finchley Childrens' Music Gp/ R R Bennett (pf)	HMV: 7″	7EG 8943 m*

Billion Dollar Brain—music from the film

J Loriod (ondes martenot)/Orch/ Dods	UNITED ARTISTS:	ULP 1183*

Calendar (for ch orch)

Melos Ens/Carewe	HMV:	ALP 2093 m*
		ASD 640*
	(reissued on ARGO ZRG 758)	

Capriccio for pf duet

R R Bennett & Musgrave (pfs)	ARGO:	ZRG 704

Clock-A-Clay

S Woolf (tr)/S Bedford (pf)	UNICORN:	RHS 316

Commedia

Philip Jones Brass Ensemble	†ARGO:	

Concerto for Guitar and Chamber Ensemble

J Bream (gtr)/Melos Ens/Atherton	RCA:	SB 6876
	[RCA:	ARL 1-0049
	(car AR 51-0049; cas ARK 1-0049)]	

Concerto for Piano and Orchestra

S Bishop (pf)/LSO/Gibson	PHILIPS:	6500 301

Dormi Jesu
  Elizabethan Singers/Halsey   ARGO: RG 446 m*
                                          ZRG 5446

Elegy for Caroline Lamb
  P Mark (vla)/NPO/Dods   HMV: CSD 3728
                            [ANGEL: SFO 36946
                   (car 8XS 36946; cas 4XS 36946)]

Far From the Madding Crowd—music
    from the film
  Orch/Dods   MGM: C 8053
                                       2315 033

Farnham Festival Overture
    Orchs of Tiffin Sch & Farnham GS/
      Bloodworth (1965 Farnham
      Festival)   WAVERLEY: LLP 1039 m*
The Fly
  S Woolf (tr)/S Bedford (pf)   UNICORN: RHS 316
The House of Sleepe
  The King's Singers   EMI: EMD 5521
The Insect World
  Finchley Children's Music Gp/
    Bennett (pf)   HMV: 7"   7EG 8943 m*
Jazz Calendar
  Ensemble/Lanchberry   PHILIPS: 6500 301
Lady Caroline Lamb—music from the film
  P Mark (vla)/NPO/Dods   HMV: CSD 3728
                          [ANGEL: S 36946
                   (car 8XS 36946; cas 4XS 36946)]

The Midnight Thief
  Choir & inst ens of W Lodge JM
    School, Pinner/Langstaff   HMV: 10"   DLP 1216 m*
Murder on the Orient Express—music
    from the film ROO/Dods   EMI: EMC 3054
Nicholas and Alexandra—music from
    the film
  NPO/Dods   BELL   BELL S 202
                          [BELL: 1103
                      car M81103; cas M51103]

One Evening (Auden)
  W Brown (t)/D Dupré (gtr)   JUPITER: JUR OA10
Out of Your Sleep Arise—carol
  John Lyon Motet Choir/Williams LYON: JL 1
Soliloquy
  C Laine/insts   FONTANA: STL 5483
The Sorrows of May
  Elizabethan Singers/Halsey   ARGO: ZRG 5499
Susanni ('A Little Child There is
    Yborn . . .')
  St Matthews Church Choir
    Northampton/Nicholas   ABBEY: LPB 655

The Bedford Singers/Walley	BBC:	REC 141
Sweet Was the Song the Virgin Sang		
St Matthews Church Choir		
Northampton/Nicholas	ABBEY:	LPB 655
[Five] *Studies for Piano*		
R R Bennett (pf)	ARGO:	ZRG 704
S Cherkassky (pf)	[FOURFRONT:	4FM 10002*]
Symphony [No 1]		
RPO/Buketoff	RCA:	RB 6730 m*; SB 6730*
That Younge Child—carol		
John Lyon Motet Choir/Williams	LYON:	JL 1
This Must Be Earth		
M Murphy (voc)/Orch/Moule	PHOENIX:	PMS 1001
Tom O'Bedlam's Song		
P Pears (t)/Joan Dickson (vlc)	ARGO:	ZRG 5418; RG 418 m*
Trio for Flute, Oboe & Clarinet		
W Bennett (fl)/P Graeme (ob)/		
G de Peyer (cl)	ARGO:	ZRG 5475; RG 475 m*
A Week of Birthdays		
R R Bennett (pf)	JUPITER: 7"	JEPOC 26 m*
Winter Music for Flute and Piano		
W Bennett (fl)/S Bradshaw (pf)	DELTA:	DEL 12005 m*;
		SDEL 18005*

BIRTWISTLE, Harrison

Nenia—The Death of Orpheus		
J Manning (s)/Matrix/Hacker	DECCA:	HEAD 7
The Fields of Sorrow		
London Sinfonietta/Atherton	DECCA:	HEAD 7
Precis		
J Ogdon (pf)	HMV:	ALP 2098 m*; ASD 645
Refrains and Choruses for Wind Quintet		
Danzi Wind Quintet	PHILIPS:	SAL 3669*
		[80274 OLY]
Ring A Dumb Carillon (words C Logue)		
M Thomas (s)/A Hacker (clar)/		
B Quinn (pf)	[MAINSTREAM:	MS 5001;
	(car M 85 001; cas M 55001)]	
Tragoedia		
Melos Ensemble	HMV:	ASD 2333*
Verses for Ensembles	Reissued on ARGO:	ZRG 759
London Sinfonietta/Atherton	DECCA:	HEAD 7

BLAKE, David

Variations for Piano		
J Ogdon (pf)	HMV:	ASD 2551*
	Reissued on	HQS 1337

BLYTON, Carey
Three Canadian Carols (arr v, clar & pf)
  Robert Ivan Foster (bar), Anthony
    Seward (clar), Nina Walker (pf)   ONSLO: OCAB-61-65 m
Six Regional Canadian Folk Songs
  Robert Ivan Foster (bar)/Nina
    Walker (pf)   ONSLO: OCAB-61-64 m
Three Welsh Folk Songs (arr v and hp)
  Robert Ivan Foster (bar)/Tryphena
    Partridge (hp)   ONSLO: OCAB-61-63 m

CAIN, David
(Various radio call signs and signature themes on BBC REC 91 are not itemised below)
Hajji Baba—incidental music
  J Bowman (c-t), Martyn Hill (t),
    E Allen (perc)
  Early Music Consort of London/
    Munrow   BBC: REC 91
The Hobbit—incidental music
  J Bowman (c-t), Martyn Hill (t),
    E Allen (perc), D Clift (tmpt)/
  Early Music Consort of London/
    Munrow   BBC: REC 91
The Jew of Malta—incidental music
  J Bowman (c-t), Martyn Hill (t), E
    Allen (perc), D Clift (tmpt)/
  Early Music Consort of London/
    Munrow   BBC: REC 91
Much Ado About Nothing—incidental music
  J Bowman (c-t), Martyn Hill (t),
    E Allen (perc), D Clift (tmpt)/
  Early Music Consort of London/
    Munrow   BBC: REC 91

CARDEW, Cornelius
The Great Learning (paragraphs 2 and
  7 *only*)   DGG: 2538 261*
Material [for harmony insts]
  L Brouwer (gtr)   DGG: Debut 2555 001*

CHAPPLE, Brian
Praeludiana
  A Wicks (org)   †DECCA:

COLE, Bruce
Autumn Cicada (ch, hp & handbells)
  Finchley Childrens' Music Group   †ARGO:

CONNOLLY, Justin
Cinquepaces
  Philip Jones Brass Ensemble
Poems of Wallace Stevens I
  J Manning (s)/Nash Ensemble/
    Connolly ⎫ ARGO: ZRG 747
Triad III
  Vesuvius Ensemble
Verse for Eight Solo Voices I and II
  John Alldis Choir ⎭

CROSSE, Gordon
Ahmet the Woodseller
  School Ch/perc & inst ens/Longstaff HMV: CLP 1893*; CSD 1616*
    reissued: XLP 40001

Ariadne—opera
  Royal Northern College of Music
    Soloists/LSO/Lancaster †ARGO:
Changes
  J Vyvyan/J Shirley-Quirk/LSO &
    Ch/del Mar ARGO: ZRG 656
Concerto da Camera
  M Parikian (vln)/Melos Ensemble/
    Downes HMV: ASD 2333*
    reissued ARGO: ZRG 759
Laetabundis
  Elizabethan Singers/Halsey ARGO: ZRG 5499
Meet My Folks!
  School Ch/perc & inst ens/Andrewes HMV: CLP 1893* m; CSD 1616*
    reissued XLP 4000

Purgatory—opera
  Royal Northern College of Music
    Soloists and orch/Lancaster †ARGO:

DALBY, Martin
The Earth Trembled
  Ch of our Lady of Grace & St
    Edward/Tamblyn APOLLO SOUND: AS 1003

DANKWORTH, John
(A very large number of jazz compositions and film scores are not listed)
Conway Suite: Lament and Wild Dance
    only
  J Dankworth Seven ESQUIRE: 5-010
Improvisations for Jazz Band and
    Symphony Orchestra (with
    M Seiber)
  Dankworth/Orchestra [ROULETTE: 52059 m; S-52059]

H 221

J Dankworth/LPO/Rignold	SAGA:	XIP 7006 m*;
	SOCIETY:	SOC 963*
	SAGA: 4123 [BOULEVARD: 4123]	

Lines to Ralph Hodgson Esqre
    C Laine/insts   FONTANA: STL 5483
Sweeney Agonistes (T S Eliot)—Globe
    Theatre 13/6/65, with music by
    Dankworth   HMV: CLP 1924 m
Tell Me the Truth About Love
    C Laine/insts   FONTANA: STL 5483
Wintertime Nights
    C Laine/insts   FONTANA: STL 5483
Zodiac Variations
    J Dankworth & his orch   FONTANA: TL 5229 m*

DAVIES, Peter Maxwell

Antechrist
    Fires of London/Davies   L'OISEAU LYRE: DSLO 2
    Pierrot Players/Davies   [MAINSTREAM: MS 5001;
                               car M 85001; cas M 5501]

Ave Maria
    Chichester Cathedral Choir/Birch   HMV: CSD 3588*; CLP 3588 m*
Ave Plena Gracia
    Elizabethan Singers/Halsey   ARGO: ZRG 5499; RG 499 m*
*Fantasia No 2 on John Taverner's 'In
    Nomine'*
    NPO/Groves   ARGO: ZRG 712
From Stone to Thorn
    M Thomas/Fires of London/Davies   L'OISEAU LYRE: DSLO 2
Hymnos
    A Hacker (cl)/S Pruslin (pf)   L'OISEAU LYRE: DSLO 2
Leopardi Fragments
    M Thomas (s)/R Phillips (a)
        Melos Ensemble/Carewe   HMV: ALP 2093 m*; ASD 640*
                          reissued: ARGO: ZRG 758
                          [ANGEL: 36387 m*; S36387]

[*Missa Super*] *L'Homme Armé*
    Fires of London/Davies   L'OISEAU LYRE: DSLO 2
Lullaby for Ilian Rainbow
    T Walker (gtr)   L'OISEAU LYRE: DSLO 3
O Magnum Mysterium
    Cirencester Sch Ch & Orch/Davies   ARGO: ZRG 5327; RG 327 m*
O Magnum Mysterium—organ fantasia
    S Preston (org)   ARGO: ZRG 5327; RG 327 m*
[*Five*] *Pieces for Piano* Op 2
    J Ogdon (pf)   HMV: ASD 645; ALP 2098 m*
Sonata for Trumpet and Piano
    G Schwarz (tmpt)/O Oppens (pf)   [NONESUCH: H 71275]

[Eight] *Songs for a Mad King*
    Fires of London/Davies   UNICORN: RHS 308
                                     [NONESUCH: H 71275]
Revelation and Fall
    M Thomas/Pierrot Players/Davies   HMV: ASD 2427 *
Taverner (opera)—Points and Dances *only*
    Fires of London/Davies   ARGO: ZRG 712
Turris Campanarum Sonantium (for
    percussion)
    Stomu Yamash'ta   L'OISEAU LYRE: DSLO 1
Vesalii Icones
    Fires of London/Davies   UNICORN: RHS 307
                                     [NONESUCH: H 71295]

DICKINSON, Peter
Winter Afternoons
    The King's Singers   EMI: EMD 5521
Extravaganzas   †ARGO:

DODGSON, Stephen
Concerto [No 1] for Guitar and
    Chamber Orchestra
    J Williams (gtr)/ECO/Groves   CBS: 72661 (Ger CBS: 77334)
                                              or in set M3X 31508
                               [AM COL·   MS 7063]
†Concerto No 2 for Guitar and
    Orchestra
    J Williams (gtr)/ECO/Groves   CBS:
Duo Concertante for Guitar and
    Harpsichord
    J Williams (gtr)/S Puyana (hpschd) CBS: 72948
                                     [AM COL: MS 31194]
Études for Guitar: Book 1 No 8 and
    Book 2 No 13 *only*
    Óscar Caceres (gtr)   ERATO: STU 70614
Fantasy Divisions
    J Williams (gtr)   CBS: 73205
Illuminare Jerusalem
    The King's Singers   HMV: HQS 1308
Partita for Guitar
    A Ponce (gtr)   ARION: 30S150
    J Williams (gtr)   CBS: SBRG 72348 (BRG 72348 m*)
                                   [AM COL: MS 6696]
[Four] *Poems of John Clare*
    W Brown (t)/J Williams (gtr)   CBS: 61126
                                   [ODYSSEY: 32160398]
Sonata for Brass
    Philip Jones Brass Ensemble   †ARGO:

String Trio No 2
  Esterhazy String Trio

MUSIC IN OUR TIME:
                    MIOTLP 2 m*

Suite for Brass Septet
  Philip Jones Brass Ensemble

ARGO: ZRG 655

Suite in D for Oboe and
    Harpsichord
  E Barbirolli (ob)/V Aveling
  (hpschd)

HMV: HQS 1298

DRUCE, Duncan
Sonata for Viola
  J Chambers (vla)

MUSIC IN OUR TIME:
         10″ MIOTLP 1 m*

FORBES, Sebastian
Gracious Spirit, Holy Ghost
  Glasgow University Chapel Ch/
    Garden

GEMINI: GM 2022

String Quartet No 1
  Allegri Quartet

ARGO: ZRG 672

GOEHR, Alexander
[Two] Choruses (1. *I had hope when
  violence was ceased*; 2. *Take but
  degree away*)
  G Shaw (bar)/John Alldis Choir/
  Alldis

HMV: ALP 2093 m*; ASD 640*
(reissued on ARGO: ZRG 758)
[ANGEL: S 36387]

Concerto for Violin and Orchestra
  M Parikian (vln)/RPO/del Mar

HMV: ASD 2810

Little Symphony Op 15
  LSO/del Mar

PHILIPS: SAL 3497

Piano Trio Op 20
  Orion Trio

ARGO: ZRG 748

[Three] *Pieces* Op 18
  J Ogdon (pf)

HMV: ASD 2551*
(reissued on   HQS 1337)

Sonata in One Movement
  J Ogdon (pf)

HMV: ALP 2098 m*; ASD 645

[Four] *Songs from the Japanese*
  M Nixon (s)/J McCabe (pf)

PYE: GGC 4105 m*; GSGC 14015
[NONESUCH: H 71209]

String Quartet No 2 Op 23
  Allegri Quartet

ARGO: ZRG 748

HARPER, Edward
Bartók Games

†[LOUISVILLE:]

HEADINGTON, Christopher
Toccata for Piano
  J Ogdon (pf)   HMV: ASD 2551*
                   (reissued on   HQS 1337)

HEDGES, Anthony
Ceremonies for Organ
  A Spedding (org)   RCA: VICS 1738*

HODDINOTT, Alun
Concerto for Clarinet and Orchestra
    Op 3
  G de Peyer (cl)/LSO/Atherton   DECCA: SXL 6513
Concerto for Harp and Orchestra Op 11
  O Ellis (hp)/LSO/Atherton   DECCA: SXL 6513
Concerto for Horn and Orchestra
  B Tuckwell (hn)/RPO/A Davis   DECCA: SXL 6606
Concerto for Piano and Orchestra No 2
  M Jones (pf)/RPO/A Davis   DECCA: SXL 6606
Divertimento for Oboe, Clarinet,
    Horn and Bassoon
  Nash Ensemble   †ARGO:
Elegy Op 18 No 3 (for piano)
  V Tryon (pf)   LYRITA: RCS 27 m
Music for Orchestra see *The Sun, the*
    Great Luminary of the Universe
Nocturnes (for piano) Op 9 *and*
    Op 16 No 1
  V Tryon (pf)   LYRITA: RCS 27 m
Piano Sonata No 1, Op 17
  V Tryon (pf)   LYRITA: RCS 27 m
Piano Sonata No 2, Op 27
  V Tryon (pf)   LYRITA: RCS 27 m
Piano Sonata No 6
  M Jones (pf)   ARGO: ZRG 761
Piano Trio
  Cardiff Festival Players   ARGO: ZRG 691
Rebecca (for choir)
  Seirol Singers/Hywell   HORIZON: HOR PR7 m
Roman Dream for soprano,
    percussion and piano
  M Price/J Lockhart/Cardiff
    Festival Players   ARGO: ZRG 691
Septet
  Nash Ensemble   †ARGO:
Sinfonietta No 3 Op 71
  LSO/Atherton   DECCA: SXL 6570
Sonata for Cello and Piano
  G Isaac (vlc)/V Tryon (pf)   ARGO: ZRG 695

Sonata for Clarinet and Piano Op 50
    G de Peyer (cl)/E Harrison (pf)   PYE: GSGC 14107
Sonata No 1 for Violin and Piano
    C Myerscough (vln)/M Jones (pf)   †ARGO:
Sonata No 3 for Violin and Piano
    J Barton (vln)/M Jones (pf)   ARGO: ZRG 761
String Quartet No 1, Op 43
    Cardiff University Quartet   PYE: GSGC 14107
The Sun, the Great Luminary of the
    Universe Op 76 [Music for
    Orchestra]
    LSO/Atherton   DECCA: SXL 6570
Symphony No 2, Op 29
    LSO/del Mar   PYE: TPLS 13013
Symphony No 3, Op 61
    LSO/Atherton   DECCA: SXL 6570
Symphony No 5, Op 81
    RPO/A Davis   DECCA: SXL 6606
Variants for Orchestra
    LSO/del Mar   PYE: TPLS 13013
Welsh Dances (for orchestra), Op 15
    RPO/Groves   HMV: ASD 2739
Welsh Dances—Suite No 2, Op 64
    National Youth Orch of Wales/
    Davison   MUSIC FOR PLEASURE:
                                           MFP 2129*

What Tidings—Carol, Op 38
    Elizabethan Singers/Halsey   ARGO: ZRG 5499

HURD, Michael
Canticles of the Virgin Mary
    Farnham Grammar Sch for Girls
    Ch & Inst/Morley
    (Farnham Festival 1965)   WAVERLEY: LLP 1039 m*

JOHNSON, Robert Sherlaw
In Carnatio   †ARGO: ZRG 722
Dum Medium Silentium
    Magdalen College Ch/Rose   ARGO: ZRG 694
Piano Sonata No 1
    R S Johnson (pf)   ARGO: ASD 2551
Piano Sonata No 2
    John Ogdon (pf)   HMV:
                      (reissued on   HQS 1337)
[Seven] *Short Pieces for Piano*
    R S Johnson (pf)   ARGO: ZRG 694
String Quartet No 2
    Allegri String Quartet   ARGO: ZRG 672

JONES, Tony Hewitt

At the Round Earth's Imagined Corners
    Exeter Cathedral Ch/Dakers   PILGRIM: JLP 154
Bring Unto the Lord O Ye Mighty—
    anthem
    RSCM Affiliated Choirs/organ
        (Royal Albert Hall 7/7/65)   ROYAL SCHOOL OF CHURCH
                            MUSIC: RRM 1m; RRS 1
A Christmas Round ('Gabriel's
    Message . . .')
Hereford Cathedral Choristers/Lloyd   ABBEY: F 648
Magnificat (for Magdalen College Oxford)
    Magdalen College Ch/A Read (tr)
    J Suter (org)/Rose   ARGO: ZRG 722

JOSEPHS, Wilfred

(Much 'mood music' and signature tunes have been omitted; a good example is 'The TV and Film Themes of Wilfred Josephs', POLYDOR 2383 294 (cas 3170 194))

Henry IV—incidental music
    Complete recording on 6s   CAEDMON: SRS M217
Samson Agonistes—incidental music
    Complete recording on 4s   CAEDMON: TC 2028

KELLY, Bryan

Cuban Suite
    LSSO/Pinkett   ARGO: ZRG 685
Evening Service—Magnificat *only*
    Chichester Cathedral Choir/
      R Seal (org)   BBC: BBC RG 16 m
    Choir of the Collegiate Church of
      St Mary, Warwick/R Scarth (org)/
      Holroyde   ABBEY: LPB 654
Washington DC—for brass band   GROSVENOR: GRS 1018
    Redbridge Youth Band/Ridgeon   (cas: GRSC 1018c)
When Christ Was Born of Mary Free
    Winchester Cathedral Choir/
      C McWilliam (org)/Neary   PHILIPS: 6833 112

LEIGHTON, Kenneth

Concerto for String Orchestra
    LPO/Snashall   PYE: TPLS 13005
Crucifixus Pro Nobis
    G English (t)/New College Choir/
      M Somerville (org)   ABBEY: ABY 702
An Easter Sequence
    D Carroll (tr)/New College Choir/
      B Wiggins (tmpt)/M Somerville
      (org)   ABY 702

Et Resurrexit, Op 49, for Organ
R Munns (org)   PYE: TPLS 13022
Give Me the Wings of Faith (Isaac Watts)
A Holst (bar)/Chichester Cathedral
Ch/R Seal (org)/Birch   HMV: CSD 3588; CLP 3588 m*
God's Grandeur
New College Choir   ABBEY: ABY 702
Let All the World (George Herbert)
Liverpool Cathedral Ch/
N Rawsthorne (org)/Woan   ABBEY: LPB 663
Worcester Cathedral Ch/
C Robinson (org)   ABBEY: 611 m
St James Parish Church Ch, Gt
Grimsby/T Allbright (org)/
Walker   ABBEY: LPB 669
Royal Sch of Church Music/
Martin How/Wrighton (Royal
Albert Hall 25 June 1970)   RSCM: RRS 4
Metamorphoses for Violin and Piano
J-L Garcia/P Wallfisch   GEMINI: GM 2014
Nocturne for Violin and Piano
J-L Garcia/P Wallfisch   GEMINI: GM 2014
Paean for Organ
Simon Preston (org)   ARGO: ZRG 528; RG 528 m*
M Somerville (org)   ABBEY: ABY 702
F Jackson (org)   POLYDOR: 2460 225
Prelude, Scherzo and Passacaglia, Op 41
D Townhill (org)   WAVERLEY: LLP 1033 m*;
      SLLP 1034*
M Cook (org)   RCA: LVL 15019

MATHIAS, William

Ave Rex (A carol sequence), Op 45
O Ellis (hp)/WNO Chorus/LSO/
Atherton   DECCA: SXL 6607
Concerto for Harp and Strings, Op 50
O Ellis (hp)/LSO/Atherton   DECCA: SXL 6607
Concerto No 3 for Piano and
Orchestra, Op 40
P Katin (pf)/LSO/Atherton   DECCA: SXL 6513
Dance Overture, Op 16
LSO/Atherton   DECCA: SXL 6607
Divertimento for String Orchestra, Op 7
ECO/Atherton   DECCA: SXL 6468
Divertimento for Flute, Oboe and Piano †ARGO:
Dy Holl Weithredoedd (chor and pf)
Cardiff Aelwyd Choir/D Hamley
(pf)/Guy   CAMBRIAN: CLP 589

[Festival] *Te Deum*, Op 28

Llandaff Cathedral Choir/ G Elliott/ Joyce	QUALITON:	QUAD 102 m; SQUAD 102
Seiriol Singers/D Hunt/Hywell	HORIZON:	HOR PR7
Guildford Cathedral Choir/ G Williams/Rose	GUILD:	GRS 7005

[Three] *Improvisations* for Harp

O Ellis (hp)	L'OISEAU LYRE: SOL 308 [S-308]

Invocation and Dance, Op 17

LSO/Atherton	DECCA:	SXL 6607

Invocations for Organ

N Rawsthorne (org)	RYEMUSE:	ALR 1204 m*; SALR 1204*
	reissued on DECCA:	
	SDD 236 [LONDON: STS 15100]	

Make A Joyful Noise, Op 26 No 2

Liverpool Cathedral Choir	ABBEY:	LPB 663

O Salutarius Hostia, Op 48

Rhos Male Voice Choir	POLYDOR:	2460 182

Partita for Organ

N Rawsthorne (org)	RYEMUSE:	ALR 1204 m*; SALR 1204
C Robinson (org)	HMV:	CLP 3646 m*; CSD 3646

Prelude, Aria and Finale

ECO/Atherton	DECCA:	SXL 6468

Processional

C Herrick (org)	VISTA:	VPS 1001

Sinfonietta

LSSO/Mathias	PYE:	GSGC 14103; GGC 4103 m

Sonata for Violin and Piano

	†ARGO:

String Quartet

	†ARGO:

Symphony No 1, Op 31

RPO/Groves	PYE:	TPLS 13023

Toccata Giocosa, Op 30 No 2

N Rawsthorne (org)	STUDIO TWO:	TWO 338

Variations on a Hymn Tune

R Joyce (org)	HMV:	CLP 3526 m*; CSD 3526*

Wassail Carol, Op 26 No 1

Elizabethan Singers/Halsey	ARGO:	ZRG 5499
Choir Of King's College, Cambridge/ Willcocks	ARGO:	ZRG 5450

Wind Quintet

	†ARGO:

MAW, Nicholas

Bulalow

Elizabethan Singers/Halsey	ARGO:	ZRG 565

Chamber Music for Oboe, Clarinet, Horn, Bassoon and Piano

Music Group of London	ARGO:	ZRG 536

Scenes and Arias
J Manning (s)/A Howells (s)/
   N Procter (c)/BBCSO/del Mar   ARGO: ZRG 622
Sinfonia
ECO/del Mar   ARGO: ZRG 676
Sonata for Strings and Two Horns
A Civil (hn)/Harper (hn)/del Mar   ARGO: ZRG 676
String Quartet
Aeolian String Quartet   ARGO: RG 565 m*; ZRG 565

McCABE, John

[Five] Bagatelles
  J McCabe (pf)   PYE: GSGC 14116
Canto for Guitar
  S Behrend (gtr)   DGG: 2530 079
Coventry Carol
  Elizabethan Singers/S Preston (org)/
    Halsey   ARGO: ZRG 5499; RG 499 m*
  Leeds Parish Church Ch/Paul
    Dutton (tr)/A Langford (org)/
    Hunt   ABBEY: XMS 697
Dies Resurrectionis
  M Cook (org)   RCA: LVLII 5019
Elegy
  E Higginbottom (org)   DECCA: ECS 626
Fear in the Night—music from the film
  Hammer City Orch/Martell   EMI: TWO A 5001
[Mini-] Concerto for 485 Penny
    Whistles, Percussion and Organ
  Audience/J Blades (perc)/G Weir
    (org)/Willcocks   ABBEY: APR 606 (m or s)
    (RCO Centenary Appeal Concert
    RAH 26 Sept 1966)
Notturni ed Alba
  J Gomez (s)/Birmingham SO/
    Frémaux   HMV: ASD 2904
Rounds for Brass Quintet
  Hallé Brass Consort   PYE: GSGC 14114
String Trio Op 37
  Cardiff Festival Ens   ARGO: ZRG 761
Symphony [No 1] 'Elegy'
  LPO/Snashall   PYE: TPLS 13005
Symphony No 2
  Birmingham SO/Frémaux   HMV: ASD 2904

MILNER, Anthony
Roman Spring
  F Palmer (s), R Tear (t), London
    Sinfonietta Chorus/London
    Sinfonietta/Atherton   DECCA: SXL 6699
Salutatio Angelica
  A Hodgson (c), London
    Sinfonietta Chorus/London
    Sinfonietta/Atherton   DECCA: SXL 6699

MUSGRAVE, Thea
Colloquy
  M Parikian (vln)/L Crowson (pf)   ARGO: ZRG 5328
Concerto for Clarinet and Orchestra
  G de Peyer (clar)/LSO/del Mar   †ARGO:
Concerto for Horn and Orchestra
  B Tuckwell (hrn)/Scottish NO/
    Musgrave   DECCA: Head 8
Concerto for Orchestra
  Scottish NO/Gibson   DECCA: Head 8
Excursions
  T Musgrave (pf)   ARGO: ZRG 704
Monologue
  T Musgrave (pf)   ARGO: ZRG 704
†*Music for Horn and Piano*
Night Music
  London Sinfonietta/Prausnitz   ARGO: ZRG 702
†*Primavera* for Soprano and Flute
Soliloquy I for Guitar and Pre-recorded
    Tape
  S Behrend (gtr)   DGG: 24530 079 (Ger: DG2530 079)
Trio for Flute, Oboe and Piano
  Mabillon Trio   DELTA: DEL 12005 m*
                                          SDEL 18005*
Triptych for Tenor and Orchestra
  D Robertson (t)/Scottish NO/
    Gibson   HMV: ASD 2279*

OGDON, John
Sonata for Piano
  J Ogdon (pf)   HMV: *in set* SLS 868 [5 rcds]
Concerto for Piano and Orchestra No 1
  J Ogdon (pf)/RPO/Foster   HMV: ASD 2709
                          [ANGEL: S 36805]
Theme and Variations
  J Ogdon (pf)   HMV: ASD 2322*

OLDHAM, Arthur
[Three] *Chinese Lyrics* (from a set of 5)
   (1. *The Herd Boy's Song*, 2. *Fishing*,
   3. *Pedlar of Spells*)
  P Pears (t)/B Britten (pf)   DECCA: 10″   LW 5241 m*
                          reissued on DECCA: ECS 545
—— 2. *Fishing*, 1. *The Herd Boy's Song*
  S Woolf (tr)/S Bedford (pf)   UNICORN: RHS 316
Hymns for the Amusement of Children
  E McLoughlin (s)/Choir/
    Kynaston (org)   WAVERLEY: LLP 1011; SLLP 1012
Laudes Creaturarum
  E McLoughlin (s)/Choir/Telfer (org)/
    Scottish NO/Oldham   WAVERLEY: LLP 1011; SLLP 1012

ORTON, Richard
Clock Farm
  York Electronic Music Studio   UNIVERSITY OF YORK:
                                        YES 2-4
Concert Music 5
  Studio Realisation by R Orton from Published on OUP 109 (an EP with
    original tape by members of the   *Approach to Music*, Book 3)
    Gentle Fire.
Cycle for Two or Four Players
  M Welsh (vlc)/R Orton (pf)   [MAINSTREAM: MS 5001;
                             car M 85001; cas M 55001]
Four Fragments of Gerald Manley Hopkins
  M White (s)/R Smalley (pf)   MUSIC IN OUR TIME: 10″
                                  MIOT LP 1 m*
Kiss for the Time Being
  York Electronic Music Studio   UNIVERSITY OF YORK:
                                        YES 2-4
Sawlo Seed—Alchemusic for Voices   YORKSHIRE ARTS
                                  ASSOCIATION: YAA 2

PATTERSON, Paul
Time Piece
  The King's Singers   EMI: EMD 5521

PERT, Morris
(Only recorded in 'pop' works with 'Suntreader'—Peter Robinson (electronic
pfs), Alyn Ross (bass), Morris Pert (perc))
From the Region of Capricorn
  (with orchestra)
Stardance
Ormoio   ISLAND: HELP 13
  (with Robin Thompson (sax))
Zin Zin

RIDOUT, Alan
Concertante Music for Orchestra
 LSSO/Ridout   PYE: GSGC 14103; GGC 4103 m*
Diversions for Two Organs and
 Percussion (excerpt)
 J Birch (org)/Peter Hurford ABBEY: LPB 665
Hymn of the Nativity (Crashaw)
 Canterbury Cathedral Ch/Wicks ABBEY: XMS 670
Let Us With A Gladsome Mind
 Canterbury Cathedral Ch/P Moore
  (org)/Wicks   ABBEY: 640 (m or s)
Modern Canticles for Congregational Singing
 (Venite-Magnificat-Nunc
 Dimittis-Te Deum-Benedictus)
 Canterbury Choral Soc/P Moore
  (org)/Wicks   ABBEY: FE 644
Nativity Processional
 Boys of Canterbury Cathedral Ch/
  W Ward (perc)/Wicks   ABBEY: XMS 670
L'Orgue Concrète
 A Wicks (org)/J Blades (perc) ABBEY: APR 606 (m or s)
 (RCO Centenary Appeal Concert,
 RAH, 24 Sept 1966)
Sacred Songs for Treble Voices
 Guildford Cathedral Ch/Organ/Rose GUILD: GRM 302 m; GRS 307
—— 2nd set
 Canterbury Cathedral Choir/
  P Moore (org)/Wicks   ABBEY: 640 (m or s)
—— 3rd set
 Guildford Cathedral Choir/
  Organ/Rose   GUILD: GRS 7005
Seven Last Words
 A Wicks (org)   HMV: CSD 3657; CLP 3657 m*
Virtue
 Boys of Canterbury Cathedral
  Choir/Wicks   ABBEY: FE 650

ROBERTS, Jeremy Dale
Capriccio for Violin and Piano
 F Mason (vln)/R Smalley (pf) MUSIC IN OUR TIME: 10″
              MIOTLP 3*

ROUTH, Francis
Sonatina for Organ
 F Routh (org)   ORYX: ORYX 735 m*

SMALLEY, Roger
Piano Pieces 1–5
 R Smalley (pf)   MUSIC IN OUR TIME: 10″
              MIOTLP 3*

STANDFORD, Patric
Autumn Grass—a jazz suite
 Continuum (inst)/with inst acc RCA: SF 8196
Epigrams for Chamber Orchestra
 New Cantata Orch of London/
  Stobart   SOUND NEWS PRODUCTIONS:
                    LP 1*

STEEL, Christopher
Bacchae of Euripides—incidental music
 Orchestra and Ch of Bradfield Coll/
  C Steel   DISCOURSES: DCL 1218

STEPHENSON, Robin
The Four Seasons
 Ealing Grammar School Ch/perc
  & pfs/John Railton   HMV: EP   7EG 8917

STEVENSON, Ronald[1]
Passacaglia DSCH
 R Stevenson (pf)   UNIVERSITY OF CAPE TOWN:
              (private limited issue)
              HMV: ASD 2321/2*

STOKER, Richard
†*Improvisation* for Guitar

TAVENER, John
Celtic Requiem
 Barton/M Lensky/Tavener/London
  Sinfonietta/Atherton APPLE: SAPCOR 20
Coplas
 M Lensky (m-s)/London
  Sinfonietta/Atherton APPLE: SAPCOR 20
Nomine Jesu
 London Sinfonietta Ch and Orch/
  Atherton   APPLE: SAPCOR 20
The Whale
 Reynolds/Herincx/Liddel/Tavener/
  London Sinfonietta & Ch/
   Atherton   APPLE: SAPCOR 15
            [APPLE: SMAS 3369]

WHELEN, Christopher
Rose Tattoo
 Queen's Hall Light Orch/Farnon CHAPPELL: C 732; LPC 729-734

[1] See also entry 281 in Bibliography.

WHETTAM, Graham
Cruel Sea
  Celebrity Symphony Orch   [HUDSON: DW2525]*
Concertino for Oboe and Strings Op 12
  C Coppens (ob)/Symphonic String
    Ens/H de Groot   [HUDSON: DW2732]*
Concerto Scherzoso for Harmonica and
    Orchestra Op 9
  J Van Viren (harmonica)/
    Symphonic String Ens/H de Groot [HUDSON: DW2732]*
Harmonic Impromptu
  Larrysons Harmonica Ensemble   [HUDSON: DW2656]*
Interlude Cantabile
  Celebrity Symphonic Ensemble   [HUDSON: DW505]*
Mood Bridges Nos 1–8
  Hudson Orchestra/H Granville   [HUDSON: DW2714]*
Nostalgic Occasion
  Hilversum Radio Orch/A Burem   [HUDSON: DW2620]*

WHITE, John
†Air for Brass
  London Gabrieli Brass Ensemble
Piano Sonatas Nos 1, 4, 5 and 9
  C Kingsley (pf)   LYRITA: RCS 18*
                                         [MUSICAL HERITAGE
                                                     SOCIETY: 7004]

Piano Sonata No 15
  I Lake (pf)   MUSIC IN OUR TIME: 10"
                                                         MIOTLP 1*

WILSON, Thomas
†The Wesling Day

WOOD, Hugh
The Horses, Op 10 [three settings of
    poems by Ted Hughes]
  A Cantelo (s)/P Hamburger (pf)   ARGO: ZRG 750
[Three] *Pieces* Op 5
  Susan McGraw (pf)   HMV: ASD 2333
                                         reissued on ARGO: ZRG 759

The Rider Victory, Op 11 [four settings
    of poems by Edwin Muir]
  April Cantelo (s)/P Hamburger (pf) ARGO: ZRG 750
String Quartet No 1 Op 4
  Aeolian String Quartet   ARGO: ZRG 565; RG 565 m*
  Dartington String Quartet   ARGO: ZRG 750
  (H Wood talks about the work
    with extracts played by the
    Aeolian String Quartet)   ARGO: EP   EAF 194*

235

String Quartet No 2 Op 13
    Dartington String Quartet   ARGO: ZRG 750

WOOLFENDEN, Guy
Dr Faustus—incidental music
    Royal Shakespeare Wind Band/
    Organ/Woolfenden   ABBEY: LPB 657
King Lear—incidental music (1968
    RSC production)
    Royal Shakespeare Wind Band/
    Woolfenden   ABBEY: LPB 657
Much Ado About Nothing—incidental
    music (1968 RSC production)
    Royal Shakespeare Wind Band/
    Woolfenden   ABBEY: LPB 657
The Revenger's Tragedy—incidental music
    Royal Shakespeare Wind Band/
    Woolfenden   ABBEY: LPB 657
Romeo and Juliet—incidental music
    (1967 RSC production)
    Royal Shakespeare Wind Band/
    Woolfenden   ABBEY: LPB 657
The Taming of the Shrew—incidental
    music
    Royal Shakespeare Wind Band/
    Woolfenden   ABBEY: LPB 657
The Winter's Tale—incidental music
    D Smith (bar)/D Motihar (sitar)/
    Royal Shakespeare Wind Band/
    Woolfenden   GROSVENOR: 7″   GR 1000
Work is a Four Letter Word—music
    from the film
    C Black (voc)/Orch/J Spence   PARLOPHONE: R 5706

Addenda

BEDFORD: *Spillihpnerak*
    K Phillips (vla)   [FINNEDAR: SR 9007]

BENNETT: *Balalow* Leeds Parish
    Church Choir/Hunt   ABBEY: XMS 727
Lute Book Lullaby Lichfield Cathedral
    Choir/Greeny   ABBEY: XMS 698
Madrigal Oxford University Schola
    Cantorum/Byrt   [RCA: LM 7043 m; LSC 7043]

BLAKE: *The Almanack* (Hatfield)
M Beverly (s); A Tilley (a);
R Orton (t); H Herford (b); York
University Chamber Choir   YORKSHIRE ARTS
                            ASSOCIATION: YAA 2

CROSSE: *Some Marches as a Ground* Op 28
Louisville Orchestra/Mester [LOUISVILLE: S 741]

DANKWORTH: *Tom Sawyer's*
Saturday R Baker (nar)/Academy
of the BBC/E Heath   HMV: CSD 3763

KELLY: *Divertimento*—March *only*
Grimethorpe Colliery Band/Howarth GROSVENOR: GRS 1022
                                   (cas GRSC 1022C)

Prelude and Fugue R Munns (org)   WEALDEN: WS 111

LEIGHTON: *Benedictus* Exeter
Cathedral Choir   EXON: EAS 5
Sanctus Exeter Cathedral Choir   EXON: EAS 5

MAW: *Our Lady's Song* Elizabethan
Singers/Halsey   ARGO: RG 446 m*; ZRG 446
(String Quartet) (Nicholas Maw talks
about the work with extracts played
by the Aeolian String Quartet)   ARGO: EP   EAF 134*

McCABE: Fanfare *Cymru* 1969 Cardiff
Searchlight Tattoo Massed Bands   HMV: CSD 3662*

MILNER: *Out of Your Sleep*
Elizabethan Singers/Halsey   ARGO: RG 446 m*; ZRG 446
The Song of Akhenaten (Heigall)
P Lloyd (s)/New Cantata Orch/
Stobart   SOUND NEWS   529/30*

OLDHAM: *Alleluia* King's College
Choir/Willcocks   HMV: ALP 2290 m*; ASD 2290
Experience does me so Surprise (Dunbar)
Scottish Festival Chorus/Oldham   HMV: CLP 2598 m*; CSD 3598*
Remember, O Moon Elizabethan
Singers/Halsey   ARGO: RG 399 m*; ZRG 5399
Variations on Sellenger's Round
(Variation 2: *Allegro con brio*)
Aldeburgh Festival Orchestra/
B Britten (Aldeburgh Festival 1953) DECCA: LXT 2798 m*
                                     [LONDON: LL 808 m*]

PATTERSON: *Jubilate* for Organ
Paul Morgan (org)   EXON: EXCATH 1
Lo He Comes With Clouds Descending
(descant by Paul Patterson) Exeter
Cathedral Choir/L Dakers   EXON: EAS 13

RIDOUT: *Scherzo* R Weddle (org)   VISTA: VPS 1021

WILSON: *Sinfonietta* City of
London Brass/Brand   RCA: LFL 15072

237

Index

The main text and the names of composers who are the subject of the section 'Other Composers' have been indexed exhaustively. The 'Select Bibliography' has been indexed very selectively (in the main only annotations and occasional items in which one composer has written on another). The 'Sources of the Music' and the 'Discography' have not been indexed at all. References to films have been made under title.

Aberystwyth University, 189
Academy of St Martin in the Fields, 106
Accademia Chigi, Siena, 196
Accademia di Santa Cecilia, Rome, 28, 32
Addison, John, 200
Aldeburgh Festival, 25, 28, 39, 116
Aleatoric processes, 138
Alexander Nevsky, 70
Alicante: Premio Oscar Esola, 196
Alwyn, William, 195
AMM Free Improvisation Group, 183
Amplified piano, 137
Amsterdam Conservatoire, 187
Apollo Contemporary Music, 187
Arden of Faversham, 46
Arnold, Malcolm, 11
Arpeggi-glissandi, 34
Aspen Fund Award, 196
Attaignant, Pierre, 73
Auden W. H., 99, 176

Bach, J. S., 33, 51, 62, 81, 90; Mass in B minor, 160
Badings, Henk, 194
Bagpipes, 38
Bangor University, 187
Banks, Don, 11, 200
Barenboim, Daniel, 49, 51
Barlow, David, 182; *David and Bathsheba*, 16; *The Selfish Giant*, 17
Barraqué, Jean, 189
Bartók, Béla, 20, 21, 27, 56, 73, 92, 146, 164
Basle Music Academy, 187
Bath Festival, 104
Bax, Sir Arnold, 37
BBC, 58, 59, 62, 100, 178, 185, 186, 187, 196, 197; Composers Competition, 191; 'Monarchy 1000 Competition', 182, 185; Northern Symphony Orchestra, 59; Symphony Orchestra, 56, 57, 190
Beatles, The, 108
Bedford, David, 11, 133ff; *An Exciting New Game for Children of All Ages*, 139; *Come in Here Child*, 137, 139; *A Dream of Seven Lost Stars*, 138, 140; *18 Bricks Left on April 21*, 140; *The Garden of Love*, 138; *Gastrula*, 140; *Its Easier Than It*

Looks, 139; *Music for Albion Moonlight*, 137, 140, 141; *Piano Piece 1*, 137; *Piano Piece 2*, 137, 139; *Piece for Mo*, 17, 136, 140; *Some Bright Stars for Queens College*, 139; *Some Stars Above Magnitude 2.9*, 134, 136; *Star Clusters, Nebulae and Places in Devon*, 15, 134ff; *Stars End*, 133, 140; *The Sword of Orion*, 140; *The Tentacles of the Dark Nebula*, 141, 142ff; *That White and Radiant Legend*, 134; *Two Poems for Chorus*, 143; *Variations on a Rhythm of Mike Oldfield*, 139; *Whitefield Music 1* and *2*, 139; *Wide, Wide in the Roses Side*, 139; *With 100 Kazoos*, 139; *You Asked for It*, 140
Beethoven, Ludwig van, 17, 25, 53, 57; 32 Variations in C minor, 57
Belfast: Queen's University, 197
Benjamin, Arthur, 86
Bennett, Richard Rodney, 13, 14, 16, 108ff, 192, 193, 196, 199; *All the Kings Men*, 111, 119; *The Approaches of Sleep*, 14; *Aubade*, 110; *The Aviary*, 119; *The Bermudas*, 119; *Commedia I–IV*, 110; *Elegy for Caroline Lamb*, 116; *Epithalamium*, 109; Horn Concerto, 109; *The Insect World*, 119; *Jazz Calendar*, 117; *Jazz Pastoral*, 117, 118; *The Ledge*, 111; *London Pastoral*, 14; *Mines of Sulphur*, 16, 111; *Nocturnall Upon St Lucies Day*, 110; Nocturnes, 110; Oboe Concerto, 109; *A Penny for A Song*, 111; Piano Concerto, 109, 110; *Soliloquy*, 117, 118; String Quartet No. 2, 109; String Quartet No. 3, 109; Symphony No. 1, 111; Symphony No. 2, 111; *Suite for Small Orchestra*, 119; *Suite Français*, 110; *Victory*, 110, 111; Viola Concerto, 109, 198; *A Week of Birthdays*, 119
Berg, Alban, 33, 55, 61, 110, 165; *Lulu*, 99; *Lyric Suite*, 57; *Wozzeck*, 99
Berio, Luciano, 188, 192, 194, 196
Berkeley, Sir Lennox, 91, 99, 108, 119, 133, 155, 185, 187, 196, 197
Berlin, 116; Hochschule für Musik, 183
Berlioz, Hector: *Harold in Italy*, 116
Billion Dollar Brain, 113
Birmingham: Midland Institute, 197; School of Music, 187, 193; University, 28

238

Birtwistle, Harrison, 11, 17, 41, 60ff, 71, 120, 185; *Cantata*, 69; *Chorales*, 70; *The Cruel Mother*, 69; *Down by the Greenwoodside*, 67, 69; *Entr'actes and Sappho Fragments*, 63; *Four Interludes from a Tragedy*, 62; *Grimethorpe Aria*, 69; *Interludes*, 63; *Medusa*, 62, 65; *Monodrama*, 63, 68; *Monody for Corpus Christi*, 65; *Narration —The Description of the Passing of the Year*, 69; *Nenia on the Death of Orpheus*, 66; *Orpheus*, 60, 69; *Punch and Judy*, 61, 62, 67, 68, 69; *Refrains and Choruses*, 64; *Ring A Dumb Carillon*, 66, 67; *A Song Book for Instruments*, 63; *Tragoedia*, 61, 67; *The Triumph of Time*, 69, 70; *Verses for Ensembles*, 64; *The World is Discovered*, 62
Blacher, Boris, 183
Blackburn (Lancs), 32
Blackheath Conservatoire of Music, 192
Blades, James, 193
Blake, David, 18, 33, 38, 120ff, 202; *The Almanack*, 125; *Beata l'Alma*, 124; *The Bones of Chuang Tzu*, 129; Chamber Symphony, 120, 123, 124; *Four Songs of Ben Jonson*, 123; *In Praise of Krishna*, 130; *It's a Small War*, 122; *Lumina*, 15, 120, 125ff; *Metamorphoses*, 128; *Nonet*, 128; *On Christmas Day*, 123; *Scenes* for solo cello, 129; String Quartet, No. 1, 122, 124; String Quartet, No. 2, 130; *Three Choruses to Poems by Robert Frost*, 123; *Toussaint l'Ouverture*, 131; *Variations* for piano, 121; Violin Concerto, 132; *What is the Cause*, 125
Blitheman, William, 167
Blues, 117
Blyton, Carey, 182
Bold, Alan, 38
The Bold Grenadier', 114
Bolt, Robert, 115
Boulanger, Nadia, 20, 99, 182, 189, 191, 197
Boulez, Pierre, 20, 41, 109, 166, 194; *Le Marteau Sans Maître*, 100
Bourgeois, Derek, 182; *Rumpelstiltskin*, 17
Bournemouth Symphony Orchestra, 197
Bradbury, Ray: *Leviathan*, 99
Bradfield College, 196
Brecht, Bertold, 47, 121
Brian, Havergal, 40
Brighton Festival, 47, 48
Bristol University, 182, 197
British Council, 192
Britten, Benjamin, 14, 28, 29, 92, 145, 146, 164, 176, 182; *Billy Budd*, 99; *Curlew River*, 16; *Nocturne*, 14; *Peter Grimes*, 99; *The Turn of the Screw*, 29; *Winter Words*, 103
Brosa, Antonia, 186
Brouwer, Leo, 13

Brown, George MacKay, 85
Bruckner, Anton: *Mass* in E minor, 147
Bryanston Summer School, 53; *see also* Dartington
Bryars, Gavin, 184
Buller, John, 18
Burgon, Geoffrey, 182
Burt, Francis, 16, 183
Bush, Alan, 188, 192, 193
'Bushes and Briars', 114
Busoni, Ferruccio, 33, 40, 121; Prize, 148
Butterworth, Arthur, 200
Byrd, William, 73, 74

Cage, John, 155
Caird Scholarship, 191, 194
Cambridge New Music Ensemble, 195
Cambridge University, 120, 182, 188, 195, 197; Christ's College, 198; King's College, 186, 187, 196, 197, 198; St Catherine's College, 195; St John's College, 7, 193, 195; Trinity College, 104, 187
Camden Festival, 182
Cannon, Philip, 183, 200, 203; *Morvoren*, 16; String Quartet, 18
Canterbury Tales, The (musical), 198
Canterbury Cathedral, 183; Choir, 194
Cape Town University, 35, 234
Cardew, Cornelius, 13, 97, 183, 184, 199, 200
Carhart, David, 185
Carl Meyer Award, 196
Carols of Today, 123
Cartoons, music for, 171
Cary, Tristram, 171ff; *Birth is Life is Power is Death is God*, 172; *January Piece*, 171; *Music for Light*, 172; *Narcissus*, 172; *Peccata Mundi*, 172; *3, 4, 5, 172*; *Winter Song*, 172
Central Tutorial School for Young Musicians, 191
Chant, Michael, 184
Chapple, Brian, 185
Cheltenham Festival, 27, 106, 183, 185
Cheskoo Karee Show, 185
Children, music for, 17, 23, 28, 76, 119, 192, 200
Christmas Carol, A, 171
Churchill Fellowship, 192
Cirencester Grammar School, 7, 73, 75, 76, 77
City of Birmingham Symphony Orchestra, 197
City of London Festival, 48
Clarke, Jeremiah, 73
Clarke, Arthur C., *The Other Side of the Sky*, 142
Clements Memorial Prize, 164, 196
Cleverdon, Douglas, 171
Coates, Albert, *Pickwick*, 16

Cobbett Prize, 191
Cockpit Theatre, 17
Cole, Ruce, 185
Cole, Hugo, 200
Collingwood, Lawrence, *Macbeth*, 16
Cologne Electronic Music Studios, 183
Come to the Edge, *see* Suntreader
Composers' Ensemble, 198
Composers Guild, 189
Connolly, Justin, 162ff, 166, 169, 173, 203, 206; *Cinquepaces*, 162, 170; *Obbliganti I*, 162; *Poems of Wallace Stevens*, 163; *Prose*, 163; *Tesserae*, 163; *Triad I*, 162; *Triad III*, 163; *Triad IV*, 164; *Verse*, 163
Cookham Festival, 191
Copland, Aaron, 77
Corder Memorial Prize, 188
Countess of Munster Award, 191
Covent Garden, 84, 159
Coward, Sir Noël, 108, 116, 117
Cowie, Edward, 185, 202
Cramb Research Fellowship, 53, 185, 192
Cranborne Chase School, 62
Cranleigh School, 182
Cross, Beverly, 105, 111, 112
Crosse, Gordon, 16, 19ff, 27ff, 202; *Ahmet the Woodseller*, 28; *Ariadne*, 31; *Changes*, 14, 28; *Concerto da Camera*, 28; *Concertante*, 27; *Corpus Christi Carol*, 27; *The Demon of Adachigahara*, 28; *For the Unfallen*, 29; *The Grace of Tod*, 29; *Meet My Folks*, 28; *Memories of Morning-Night*, 30; *Purgatagory*, 29; *Some Marches on a Ground*, 29; *The Story of Vasco*, 27, 29; *Violin Concerto No. 2*, 28, 30
Cruft, Adrian, 200
Cuckston, Alan, 38

Dalby, Martin, 185, 188
Dallapiccola, Luigi, 11, 20, 146, 179, 194
Dameron, Tadd, 116
Dankworth, John, 186
Darmstadt, 20, 168, 196
Dartington Hall, 53, 183, 189, 191
Davidson, John, 35, 38, 40
Davies, Hugh, 193
Davies, Peter Maxwell, 7, 11, 12, 17, 27, 41, 48, 61, 62, 71ff, 97, 120, 165, 167, 173, 199, 200; *Alma Remptoris Mater*, 72; *The Boyfriend*, 85; *The Devils*, 85; *Eight Songs for a Mad King*, 84; *First Fantasia on Taverner's 'In Nomine'*, 77; *Five Canons*, 73; *Five Klee Pictures*, 74; *Five Motets*, 77; *Five Pieces for Piano*, 71; *Frammenti di Leopardi*, 42, 75; *From Stone to Thorn*, 85; *Hymn to St Magnus*, 85; *Missa Super L'Homme Armé*, 84; *Miss Donnithorne's Maggott*, 84; *O Magnum Mysterium*, 74; *Prolation*, 72; *Resurrection*, 84; *Revelation and Fall*, 84; *Ricercar and Doubles*, 74; *St Michael*, 72, 77; *Second Fantasia on John Taverner's 'In Nomine'*, 75; *Sinfonia*, 75; *Sonata for Trumpet and Piano*, 71; *Stone Litany—Runes for a House of the Dead*, 85; *String Quartet*, 75; *Taverner*, 71, 77, 79; *Vesalii Icones*, 84
Dean Close Junior School, 189
Debussy, Claude, 51, 177
Delius, Frederick, 36, 118, 130
Demuth, Norman, 184
Dennis, Brian, 184, 198
Deutsch, Max, 190
Dickinson, Meriel, 186
Dickinson, Peter, 186, 208, 210
Dr Who, 171
Dodgson, Stephen, 186, 200
Dorow, Dorothy, 17
Dorward, David, 186; *Tonight Mrs Morrison*, 17
Dowland, John, 74
Drew, David, 178
Druce, Duncan, 186
DSCH, 33, 35
Du Pré, Jacqueline, 48
Dunstable, John, 72, 74
Durham University, 169, 190

East of the Sun and West of the Moon, 171
Edinburgh: Festival, 182; St Mary's Cathedral, 193; University, 20, 147, 188, 193
Eisenstein, Sergei Mikhailovich, 42
Eisler, Hans, 121, 122, 124; *Chamber Symphony*, 124; *Einheitsfrontlied*, 121; *Lob des Kommunismus*, 121; *Palmström*, 121
Electric Candle, The, 7
Electronic Music, 65, 168, 171, 190, 192, 193, 197
Elgar, Sir Edward, 57
Elguera, Amalia, 25
Eliot, T. S., 36; *The Rock*, 148
Ellis, David, 18, 177ff; *Elegy*, 177; *Piano Sonata*, 177; *Symphony*, 177; *Violin Concerto*, 177
English Chamber Choir, 8
English Chamber Orchestra, 49, 106
English National Opera, 131
English Sinfonia, 193
Experimental Music Catalogue, 184
Expo '67, 172

Far From the Madding Crowd, 113
Fellowes, E. H., *Tudor Church Music*, 78
Ferguson, Howard, 108, 183
Ferneyhough, Brian, 187
Figures in a Landscape, 113
Film, 108, 109, 112, 113, 171
Finissy, Michael, 187
Finzi, Gerald, 173

Fires of London, 18, 62, 84, 187; *see also* Pierrot Players
Florida International Festival, 191
Folksong, 38, 113
Forbes, Sebastian, 187
Free-tempo notation, 26
Fricker, Peter Racine, 184, 185, 192, 194
Fried, Erich, 46
Furneaux, Mark, 185

Gabrieli, Giovanni, 45, 73; *Canzon Noni Toni*, 77
Gál, Hans, 20, 194
Garioch, Robert, 38
Garvald School, 36
Genet, Jean: *Notre Dame des Fleurs*, 159, 160
Gentle Fire, The, 193
Gerhard, Roberto, 56, 57
Gersh, Stephen, 188
Gershwin, George, 108, 116
Gibbons, Orlando, 74; *The Cries of London*, 47
Gilbert, Anthony, 188
Glasgow: Educational Trust, 194; University, 192, 198
Glyndebourne, 104
Godowsky, Leopold, 33
Goehr, Alexander, 44ff, 61, 71, 120, 185, 188, 196, 200; *Arden Must Die*, 46; *Capriccio*, Op. 6, 41; *Chaconne*, 52; *Concerto for Eleven*, 51; *The Deluge*, 17, 42; *Fantasias*, Op. 3, 41; *Four Songs from the Japanese*, 42; *Hecuba's Lament*, 42; *Konzertstück*, Op. 26, 49, 51; *Little Music for Strings*, 45; *Little Symphony*, Op. 15, 44, 50; *Lyric Pieces*, 52; *Metamorphosis/Dance*, 52; *Naboth's Vineyard*, 47, 48; *Nonomiya*, 48; Piano Concerto, 49, 51; *Piano Sonata*, Op. 2, 41; *Piano Trio*, 45; *Romanza*, 48, 49, 51; *Shadowplay-2*, 48; *Sonata About Jerusalem*, 48; String Quartet No. 2, 17, 45; *Suite*, Op. 11, 43; *Sutter's Gold*, 15, 42; *Symphony in One Movement*, Op. 29, 50; *Three Pieces for Piano*, 44; *Three Pieces from Arden*, 43; *Two Choruses*, Op. 14, 43; *Variations for flute and piano*, 42; Violin Concerto, 43, 49
Goehr, Walter, 41, 44
Goldsmith's College, 186, 195
Goossens, Eugene, 16
Gow, Neil: *Repository*, 38
Grainger, Percy, 36
Granada Fellowship in Creative Arts, 122, 184
Green, Gordon, 192
Grimethorpe Colliery Band, 190
Gruenberg, Erich, 102
Guildhall School of Music, 182, 190, 196, 198

Guitar, electric, 140
Gulbenkian Dance Award, 191
Gurney, Ivor, 15
Guy, Barry, 18

Hacker, Alan, 18, 61
Hadley, Patrick, 114
Hall, John, 188
Hall, Richard, 41, 61, 192
Hamilton, Iain, 11, 53, 192, 200
Harewood, Lord, 52
Harkness International Fellowship, 62, 77, 191, 194
Harper, Edward, 188
Harrison, Frank, 28
Harrogate Festival, 38
Hart, Roy, 85
Hatfield, John, 125
Harvey, Jonathan, 18, 164ff; *Cantata I*, 164, 165; *Canata III*, 165; *Inner Light I*, 166; *Ludus Amoris*, 15, 165, 166; *On Vision*, 166; *Persephone Dream*, 166; Piano Sonata, 165; String Quartet, 164; Symphony, 165; Variations for violin and piano, 164
Headington, Christopher, 175ff; Oboe Sonatina, 176; Piano Sonata, 176; *Reflections of Summer*, 175; *Three Poems of Rainer Maria Rilke*, 176; *Toccata*, 176; *Transformations of 'Love Bade Me Welcome'*, 165; Violin Concerto, 175
Hedges, Anthony, 188
Hellewell, David, 187
Herrick, Robert, 109, 118
Hewitt-Jones, Anthony, 189
Hill, Alec, 184, 198
Hindemith, Paul, 92, 97, 146, 148; *Ludus Tonalis*, 148
Hobbs, Christopher, 184, 198
Hoddinott, Alun, 86ff, 200; *The Beach of Falesá*, 90; Horn Concerto, 89; Piano Concerto, No. 2, 87; Piano Sonata No. 6, 88; Sinfonietta No. 3, 90; String Trio, 86; *The Sun, the Great Luminary of the Universe*, 90; Symphony No. 1, 86; Symphony No. 3, 88; Symphony No. 5, 90; *The Tree of Life*, 15
Hold, Trevor, 16, 189; *The Unreturning Spring*, 14
Holden, Margaret, 37
Hollingsworth, John, 110, 113
Holloway, Robin, 18, 176ff; Concertinos, 176; Concerto for Orchestra, 176; *Domination of Black*, 177; *Evening with Angels*, 177; *Liederkreis*, 176; *Melodrama*, 176; Organ Concerto, 176; *Souvenirs de Schumann*, 176
Holme, Christopher, 171
Holst, Gustav, 56
Holst, Imogen, 183

Hopkins, Bill, 189
Howarth, Elgar, 71, 190
Howells, Herbert, 185
Huber, Klaus, 187
Huddersfield Music School, 197
Hughes, Ted, 29, 57
Hull University, 189
Humberside, Radio, 18

Illinois University, 194
Intermodulation, 168, 196
Ireland, John, 146, 175
Isaac, Heinrich, 62
Isaacs, Harry, 185
'I Sowed the Seeds of Love', 114
Ives, Charles, 24

Jacob, Gordon, 183, 188
Jacobs, Arthur, 102
Japanese Noh Theatre, 48
Jazz, 18, 56, 109, 110, 117, 177, 186, 192, 193
Jeannetta Cochrane Theatre, 101
Jersild, Jorgen, 182
Johnson, Robert Sherlaw, 18, 190
Jones, Raymond, 196
Jones, Sidney: The Geisha, 111
Jones, Tony Hewitt, see Hewitt-Jones, Tony
Jonkers, Ingrid, 35
Joplin, Scott, 108
Josephs, Wilfrid, 190
Joyce, James, 90; Ulysses, 57
Juilliard School of Music, 186

Keller, Hans, 32, 108
Kelly, Bryan, 16, 191, 200
King's Singers, 116
Kitt, Eartha, 116
Knussen, Oliver, 191
Kodaly, Zoltan, 36, 37

Laclos, Pierre de, Les Liaisons Dangereuses, 179
Lady Caroline Lamb, 115
Lady Killer, The, 171
Laine, Cleo, 117, 186
Laird Scholarship, 185
Lambert, Constant, 116
Lambert, John, 191
Lancaster University, 185, 186; Violin Competition, 189
La Scala International Composition Competition, 190
Leeds: Triennial Festival, 42, 52, 125; University, 52, 186
Leeuw, Ton de, 187
Lefanu, Nicola, 191; Antiworld, 17
Léhar, Franz: The Merry Widow, 108
Leicester University, 189
Leighton, Kenneth, 145ff; Concerto for

organ, timpani and strings, 147, 149; Concerto for string orchestra, 149; Conflicts, 149; Crucifixus Pro Nobis, 147; Dance Suite No. 2, 147; Fantasia Contrappuntistica, 148; God's Grandeur, 147; The Light Invisible, 148; Piano Concerto No. 2, 149, 150; Piano Concerto No. 3, 149, 150; Piano Sonata No. 1, 146; Second Service, 147; Sonatinas for piano, 146; Sinfonia Mistica, 149; Symphony No. 1, 149, 150
Lennon, John, 122
Leverhulme Scholarship, 190
Lewis, Alun, 99
Liebenthal, Tertia, 37
Limpus Prize, 189
Lion Roarer, 49
Lipkin, Malcolm, 192
Little Island, The, 171
Liverpool, 53; Mozart Orchestra, 198; University, 189
Lloyd, George, 192
Lloyd Webber, W. S., 53
Local radio, 18
Logue, Christopher, 53, 54, 57, 66
London Chorale, 193
London College of Music, 196
London County Council, 101
London Polytechnic, 184
London School of Contemporary Dance, 187
London Sinfonietta, 17, 56, 190
London Symphony Orchestra, 190, 191
London University, 23; Institute of Education, 196
Lord, David, 192
Losey, Joseph, 113
Louther, William, 85
Lumsdaine, David, 155
Lumsden, David, 196
Lutoslawski, Witold, 185, 196
Lutyens, Elizabeth, 97, 195, 198

Maderna, Bruno, 192, 194
Mahler, Gustav, 62, 70, 176, 177; Das Lied von der Erde, 153
Malipiero, Francesco, 196
Manchester New Music Group, 61, 71
Manchester University, 71, 146, 190
Manning, Jane, 17
Manson Ensemble, 193
'Mariachi' band, 30
Mark, Peter, 25
Marx, Karl (composer), 148
Massachusetts Institute of Technology, 197
Mathias, William, 86, 91ff; Ave Rex, 96; Concerto for Orchestra, 94; Culhwch and Olwen, 96; Dance Overture, 95; Divertimento, 92; Harp Concerto, 96; Invocation and Dance, 95; organ Partita

Mathias, William—*cont.*
93; Piano Concerto No. 2, 92; Piano
Concerto No. 3, 96; Piano Sonata
No. 1, 94; *St Teilo*, 96; Sinfonietta, 95;
String Quartet, 93; Symphony No. 1,
94
Matthay School of Music, 195
Maw, Nicholas, 14, 97ff, 200, 201;
Chamber Music, 101, 106; *Chinese Songs*,
14, 97, 100; *Concert Music*, 106; *Essay
for Organ*, 100; *Life Studies*, 98, 106,
107; *Nocturne*, 14, 98ff; *One Man Show*,
101, 104; *Personae*, 107; *Requiem*, 97;
The Rising of the Moon, 15ff, 104ff;
Scenes and Arias, 100ff; *Serenade*, 106;
Sinfonia for small orchestra, 103,
106; *Six Interiors*, 103; Sonata for
Strings and Two Horns, 98, 104;
Sonatina for flute and piano, 97, 98,
100; String Quartet, 98, 102, 103, 104;
The Voice of Love, 103, 104
Mayerl, Billy, 116
McCabe, John, 18, 145, 150ff; *Aspects of
Whiteness*, 152, 153; *The Castle of
Arianrhod*, 153; *Fantasy on a Theme of
Liszt*, 153; *The Lion, the Witch and the
Wardrobe*, 153; *Notturni ed Alba*, 153;
Partita for string quartet, 151;
Symphony No. 1, 152; Symphony
No. 2, 150, 152; *The Teaching of Don
Juan*, 153; *Time Remembered*, 153;
Variations for piano, 153; *Variations on a
Theme of Hartmann*, 152; *Voyage* 153
McCartney, Paul, 122
McCormack, John, 32
MacCrimmon, Patrick Mor, 34
McDiarmid, Hugh, 36, 37
MacLean, Sorley, 37, 38
Medieval music, 27, 62, 74
Mendelssohn Scholarship, 121, 187, 191,
196
Mellers, Wilfrid, 108
Melos Ensemble, 43
Menuhin, Yehudi, 40
Messiaen, Olivier, 41, 61, 71, 155, 159,
164, 165, 179, 189, 190; *Cinq Rechants*,
43, 123; *Turangalîla*, 198
Microtones, 37
Miles, Maurice, 187
Milhaud, Darius, 73
Milner, Anthony, 53, 173ff, 198, 200;
*Cast Wide the Folding Doorways of the
East*, 174; *City of Desolation*, 174; *The
Harrowing of Hell*, 174; Mass, 173;
Oboe Quartet, 173; *Our Lady's Hours*,
174; *St Francis*, 174; *Salutatio Angelica*,
173; Symphony, Op. 23, 175; Varia-
tions for Orchestra, 174; *The Water and
the Fire*, 175
Milner, Arthur, 190
Mime, 185

Mitchell, Donald, 109
Mitchell, Ian, 185
Monteverdi, Claudio, 73; *Il Combatti-
mento di Tancredi . . .*, 48; *Sonata Sopra
Sancta Maria*, 75; *Vespers of 1610*, 75
Morgan, David, 192; Violin Concerto, 14
Morley College, 53, 173, 184, 188, 192,
195; Concert Society, 15; Symphony
Orchestra, 198
Mozart, W. A., 33, 57; *Die Zauberflöte*, 129
Murder on the Orient Express, 119
Musgrave, Thea, 16, 19ff, 200; *The
Beauty and the Beast*, 25; *Cantata for a
Summer's Day*, 21; Chamber Concerto
No. 1, 22; Chamber Concerto No. 2,
20, 23, 24, 26; Chamber Concerto No.
3, 20, 23, 24, 26; Clarinet Concerto,
24; *Colloquy*, 21, 22; Concerto for
Orchestra, 23, 24, 26; *The Decision*, 20,
23, 27; *Elegy*, 25; *Five Ages of Man*, 23;
From One to Another, 25; Horn Concerto,
25; *Memento Vitae*, 25; *Monologue* for
piano, 22; *Night Music*, 23, 24, 25, 26;
Phoenix and the Turtle, 23; *Scena—A
Song for Christmas*, 21; *Serenade*, 22;
Soliloquy I, 25; String Quartet, 20, 22;
Trio, 21, 22; *Triptych*, 21, 22; Viola
Concerto, 23, 24, 25; *The Voice of
Ariadne*, 20, 25, 26, 27
Musical Times, 179
Music Theatre, 17, 48, 84
Music Theatre Ensemble, 47, 48, 130

National Youth Orchestra, 185
Nelsova, Zara, 56
Newson, George, 192
Nicholas and Alexandra, 113, 114
Nielsen, Carl: Fifth Symphony, 145
Noble, Morag, 57
Nono, Luigi, 133, 189, 190
Northcott, Bayan, 46
Norwich Triennial Festival, 23
Nottingham University, 189
Number Games, 198
Nyman, Michael, 69

Ogdon, John, 18, 71, 192
Oldham, Arthur, 193
Old Vic, 191, 197
Ondes Martenot, 113
Opera, 15ff
Ord, Boris, 195
Orton, Richard, 193
Osborne, John: *The World of Paul
Slickey*, 197
Osborne Letters, 104
Oundle School, 53
Oxford Bach Festival, 110
Oxford University, 184, 188, 189, 191,
196; Brasenose College, 194; Christ
Church, 188; New College, 53

Parikian, Manoug, 56
Paris, 20, 41, 100, 109, 171, 197
Parsons, Michael, 183, 184
Patchen, Kenneth, 134, 137, 141
Patterson, Paul, 193
Payne, Anthony, 29, 169ff, 204, 206, 208, 210, 212; *Concerto for Orchestra*, 171; *Paean*, 171; *Paraphrases and Cadenzas*, 170; *Phoenix Mass*, 169; *Sonatas and Ricercars*, 171; *Two Songs Without Words*, 170
Pears, Peter, 39
Pert, Maurice, 193
Peter Stuyvesant Fund, 191
Petrassi, Goffredo, 28, 72, 146, 183, 191, 196
Pierrot Players, 62, 63, 68, 69, 84; *see also* Fires of London
Pollini, Maurizio, 12
'Pop' music, 18, 108, 109, 116, 122, 133, 138, 140, 168
Porter, Cole, 116, 117
Porter, Peter, 103
Portsmouth College of Art, 184
Pound, Ezra, 36, 120, 125
Prague Academy of Music, 192
Promenade Concerts, 23, 54, 56, 101, 132
Promenade Theatre Orchestra (PTO), 184, 198
Pruslin, Stephen, 68
Purser, John, 194; *The Bell*, 17; *The Undertaker*, 17

Quarter tones, 143
Queen Elizabeth Hall, 63

Radcliffe Music Award, 190
Radio, 171
Rainier, Priaulx, 195
Rands, Bernard, 194; *Serena*, 17
Rawsthorne, Alan, 93
Raybould, Clarence: *Sumida River*, 16
Read, Herbert, 99, 124
Recorder, 36, 139
Redcliff Concerts, 195
Richardson, Arnold, 195
Riddle, Frederick, 185
Ridout, Alan, 194
Rifkin, Joshua, 108
Roberts, Jeremy Dale, 195; *Sinfonia da Caccia*, 14
Roberts, Wesley, 195
'Rock', 185, 193
Rodgers, Richard, 116
Roman Catholic Church, 79
Rose, Bernard, 189, 196
Round House, 57
Routh, Francis, 195, 200
Rowland, David, 18
Roxburgh, Edwin, 188, 195

Royal Academy of Music, 53, 60, 97, 108, 109, 113, 133, 155, 183, 184, 185, 186, 187, 188, 190, 191, 192, 193, 195, 197; Manson Fellowship, 193; New Music Club, 187
Royal College of Music, 182, 183, 184, 185, 186, 187, 188, 191, 192, 193, 194, 195, 196, 198
Royal College of Organists, 189
Royal Festival Hall, 192
Royal Liverpool Philharmonic Orchestra, 56
Royal Manchester College of Art, 60
Royal Manchester College of Music, 32, 37, 41, 71, 188, 190, 192
Royal Navy, 171, 186
Royal Philharmonic Orchestra, 133, 190, 192
Royal Philharmonic Society, 196; Prize, 188, 194
Royal Scottish Academy of Music, 189, 194
Royal Shakespeare Company, 198
Royal Signals Band, 189
Rubbra, Edmund, 145, 189, 196
Russell, Ken, 85

Sadie, Stanley, 111
Sadlers Wells Opera, 27, 195
St Andrew's University, 186
St Catherine Singers (Blackpool), 36
St Philip's Church, Earls Court Road, 195
St Vedast Church, Foster Lane, 191
Salzedo, Leonard, 200
Sammy Going South, 171
Satie, Eric, 73
Saxton, Robert, 195
Schehade, George, 29
Schoeck, Othmar, 57
Schoenberg, Arnold, 12, 19, 20, 41, 46, 51, 53, 54, 55, 56, 121, 165, 179; *Chamber Symphony*, Op. 9, 45; *Erwartung*, 99; *Pierrot Lunaire*, 62; String Quartet No. 2, 122
Schuller, Gunther, 191
Schumann, Robert, 176, 177
Schwarz, Rudolph, 197
School orchestra, music for, 17, 73, 139
Scott, Francis George, 37, 38
Scottish Arts Council, 194, 198
Scottish Festival Chorus, 193
Scottish Music Archive, 36, 213
Scottish Opera, 193
Scottish Theatre Ballet, 25
Scratch Orchestra, 13, 183, 184
Shaw, Christopher, 178ff; Clarinet Sonata, 178; *Four Poems by James Joyce*, 178; *In Memoriam Jan Palach*, 180; *A Lesson from Ecclesiastes*, 179; *Les Liaisons Dangereuses*, 179; *Peter and the*

Shaw—*cont.*
  Lame Man, 178, 180; *Sonnet*, 179; *To the Bandusian Spring*, 179; *Trio*, 179
Shaw, Francis, 196
Shirley-Quirk, John, 128
Shostakovitch, Dmitri, 33, 93, 129
Shrapnel, Hugh, 184, 198
Simpson, Robert, 11
Skempton, Howard, 183, 184
Smalley, Roger, 18, 166ff, 196, 198, 202, 205; *Beat Music*, 168; *Elegies*, 167; *Gloria Tibi Trinitas I* and *II*, 169; *Missa Brevis*, 167, 168; *Missa Parodia I* and *II*, 167, 168; *Monody*, 169; *Piano Pieces I–V*, 166, 233; *Pulses for 5 × 4 Players*, 168; *Septet*, 167; *The Song of the Highest Tower*, 168; *Strata*, 169; *String Sextet*, 167; *Transformations I*, 168; *Two Poems of D. H. Lawrence*, 166; *Zeitenbenen*, 169
Smith, Monica, 153
Searle, Humphrey, 97, 187
Second Viennese School, 11, 41, 55, 71, 120
Secret Ceremony, 113
Seiber, Mátyás, 53, 188, 192, 195
Semple, Margaret, 197
Serialism, 13, 55, 97, 129
Sets, 80
Society for the Promotion of New Music, 191
Souster, Tim, 196, 204
Soutar, William, 36, 38
Southampton University, 185, 196
Spectrum, 8
'Spring Song', 63
Sprague Coolidge Medal, 197
Standford, Patric, 196
Steel, Christopher, 196; *Odysseus*, 17
Stephenson, Robin: *The Four Seasons*, 14, 234
Sterling, William: *Cantus Partbook of 1639*, 37
Stevens, Bernard, 187, 198
Stevenson, Ronald, 32ff, 38; *Ae Gowden Lyric*, 36; *Anger Dance*, 32; *Anns an Airde as an Doimhue*, 38; *Berceuse Symphonique*, 33; *Border Boyhood*, 39; *Calum Salum's Salute to the Seals*, 38; *Canonic Caprice on 'The Bat'*, 33; *Cello Concerto*, 32; *Choral Symphony*, 32, 37, 40; *The Continents* (Piano Concerto No. 2), 32, 35, 36; *Day is Dune*, 36; *Eclogues*, 33; *Haiku*, 38; *Harpsichord Sonata*, 38; *Heroic Sang*, 37; *The Infernal City*, 39; *Keening Sang for a Makar*, 37; *A Mediaeval Scottish Triptych*, 38; *Ne'erday Sang*, 37; *One and All*, 36; *Passacaglia on DSCH*, 34, 36; *Peter Grimes Fantasy*, 33; *Piano Concerto No. 1*, 32, 33; *Prelude, Fugue and Fantasy*, 33; sonatinas for piano, 34; *Scots Dance Toccata*, 38; song cycles, 32; songs, 39; *Songs into Space*, 35; *Songs of Innocence*, 38; *Songs of Quest*, 35, 40; *Sounding Strings*, 36; *Three Scots Fairy Tales*, 36; *To the Future*, 36; *A Twentieth Century Music Diary*, 33; *Variation-Study on a Chopin Waltz*, 33; *Vietnamese Miniatures*, 38; *Violin Concerto*, 40; *Violin Sonata*, 33; *A Wheen Tunes for Bairns to Spiel*, 36; *The Young Pianist's Grainger*, 36
Stockhausen, Karlheinz, 20, 155, 165, 168, 169, 188, 196, 199; *Carré*, 183
Stoker, Richard, 197, 202
Stomu Yamash'ta, 193
Stow, Randolph, 84
Stravinsky, Igor, 15, 20, 48, 56, 73, 97, 155, 158, 179; *Ave Maria*, 74; *Canticum Sacrum*, 155; *Octet*, 51; *Pater Noster*, 74
Sullivan, Sir Arthur: *Trial by Jury*, 108
Suntreader, 193
Surrey University, 187

Tanglewood, 191
Tape, pre-recorded, 25
Tavener, John, 155ff, 197; *Cain and Abel*, 156; *Celtic Requiem*, 156, 157, 158; *Coplas*, 157, 160; *In Alium*, 158; *In Memoriam Igor Stravinsky*, 156; *Introit*, 160; *Nomine Jesu*, 157, 158; *Requiem for Father Malachy*, 156; *Responsorium in Memory of Annon Lee Silver*, 156; *Saint Thérèse*, 159; *Three Holy Sonnets*, 156; *Ultimos Ritos*, 156, 160; *The Whale*, 156, 157, 158, 160
Taverner, John, 78, 167
Tchaikovsky, Peter, 62; Tchaikovsky Prize, 192
Television, 171
Tennyson, Charles, 177
Thaxted Festival, 15
Thomas, Mary, 17
Three Choirs Festival, 165, 182, 191
Tilbury, John, 183
'The Tinker's Song', 114
Tippett, Sir Michael, 56, 60, 92, 95, 99, 173, 176, 194; *The Midsummer Marriage*, 101, 175; Symphony No. 2, 44
To Many a Well (carol), 73
Traherne, Thomas, 123, 163
Trinity College of Music, 182, 185
Twentieth Century Ensemble of London, 195

Ulster Orchestra, 197

Van Dieren, Bernard, 33
Varèse, Edgar, 65, 162
Vaughan, Henry, 156
Vaughan Williams, Ralph, 56, 114, 146, 173, 183; *Tallis Fantasia*, 165

Verdi, Giuseppe, 105
Victoria, Thomas Luis de, 74, 155

Wagner, Richard, 176, 177; *Parsifal*, 175; *Tristan and Isolde*, 57, 169
Wales, Roy, 193
Wales, University of, 194; University College of South Wales, 86
Walker, Timothy, 140
Walton, Sir William, 86, 89, 92, 116, 146, 149
Ward, Anthony, 131
Warlock, Peter, *The Curlew*, 163
Warren, Raymond, 197
Warwickshire Symphony Orchestra, 198
Watney-Sargent Award, 191
Webern, Anton von, 20, 27, 55, 61
Weill, Kurt, 116, 122
Weir, Judith, 197
Wellesz, Egon, 189
Welsh, Moray, 129
Wess, Thomas, 184
Western Theatre Ballet, 198
Whelen, Christopher, 197
Whettam, Graham, 197, 200
White, John, 184, 198

Williams, Richard, 171
Williamson, Malcolm, 11, 16, 200
Wilson, Thomas, 198; *Confessions of a Justified Sinner*, 17
Wood, Hugh, 14, 53ff, 120, 200, 202, 206; Cello Concerto, 56; Chamber Concerto, 56, 57; *The Horses*, 58; *Logue Songs*, 53, 54, 56; *The Rider Victory*, 58; *Scenes from Comus*, 54, 56; String Quartet No. 1, 53, 54, 56; String Quartet No. 2, 58; *Three Pieces for Piano*, 56; Trio, 53; Variations for viola and piano, 53, 57; Violin Concerto, 56, 57
Wood and Metal Orchestra, 184
Woodward, Roger, 18
Woolfenden, Guy, 198
Woolverstone Hall School, 197
Workers' Educational Association, 28, 53
The World Assured, 113

Yeats, W. B., 29, 57
York Festival, 29, 57
York University, 122, 193; Electronic Studio, 193
Young, Douglas, 198